EVERYDAY
WATERCOLOR

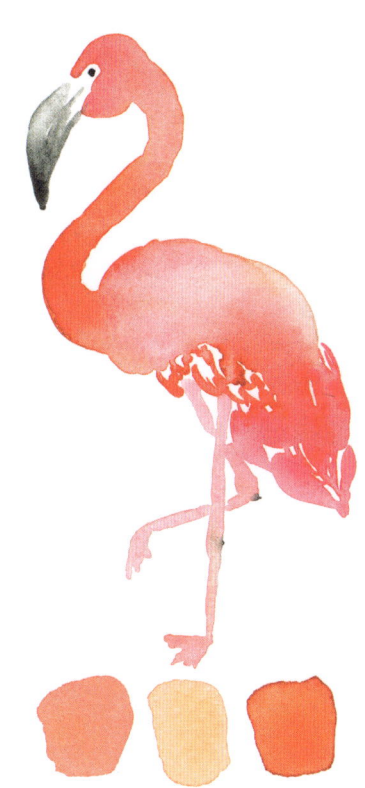

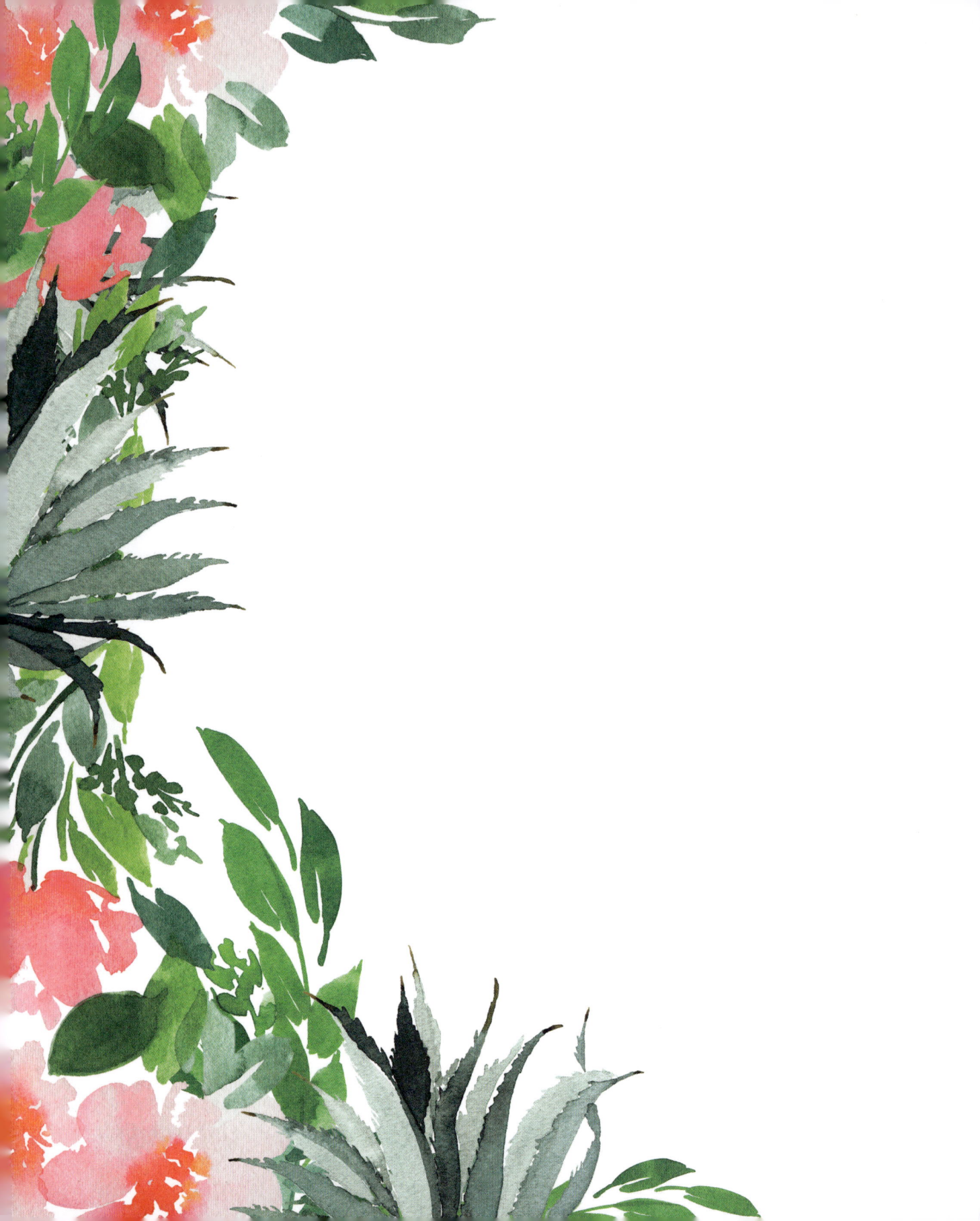

EVERYDAY WATERCOLOR

LEARN TO PAINT WATERCOLOR IN 30 DAYS

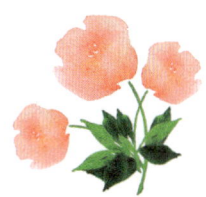

Jenna Rainey

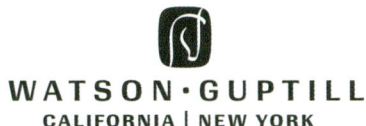

WATSON·GUPTILL

CALIFORNIA | NEW YORK

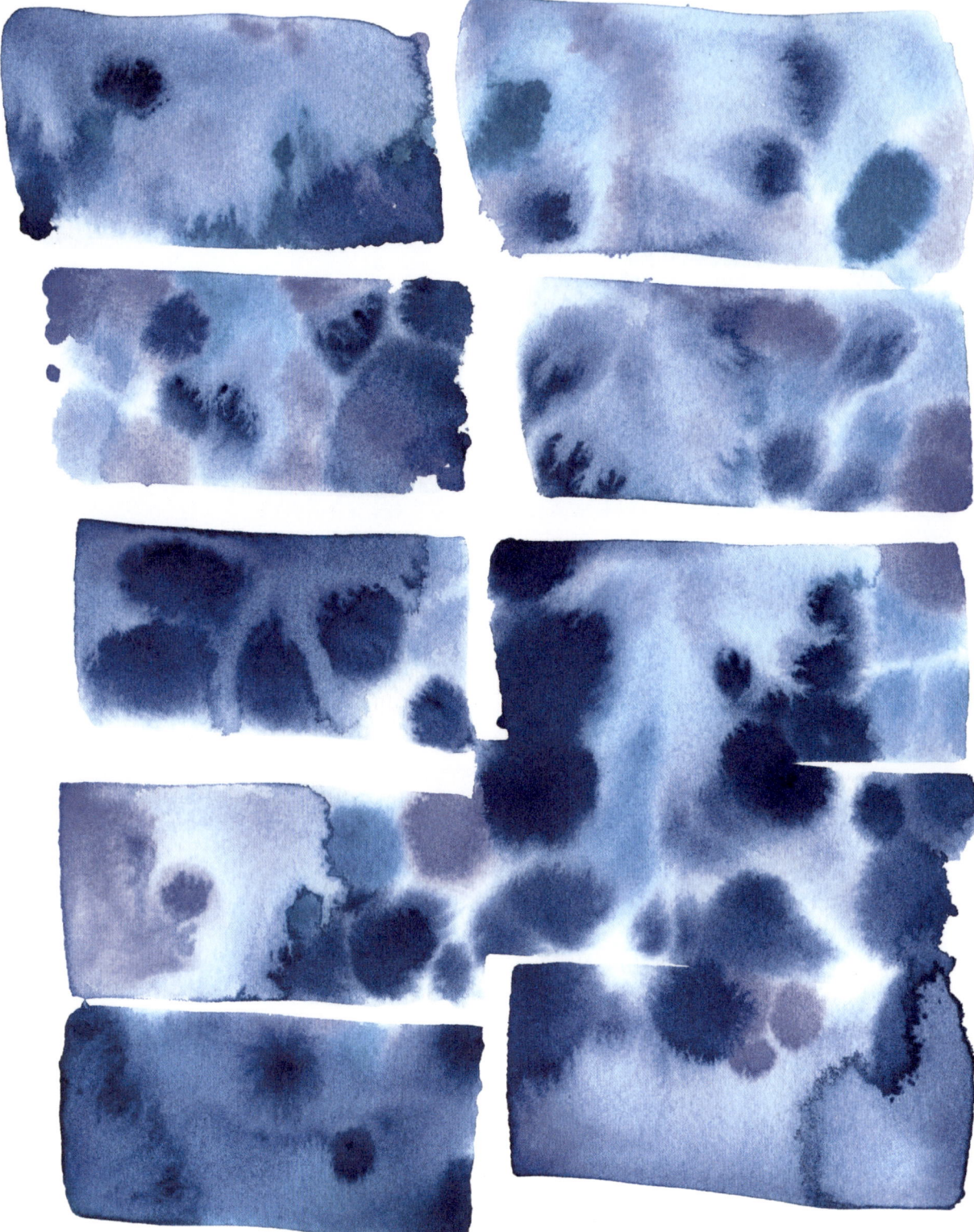

CONTENTS

1   INTRODUCTION

Section One
TECHNIQUE 17

18   DAY 1   STROKES
24   DAY 2   CURVES AND CIRCLES
32   DAY 3   STRAIGHT LINES AND TRIANGLES
38   DAY 4   LAYOUT
44   DAY 5   COMPOUND STROKES
50   DAY 6   COMPLEX CURVES

Section Two
FORM, PERSPECTIVE, AND LIGHT 55

56   DAY 7   LIGHT TO DARK LAYERING
62   DAY 8   BACKGROUND AND FOREGROUND
66   DAY 9   PATTERN
72   DAY 10   LIGHT SOURCE AND SHADING
76   DAY 11   VARIED HUE BLENDING
82   DAY 12   CAST SHADOW

Section Three
COMPLEX SHAPES AND FORMS 89

90   DAY 13   ANGLES AND FOLDS
96   DAY 14   PAINTING IN SECTIONS
102 DAY 15   COMPLEMENTARY COLORS
106 DAY 16   FINE LINES
110 DAY 17   HIGHLIGHTS, MID-TONES, AND SHADOWS
118 DAY 18   GESTURE

Section Four
VALUE, VOLUME, AND DEPTH 125

126 DAY 19   MOVEMENT
132 DAY 20   VALUES
138 DAY 21   SUBJECT IN A LANDSCAPE
146 DAY 22   ATMOSPHERIC PERSPECTIVE
154 DAY 23   GRAYSCALE VALUE
160 DAY 24   VOLUME

Section Five
APPLICATION 171

172 DAY 25   WIDE LANDSCAPE: DESERT
180 DAY 26   WIDE LANDSCAPE: JUNGLE
186 DAY 27   FINAL DESERT PIECE: PART ONE
192 DAY 28   FINAL DESERT PIECE: PART TWO
198 DAY 29   FINAL JUNGLE PIECE: PART ONE
206 DAY 30   FINAL JUNGLE PIECE: PART TWO
210 DAY 31 AND BEYOND

212 ACKNOWLEDGMENTS
213 ABOUT THE AUTHOR
215 INDEX

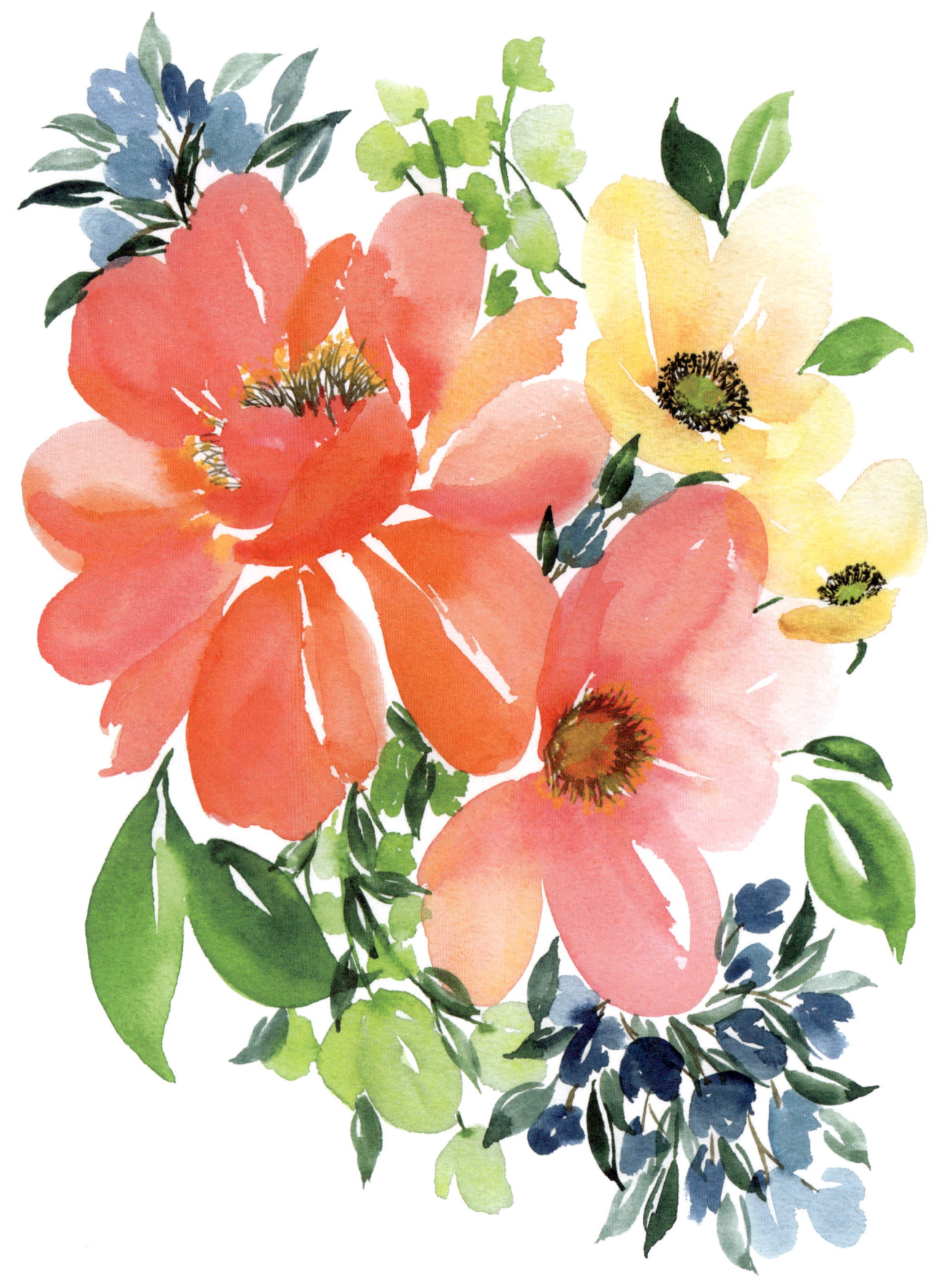

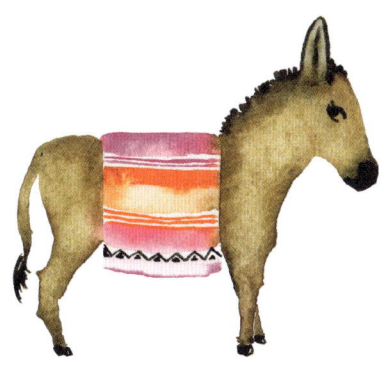

Introduction

Ah, watercolor. Its beautiful luminous quality is pure delight. Watercolor is wildly uncontrollable and at the same time containable. It's a visual medium that moves around with ease, exploding and bursting into surrounding strokes, creating texture and depth that can't be found in any other type of media.

You know the feeling when you've fallen in love and you can't stand to be away from that person? This was my story with watercolor. I know—dramatic, right? Well, it's true. I became obsessed. When I wasn't painting, I was thinking about painting. I fell in love with watercolor and began to study it. I put in countless hours discovering all the ins and outs.

My mom and both of my grandmothers were acrylic painters, and although I'd tried my hand at painting a few times, I would definitely have considered myself OK at best. And sure, I'd dabbled with watercolor in elementary school. But when my profession as a calligrapher and designer began to take off, I came across the right watercolor supplies—and something changed for me. With the correct materials, the process was so enjoyable that I wanted to learn more.

This infatuation rapidly turned into an important part of my career as an artist and designer. I've been able to work with clients from all over the globe, using watercolor to provide illustrations for large brands, as well as creative stationery for events like beautiful high-end weddings. I've also been able to travel and teach my watercolor classes to thousands of students over the years. With my teaching experience, I've learned how to communicate with beginner and developing watercolorists, to break down complicated subjects into something simpler and easier to grasp. I'm able to share what I've learned the hard way through experience and mistakes. I've come to discover that watercolor painting is about learning from the failed attempts and continuing to develop muscle memory and technique.

In the beginning, I challenged myself to paint subjects more complex than what I thought I could manage. I incorporated my knowledge of basic sketching and shading techniques into more complex subjects. At each stage of my relationship with watercolor, I was accepting of where I was—not discouraged with the outcome, but learning to enjoy the process and seeking to understand more of why watercolor does what it does and how to master it.

Being a self-taught watercolor artist has allowed me to break rules and learn the hard way. I've written this book to help you do just that (and perhaps avoid some of the hard parts I encountered). So here's my advice at the outset: Allow yourself to be challenged. Paint differently than you think you should, and ask yourself what you enjoy about it. Like anything, becoming a better watercolorist takes work, dedication, practice, and most of all, patience. Patience with yourself to look at subjects with new eyes—the eyes of an artist. But first, you must allow yourself to start small and work your way up, adding more detail and complexity as you go. Jumping straight into painting a detailed flower or a toucan before practicing brush technique will usually lead to disappointment—you need to build basic skills before you tackle form and structure.

Throughout this book, we're going to develop muscle memory and train our eyes to look for basic shapes and curves in every subject. No matter how complex and detailed a subject may seem on the surface, everything you paint or draw can be broken down into very simple shapes, like circles and ovals. We'll start developing good brush and painting technique by practicing these basic shapes, training our eyes to look for unifying color palettes, and following rules of composition. We will define and create

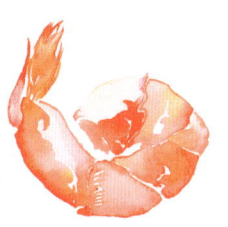

more complex shapes as we move through our thirty days together, building upon our foundation to continually instill confidence in your painting. Knowing where and how to start with any subject is a crucial part of the process, and this book will show you just that.

I hope you love getting to know more about watercolor over these next thirty days and you are inspired to continue painting with a new appreciation for this medium and for yourself as a creative individual. Once you have a strong foundation, you can develop your own style. Accept each step of the process, even your less successful attempts, as an opportunity for growth. Watercolor can be unpredictable, yet incredibly manageable too. If you're up for the challenge to #everydaywatercolor, I'm sure you'll be surprised by the creativity that is naturally in you— sometimes it just takes looking at things from a different angle. Throughout your journey through this book, I would love to see some of your favorite pieces you've created. If you're on social media, use the hashtag #everydaywatercolor to add your own paintings. I'd enjoy seeing your transformation over the course of these daily painting exercises.

Let's get started with the foundations, shall we?

SUGGESTED TOOLS AND MATERIALS

When I tried my hand at watercolor for the very first time many years ago, I was in, I don't know—kindergarten? The teacher pulled out these cheap trays of watercolor that resembled dusty old eye shadow. Our brushes were coarse, and the plastic handle seemed to squeeze the hairs of the brush so tightly that they puffed out in every direction. The paper probably came straight from the copy machine. The masterpieces we created that day surely were displayed on fridges by proud parents, with a few fond chuckles—and soon replaced with finger paint and crayon art.

My experience with watercolor materials later in life was much different. This medium is addicting once you discover the proper materials for you and find a groove in your practice—indeed, it can be hard to stop! It's life changing, I tell you. And I'm excited to share with you my list of most-loved supplies and why they can be so effective in your paintings.

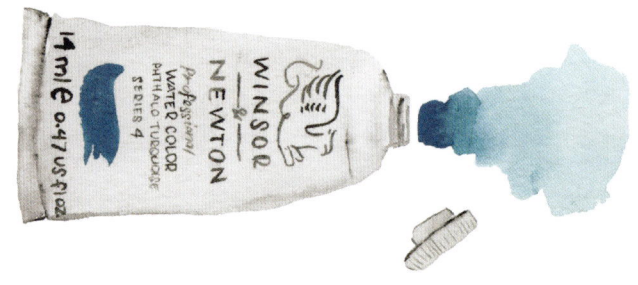

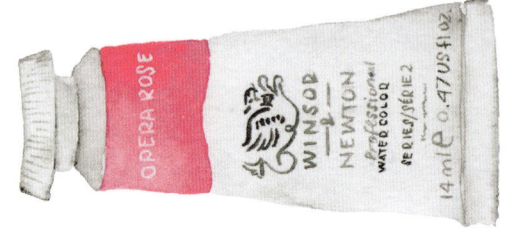

PIGMENTS

Watercolor paint is a mixture of finely ground pigment powder combined with gum arabic. Gum arabic is a water-soluble binder, so when more is added to a particular tube or pan, the paint mixture can be sold for less money—but the purity and permanence of the pigment is degraded. I've found that the student-grade paints, which contain more binder, have a duller look, whereas professional-grade paints are higher quality when it comes to transparency, permanence, and color. Your eyes will light up when you see the difference these paints make in your art. I'm convinced it's always better to invest from the beginning in professional-grade watercolor paints. You will also find that your colors become less muddy with professional grade than with student grade—and let me tell you, muddy colors for watercolorists are like death (more on this later).

My palette consists of a beautiful range of Winsor & Newton professional-grade watercolor paints, including these shown below.

Mars Black, Ultramarine Violet, Prussian Blue, Cobalt Blue, Phthalo Turquoise, Winsor Green, Sap Green, Olive Green

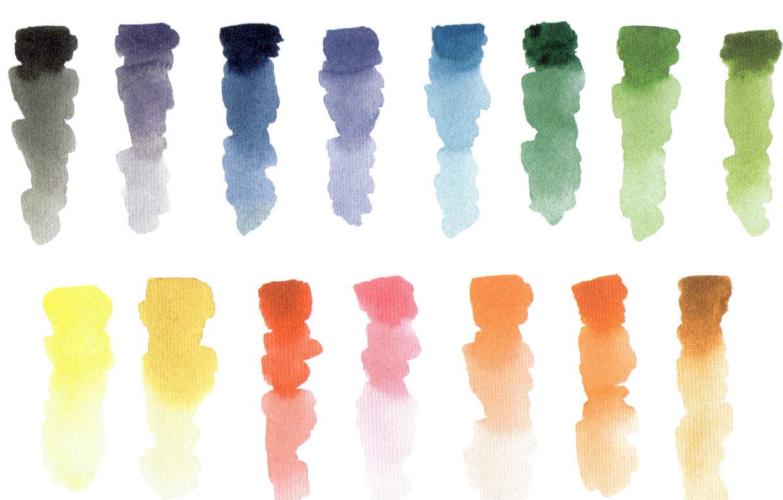

Lemon Yellow Deep, Yellow Ochre, Scarlet Lake, Opera Rose, Cadmium Orange, Winsor Orange (red shade), Burnt Umber

The number of paints in each artist's palette will vary. Some prefer to have fewer options; others may prefer to have many more. This just depends on how the artist likes to mix and add hue variety to the palette. For example, when mixing up the color green, the hue will look much different if you use Prussian Blue and Lemon Yellow Deep than Phthalo Turquoise and Lemon Yellow Deep. I recommend going to your local art supply store to see these tubes and test out a couple of different types. If you purchase Winsor & Newton, the value of the pigment is rated by series numbers 1 to 4. The higher the series number, the higher the value of the pigment (and the cost). If you see the word "hue" in the name of a specific color—like "Lemon Yellow Hue" instead of "Lemon Yellow Deep"—that means the manufacturer is mixing two or more different and cheaper pigments together to emulate the hue of a specific pigment, without having to use that particular pigment itself. While this makes a less expensive version of that color, the result is muddied colors, and you all know how we feel about muddy colors . . . .

Note: You may have noticed that my palette of colors does not contain any white paint. I prefer to lighten my colors by loading more water on my brush. For this reason I always have two cups of water out when I paint—one cup to rinse out all the paint from my brush and a cup of clean water to load up the brush before grabbing a different color. I'll have more to say on this in the next section.

PAPER

Watercolor paper is offered in three different types: hot-pressed, cold-pressed, and rough. Hot-pressed paper has a smooth surface that doesn't have much *tooth*—that is, the bumpiness and texture found in rougher papers. I prefer not to use this type of paper for watercolor, as it tends to not hold water and pigment in place while it dries. I prefer cold-pressed, because it has a nice toothy texture perfect for soaking up strokes and holding applied paint in place. It's not too toothy, as rough paper can tend to be, which makes it difficult to create smooth strokes. The variation in how your paint dries on cold-pressed versus how it dries on hot-pressed can make a substantial difference to your piece.

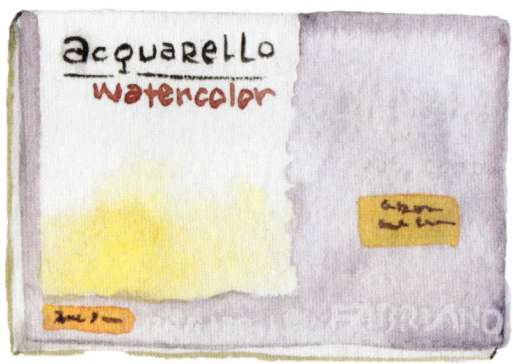

Another important note about watercolor paper is its thickness, indicated by weight. This is measured in both pounds per ream (lb) and grams per square meter (gsm). I think any paper less than 140 lb/300 gsm is too light, because it becomes wavy when the paint dries. You don't have to use paper thicker than 140 lb, but it can help with absorbency. My two preferred brands of watercolor paper come in blocks by Fabriano or Stonehenge Aqua by Legion Paper, 100% cotton 140 lb/300 gsm in "extra white." Painting on a block of paper, instead of individual sheets, guarantees that the paper has been stretched beforehand. If watercolor paper is less than 300 lb and isn't stretched, it's almost guaranteed to buckle and warp when water and pigment are added. Because blocks are glued on all four sides, I can leave a painting in the block while it dries—this keeps it completely flat. If you paint using a block of paper, when it's dry you should use a ruler or a canvas bone to peel up your finished painting from the rest of the sheets in the block. These tools will help prevent your piece from tearing when you're trying to remove just one sheet. If you have only sheets of paper, I recommend taping down all four sides with artist tape, which will mimic the benefits of a block.

BRUSHES

When it comes to materials, the biggest game changer for me was changing the type of brushes I use. For the longest time, I was using coarser-haired brushes (like goat and camel or mixed hair); once these are loaded up with water, the brush flops over like a wet mop.

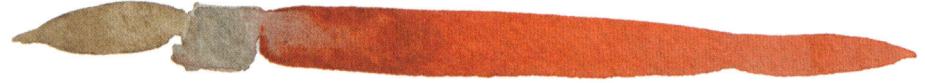

It is essential that your watercolor brushes be able to hold their form and flexibility when wet. You want brushes that, when loaded up with water and pigment, can lift and rebound easily between strokes. The best types for watercolor are made from sable hair. Kolinsky sable hair is the most coveted type for brushes. Because of how well they hold pigment and their flexibility, these brushes are quite expensive. If Kolinskys are just too pricey for you, Princeton synthetic sable hair brushes are great brushes that won't break the bank. These brushes hold pigment really well and are quite flexible.

The sizes and types of brushes that I use include the following:

Round size 2 | Round size 6 | Round size 16

I use only round-tip brushes because of their versatile two-in-one nature—perfect for the type of work I do. I tend to paint quickly, constantly shifting between broader strokes and finer details, and round-tip brushes allow me to do this without having to pick up a different brush between strokes. As you grow as a watercolorist, you may find that your style is best served by filbert brushes (with rounded ends) or flat brushes, and so on. Feel free to experiment with other materials and tools and find out what works best for you.

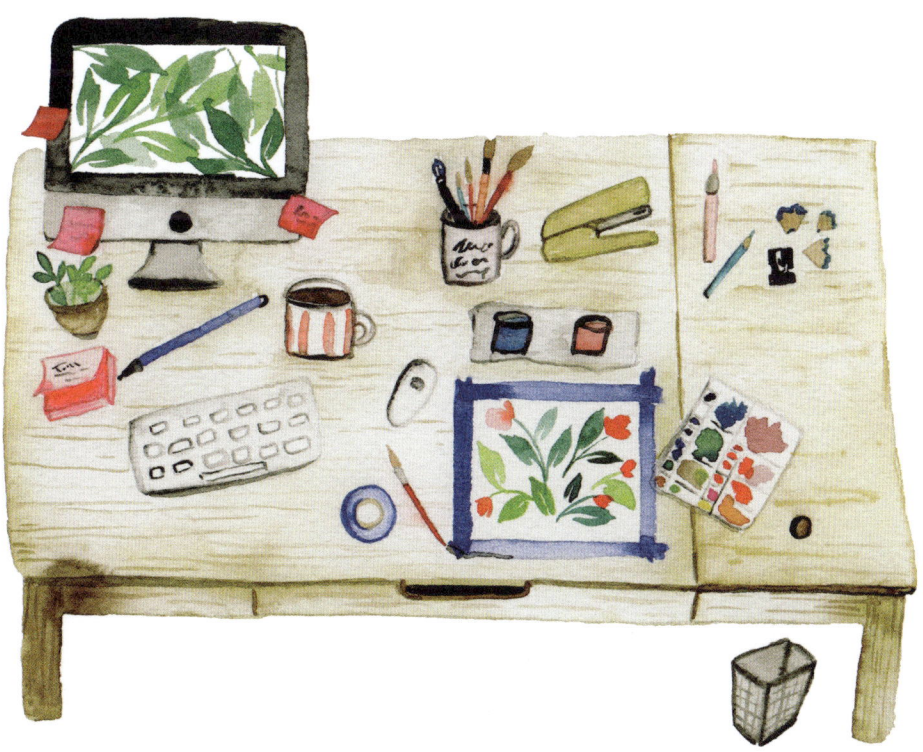

OTHER RECOMMENDED MATERIALS

When I'm painting more detailed subjects, I always use an HB graphite pencil to first create a faint sketch. Art pencils or graphite pencils are ranked on a scale from hardness (H) to softness (B) to indicate what type of shade and line work you'll be able to achieve. HB is my favorite lead for sketching before watercolor, as it creates lighter marks with my preferred amount of pressure. One of my favorite sketching tools is the Staedtler mechanical pencil with HB lead. I also always have on hand a hi-polymer eraser, paper towels, and, as mentioned earlier, two cups of water—one to rinse paint from my brush, the other to pick up clean water before going to a different color. I use a traveler's palette with twenty-eight smaller dishes for pigment. I distribute about one-third of a 14 ml tube of wet paint into each small well of my palette and let it dry overnight; this helps me to not waste paint! Because I'm using true pigment, wasting paint makes me cringe. It's easy to swipe up too much paint on your brush when loading up with gooey wet paint, and with watercolor, a little bit of pigment can go a very long way.

COLOR THEORY

All right, now that you've got the lowdown on all the materials I use, here's another important piece to understanding watercolor (and all media that involve color, for that matter): color theory.

Whether I'm painting or designing, color plays a huge role in what I do. The use of color can be either incredibly captivating and powerful or disharmonious and confusing. Our brains respond strongly to unity and harmony, so when the colors on your paper convey these in a composed manner, your viewers' eyes will thank you! I'm going to start with the very basics of color theory, using the color wheel to explain how colors are formed and how they work together.

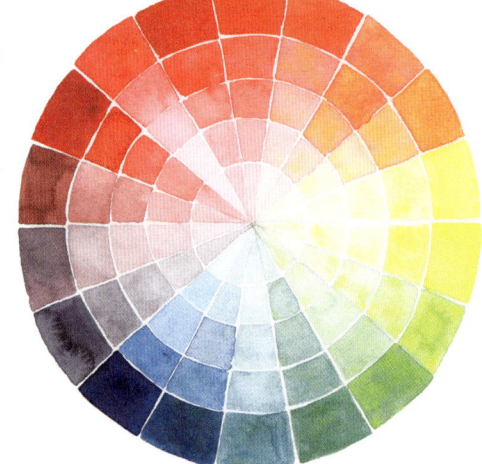

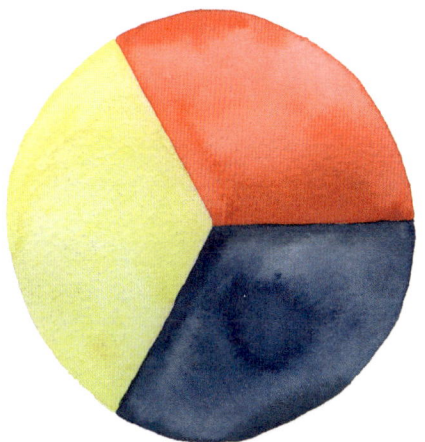

PRIMARY COLORS

Red, blue, and yellow
These are the three colors that cannot be formed by using or combining any other colors. If these three colors are all combined in equal parts, you will get black. All other colors are derived from a combination of these primary colors.

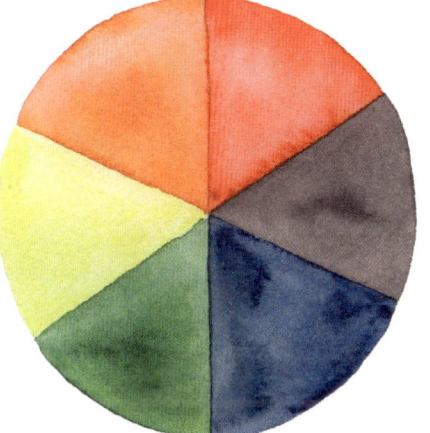

SECONDARY COLORS

Orange, green, and purple
These are the colors that each result from an equal parts mixture of two primary colors. Red and yellow make orange, blue and yellow make green, and blue and red make purple.

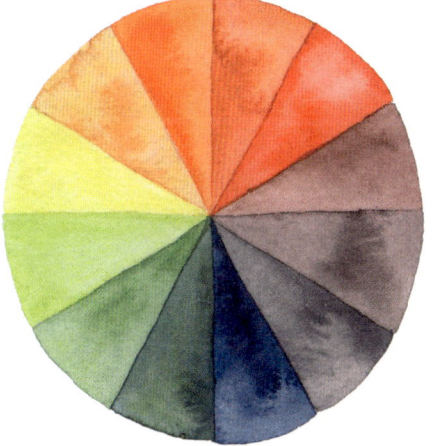

TERTIARY COLORS

Yellow-orange, red-orange, yellow-green, blue-green, blue-purple, red-purple
These are the colors that are created using a primary color and a secondary color—thus the hyphenated names.

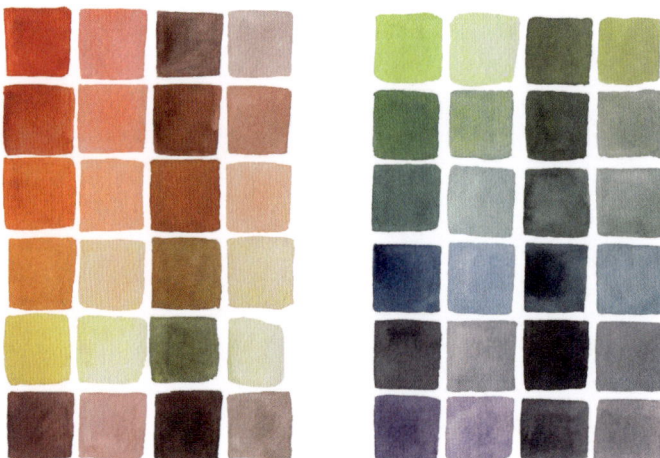

Each of these colors has four main characteristics:

- **Hue** (first column of each grid above): Twelve of the purest forms of color as seen on a tertiary color wheel. These colors do not contain any desaturation or lightness.

- **Tone** (second column): Created by adding gray to a hue. Each tone is a more subtle version of each hue.

- **Saturation/Desaturation or Shade** (third column): Describes a color's intensity. When the color's value is altered, the saturation decreases and becomes less brilliant. Adding black lessens the saturation of a color or creates its shade.

- **Value** (fourth column): Refers to a color's lightness or darkness. The more water is added to the pigment, the lighter or more transparent the hue will be. The less water is added, leaving a thicker, less diluted amount of pigment on the brush, the deeper and richer the value will be.

Before we move on, here is a very helpful tip for recognizing a color's value. I'll be bringing up highlights, mid-tones, and shadows quite a bit throughout this book, so before we get there, read through the following helpful information!

THE VALUE SCALE

While we want highlights to be the lightest versions of a color and shadows the darkest, there are many more shades in between that can help give your paintings even more form and dimension. Create a value scale of your own to use for reference throughout your journey through this book! Let's use the value scale here as an example:

This scale starts with Winsor & Newton Mars Black at its full intensity at number 9 on the right. For each succeeding swatch, continually lighten the pigment with water just a touch until it reaches number 1 on the left—or pure white paper. You can create a value scale swatch card by painting this yourself, then cut out the strip of paper and use it as a practical guide for discovering the value number in a photo or real-life subject. To decipher the intensity of each value in a subject (real-life or in a photo) that you're painting from, you can just hold this scale up to it.

Gaining a good understanding of color theory will strengthen your ability to choose harmonious color palettes. As you become more aware of color harmony and the importance of each combination, you'll be able to create more striking and effective pieces. It's important in each piece to strike a balance between unity and stimulation with color and composition. Now let's look at a few arrangements and examples of harmonious palettes that will be helpful to refer to as we make this daily journey together:

Monochromatic: One hue, with variations in value/intensity/temperature.

Analogous: Any three or four hues next to each other on the color wheel.

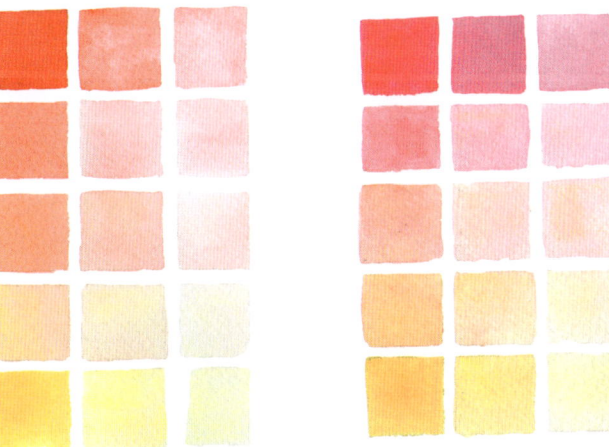

In the swatches on the previous page, we lay out the range of color, working from top to bottom, by starting with two primary colors (or with the pink example, starting with Winsor & Newton Opera Rose and yellow), and gradually adding little bits at a time of Winsor & Newton Lemon Yellow Deep to Scarlet Lake or Opera Rose. This shows the subtle change in hue from one pure color to the next: in the left grid, red to yellow; in the right grid, pink to yellow. The range between the columns shows the alteration of value or lightening of each color, left to right, by gradually adding more water to the mixture.

Complementary: Any two hues opposite each other on the color wheel.

Complementary colors deliver the highest amount of contrast and can be pretty straining to look at if used improperly. To create more harmony and subtlety, try combining a palette, like in the example below. The two complementary colors are blue and orange. Note the range of blues with a softer value, helping create balance and a break for the eyes. Yellow is also a great color for this palette; it is mixed with both the blue and the orange, helping to merge the two opposing/contrasting complementary colors a bit more.

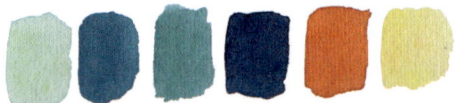

Split-complementary: Any primary, secondary, or tertiary hue, plus the two colors on either side of its complement.

An example would be red, plus the two hues on either side of its complement (green): yellow-green and blue-green. Similar to the blue-orange swatches, this palette (below) contains blended colors that help soften and merge the range between the more contrasting colors. Split-complementary palettes aren't as high contrast as pure complementary colors, but they can still be off-putting. In this example, the hue on the far left is a violet, bringing in hints of blue from the blue-green end of the palette.

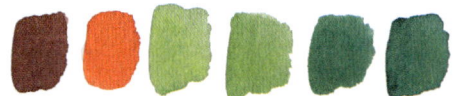

COMPOSITION

Now that we've covered the essence of color theory—it's a huge topic, but you've got the basics—let's find out how to take balance and harmony even further, with the basic rules of composition.

TIP 1: RULE OF THIRDS

Every painting must help direct a person's eyes to its focal point. This is where the rule of thirds comes in handy! Imagine taking your ruler and pencil and sectioning off your paper into thirds, horizontally and vertically. You should be directing people's eyes to one or more of these four intersection points as the focal point. A focal point could be an intense burst of color, a striking color combination, a horizon line, and so on. Think of what your areas of focus or impact could be, and be mindful of placing these on these intersection points in odd numbers. I'll explain why with the next tip.

TIP 2: NUMBER OF ELEMENTS

Think of the painting you're about to create, with the different colors and values you want to incorporate. In choosing the types of elements, variations, and perspectives you'll include, it's crucial to keep in mind that they should all be grouped in odd numbers. If you arrange elements in even numbers, your viewer's eyes will begin grouping things in pairs. This creates a static feeling, so once they have matched up all the pairs, they'll be looking in vain for more. Instead, you want your viewer's eyes to keep moving around the field, from one striking element or color to the next. Odd numbers will help create movement through your piece; symmetry and pairs will appear static and rigid.

TIP 3: WARM VERSUS COOL DOMINANCE

When you include both cool and warm colors in the color palette of a piece, make sure either cool colors or warm colors are dominant—they should not have equal value. If you're struggling with how to create a harmonious color palette for your piece, refer back to pages 11–12 (on color harmonies) to help create balance!

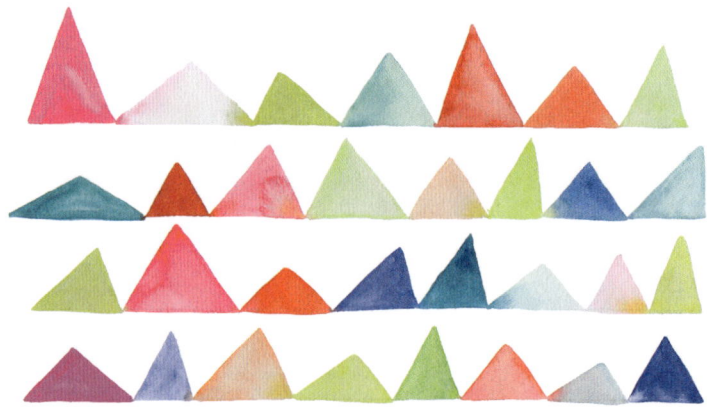

You'll need to keep in mind both color harmonies and compositional tips and tricks. If the composition is on point but the color palette is not working, viewers will move on.

PAINTING TECHNIQUES

With watercolor, there are two different ways of applying paint: wet on wet and wet on dry. It's important to know the difference between these two, as they provide very different results.

WET ON WET

Wet on wet is the technique of applying wet paint to a wet surface to create a soft, diffused edge or a bleed. This method is great when building from light to dark, adding darker pigment to a lighter surface, and creating a soft blend and smooth transitions between colors (see examples below).

WET ON DRY

Wet on dry is the technique of applying wet paint to a dry surface. This could mean directly to the paper or also wet paint layered on top of already dried sections of paint. You'll use this method when you want to give a subject hard, clean edges or add dimension and depth with layers (opposite, top).

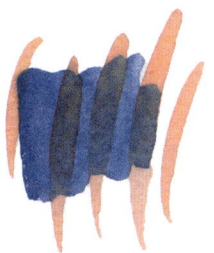 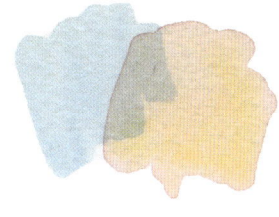

Note: Throughout the rest of the book I will refer to these two terms quite a bit. So instead of typing them out each time, I am going to affectionately call them by the abbreviations WOW and WOD.

I hope the list of supplies and these foundational tips are getting you excited to paint for yourself! Once we start painting together, we'll be defining these foundations even more, and they will become easier to grasp. When I first began with watercolor, I didn't have an in-depth knowledge of color theory, nor did I know anything about composition. I poured countless hours into studying the foundations, and without knowing it at the time, I was giving myself a very important gift: muscle memory. Every day I would come home from my 9-to-5 office job and paint. As I became more comfortable with how the brushes worked and forming basic shapes, I started building on the basics, creating forms and pieces that were more complex. I was able to develop as an artist by falling in love with daily practice.

I hope that you, too, fall in love with watercolor. If you think you're not creative or not a painter, crumple up that lie and throw it in the trash, because we all are made to be creators. All it takes is practice, a lot of passion, dedication, and most importantly, patience and confidence that with effort you will get better each day. With that said, I challenge you to paint something every day with me. If you're disappointed in the outcome of any particular day, do it again or come back to it later. This book doesn't guarantee thirty masterpieces in thirty days, but if you enjoy the process of painting daily, you may surprise yourself with the outcome when you get there. Remember to use the hashtag #everydaywatercolor on social media to help track your progress; I am looking forward to seeing your paintings and practice! Enjoy each moment, soak up every word, and push through your mistakes. I'm excited to help guide you through this process.

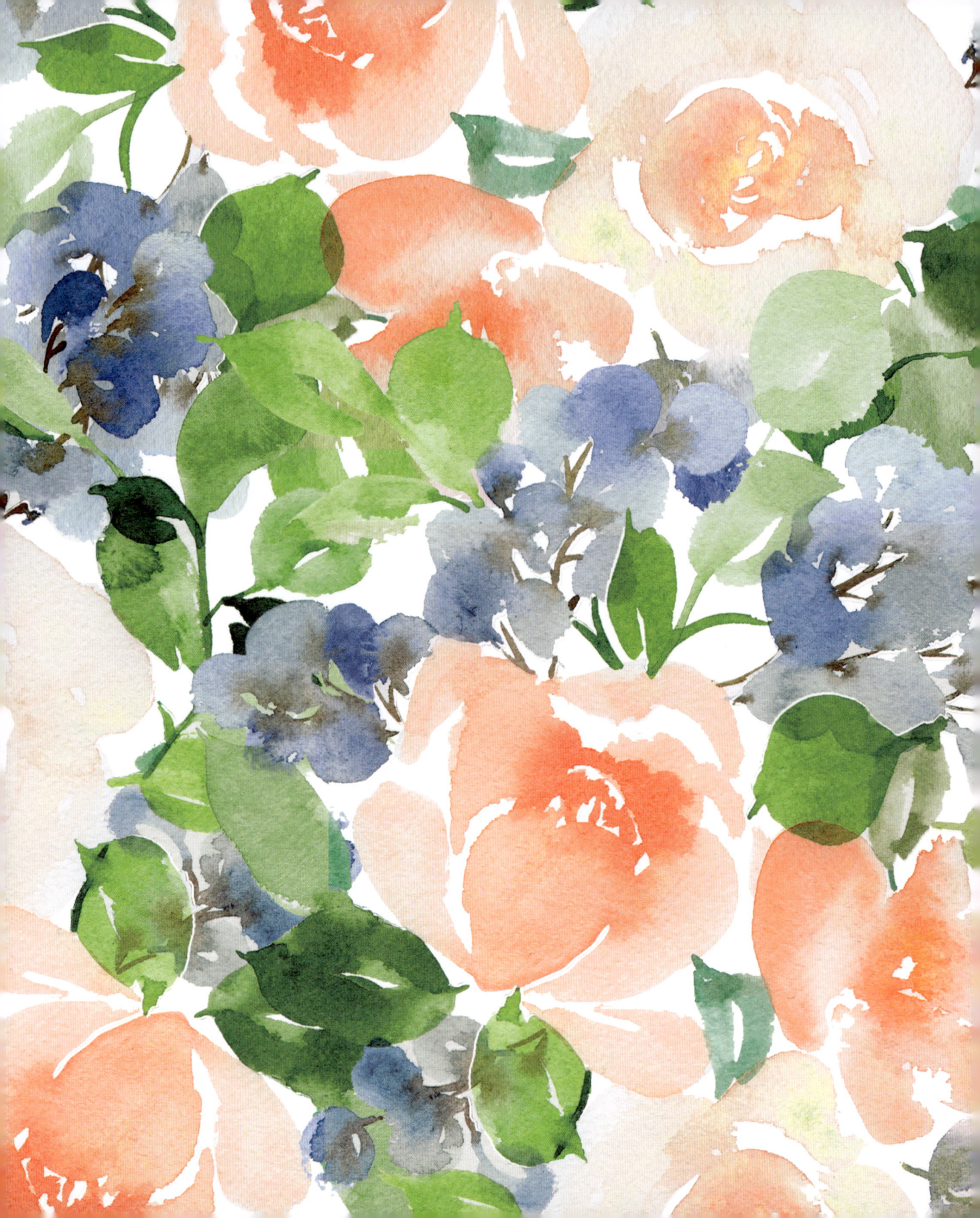

Section One

TECHNIQUE

This section provides the essentials for you to gain basic watercolor knowledge and practices. Each day we'll cover a stroke or shape and unpack color harmonies and combinations that will take your pieces from ordinary to striking. On day 1, you'll begin to develop muscle memory and familiarity with strokes that you will apply to everything you paint from here on out. We'll start with painting with cool colors on days 1 and 2, then move to warm colors and mixed palettes on days 3 and 4. As you move along through this section, you'll find yourself practicing compound brush strokes and developing an eye for color harmonies. Before you sit down and paint each day, I recommend clearing a good amount of space on a flat surface to paint on, with plenty of light (natural, if possible), and putting on some good tunes (or enjoying peace and quiet, if that gets your creative juices flowing). Let's get started!

Day One

STROKES

Use basic strokes to create an abstract piece with swatches. Learn how to choose a color palette, basic composition, and the WOW technique.

Estimated time: 15 to 25 minutes

STEP ONE:

Warm up with lightening a hue

For the very first daily painting, you will be making basic marks on the page, called *swatches*. The idea is to go back and forth in a parallel angle or zigzag motion until the painted area is roughly one-half inch square. Using the belly or width of your round brush will cover a larger area much faster than using just the tip. The example here is a swatch of Winsor & Newton Prussian Blue.

Before applying any paint to paper, always make sure your brush is fully soaked in water. Swish the brush around in your clean water cup and swipe the tip across the rim of the glass two or three times to get rid of any excess water.

Then load up your brush with Prussian Blue or another full-strength color of your choosing. To do this, roll the belly of the brush in the paint three or more times, stopping once the hairs are coated in thick pigment. Apply the first swatch to the paper, then swish the brush back and forth two or three times in your dirty water cup to release some pigment before the next swatch. The more vigorously you wash off the brush, the more paint you will remove; for this exercise you want to retain some paint, so don't be too thorough, and always swipe your brush across the rim of the cup or even dab it on a paper towel to get rid of any excess water. Do this before and after each swatch so the row of swatches goes from dark to light—in this case, a deep blue to a pale blue.

STEP TWO:
Choose a color palette and learn WOW

For our very first piece together, we're going to focus on the most simple color combination when it comes to mixing color: monochromatic. Add variations to the piece with shade and tone, by lightening your base hue with water, darkening it with black, or using it in full saturation by picking up lots of pigment on your brush. This color scheme can be quite striking with the right composition. Reminder, I never use white to lighten my colors, as I think this makes them look dull. Just rinse pigment off your brush in water—it works like a charm!

Start with applying one swatch—maybe a thick amount of Prussian Blue with a touch of black mixed in to make it a midnight blue. Once that first swatch is finished, rinse your brush to remove most of the pigment, so what's left on the brush is a pale blue wash. Now, start away from your first swatch and work the brush toward it, touching it with just the tip with the pale wash, and watch the colors explode into one another. Make sure to work quickly enough that the colors are still wet and can bleed into one another.

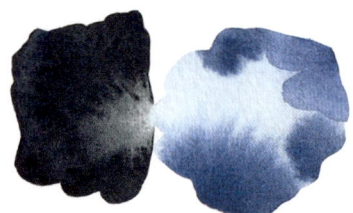

To add character and a feeling of excitement to your piece, add parallel lines or hash marks that vary in height and weight. If you're using a more calm color palette, it's best to keep these markings at a minimum—but try it out.

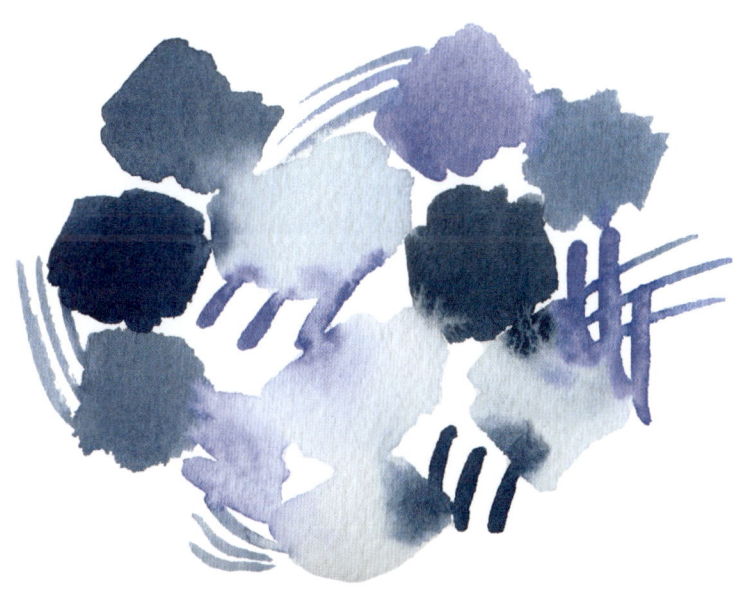

STEP THREE:

Put paint to paper

For composing an abstract piece, it's easiest to start from the top left or right corner (depending on your handedness) and work your way down. Try not to spend too much time in the center, as this tends to throw off the balance of the piece. Starting at the top, you can take steps back to analyze as you work your way through the piece. It's also important with abstracts to stay loose and not overthink your next moves. Simply using the right colors and allowing for areas of contrast is surprisingly effective. Use the WOW technique to add bursts, texture, depth, and bounce. Stick with one hue, adding multiple variations in tint and shade.

Day Two

CURVES AND CIRCLES

Apply previous techniques to circles.
Develop muscle memory for curves, and
practice brush technique with different
stroke widths.

Estimated time: 20 to 30 minutes

STEP ONE:

Warm up with "C" curves and circles

To get started, we're going to draw the outlines of circles. This will help you learn how to use the fine point of your round brush for a thinner line and get used to using your arm to help create steady lines. To start, load up your size 6 brush with water and paint. I used Winsor & Newton Phthalo Turquoise for this example. Make sure your brush is relatively vertical, as shown, with the tip of the brush pointed down and the end of the brush about 75 to 90 degrees away from the paper.

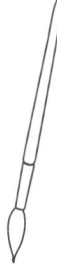

This will focus the fine tip of the brush so that you can achieve a nice thin line. With your brush in this position, start outlining a couple-different-sized "C" curves and circles.

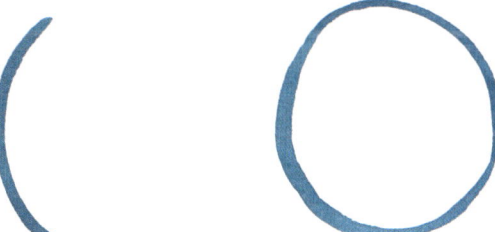

Move your brush around the entire shape by moving your arm and wrist, keeping your fingers' grasp of the brush handle stable and relaxed. Pivot from your bent elbow so your forearm is steady, rolling your wrist around the circle. You can rotate the paper as you work if you need to for a better angle. If you move your fingers on the brush, changing your grip as you trace it around the shape, your lines will tend to be shakier and you won't be able to control the amount of pressure you're applying. With added pressure, the hairs will fan out, creating a wider stroke. For these shapes, you want a crisp, clean, smooth line. Practice getting used to the form of circles and creating steady outlines with your arm until you feel comfortable. If your lines are looking unsteady, don't fret! This takes some practice—but remember to rely on your arm.

Tip: When trying to create steady lines, lay off the coffee! Too much caffeine can cause shakiness. Trust me; I've been there.

Next, we're going to practice how to achieve an even blend throughout an entire shape. Begin by outlining a circle using your size 6 brush. Try not to linger or go too slowly, as you'll want the outline to be wet when you move paint into the middle of the shape. Next, working quickly, grab a little water on your brush, then with your brush tilted to about a 35-degree angle from the paper surface, drag it along the inner edge of the outline and into the middle area of the circle.

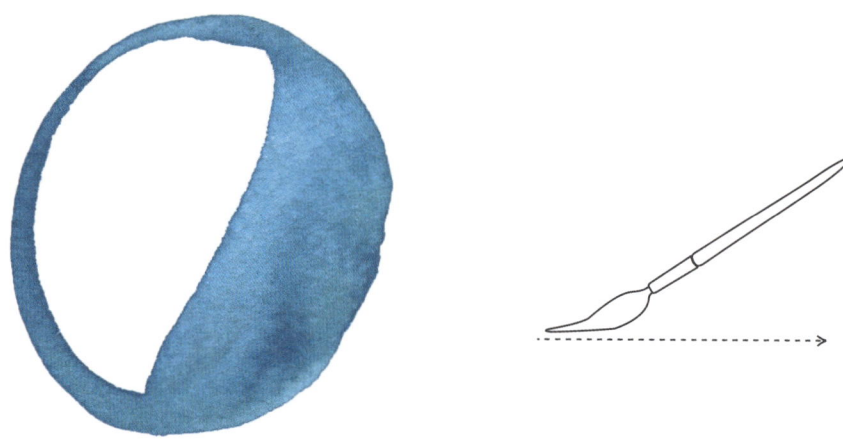

Continue this to create a smooth blend throughout the shape. Make sure you're doing this quickly so the shape stays wet when you paint the next circle.

If you don't act rapidly between laying down the outline and applying color to fill in the shape, you'll get unwanted hard lines—an obvious line or contrast between the outline and the rest of the shape:

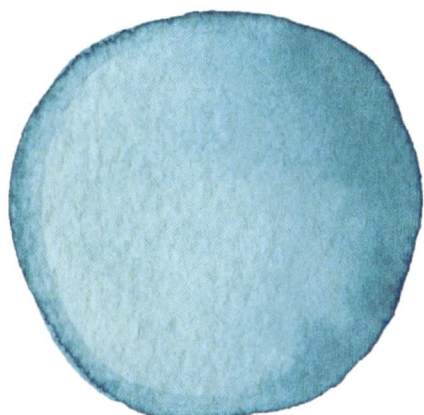

The left side of the circle has an obvious hard line, while the right side is a smooth even blend from the outline well into the interior.

Once your first circle is done, wash your brush off quickly and completely and load up with just water. We're going to add a neighboring circle to create a bleed, using WOW.

Bring your loaded brush to your paper and outline and fill in a circle of plain water next to your first circle, making sure not to touch the two shapes just yet. Once your second circle is fully wet, take the point of your brush and increase the size of this second circle by outlining it wider and closer to that first, filled-in blue circle you've just painted. Eventually let the two shapes "kiss." If your first circle is still wet or damp, you should see an explosion of color blossoming into the new wet circle. This is called *bleeding*. This method works best when the two colors that are touching contrast strongly with each other. So the circle with just water in it is either bleeding a bloom of lightening water into the darker turquoise circle, or turquoise is bleeding into the circle with just water, adding a little burst of color.

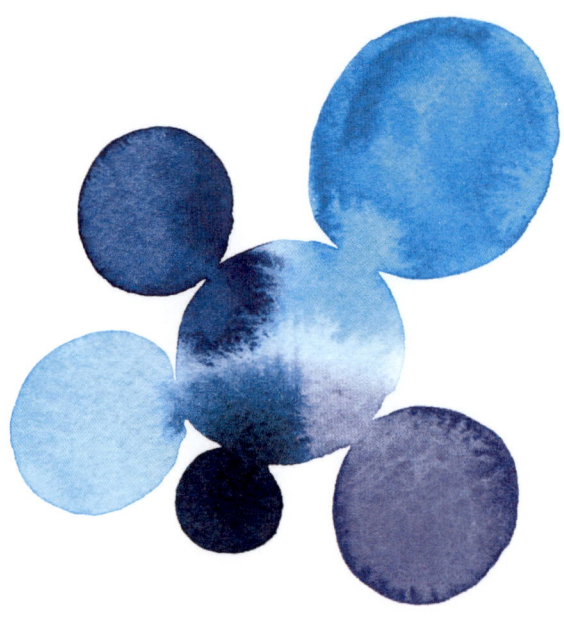

Add more neighboring circles and watch the colors explode and bleed! Keep in mind that too much overlapping will create muddiness. When your two shapes are about to touch, make sure they barely come into contact. That's why it's called a kiss! No one likes a sloppy wet kiss, am I right?

STEP TWO:

Choose a color palette

For our second piece together, we're going to start adding more color by using an analogous color scheme. For yesterday's piece, we talked about adding contrast to a single hue with value and saturation; today we'll be adding a range of hues. The analogous color scheme uses adjacent colors on the color wheel (see page 11), so the changes between hues is more subtle. This color palette creates a serene and harmonious effect in your piece.

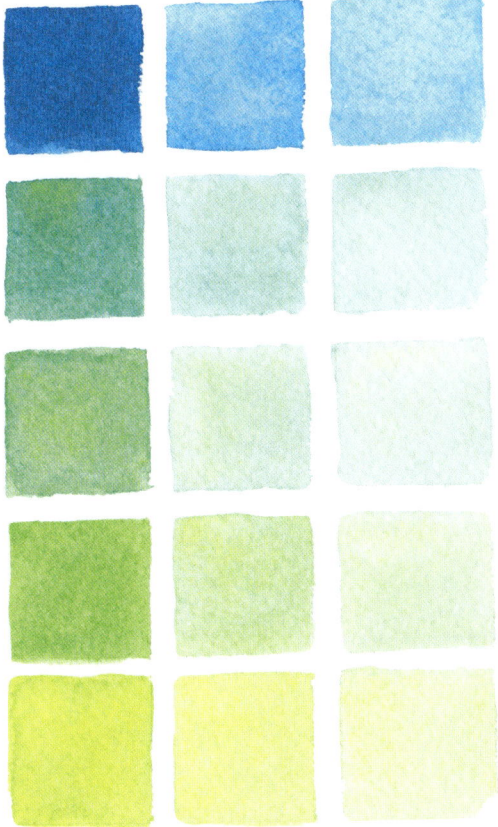

For today's piece I recommend sticking with two or three different hues and varying their value and saturation throughout, like we did on day 1 with Prussian Blue. Using the full range of possible hues can be quite overwhelming, so for my example piece I've chosen to paint using the range from turquoise to green and yellow-green. Instead of using Prussian Blue and Winsor & Newton Lemon Yellow Deep to mix up my hues, I've used turquoise to create a more vibrant, eye-catching green. As you can see, Prussian Blue and yellow produce a very different green from what you get with turquoise and yellow.

Let's give it a try!

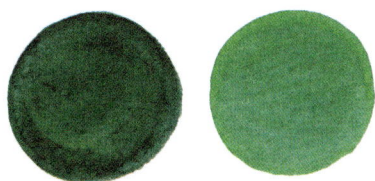

STEP THREE:

Put paint to paper

Now it's time to put these practice shapes to the test! Even for abstract, basic shape pieces I prefer to visualize my painting on the paper before actually putting paint down. I choose my overall color palette, decide what kind of focal points I want to create, and consider how I'm going to add variety to the piece with sizes, colors, and value. Once I'm ready to begin, I'll structure the composition of the piece the same way we did in day 1: from the top left corner down to the bottom right corner. Try this out with the piece shown here as a reference. Don't be intimidated by the myriad of circles here—have fun with it! A lot of unexpected surprises can happen when you're just playing and practicing. Get used to how your brushes work to form basic shapes, and take note of color balance and different mixtures and how they work together. You'll thank yourself later for this practice. If your shapes are looking wonky or oddly shaped because you're rushing to paint, remember that this is practice, and refinement will come with time.

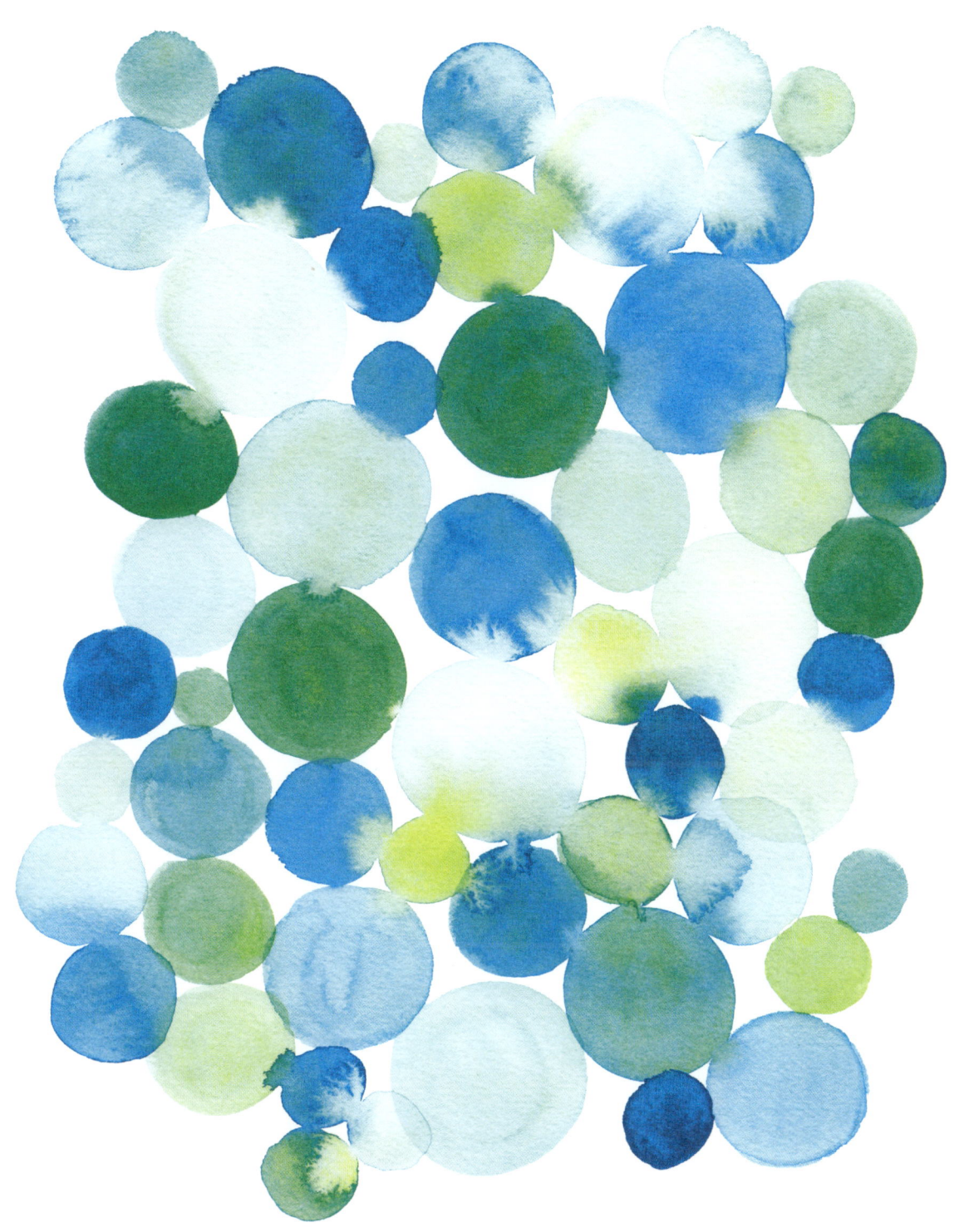

Day Three

STRAIGHT LINES AND TRIANGLES

Apply previous techniques to triangles. Develop muscle memory for straight lines, and practice layering shapes using the WOW technique.

Estimated time: 20 to 30 minutes

STEP ONE:

Warm up with straight lines and triangles using different stroke widths

Today, our first step will be developing confidence and muscle memory for straight lines and triangles. Many people struggle with how to achieve steady lines, so today's exercise will help with that. Similar to yesterday, we're going to start with just lines. Try them out in different angles, and take your time with this step—especially if you have shaky lines! Just as you drew circles, you'll create a thin line by pointing the tip of the brush straight down with the handle pointed to the sky and a light pressure that doesn't spread the tip.

To gain confidence with painting straight lines, practice painting steady lines by creating triangles. Start with just outlines of triangles first, then after a few of these, paint filled-in triangles. Refer back to step one of the previous day to refresh your memory if needed. Remember to move your arm for steady outlines and use the belly of the brush to fill in shapes quickly. Try out different sizes and widths, lighter and darker triangles, and so on to get comfortable with the shape and to develop muscle memory.

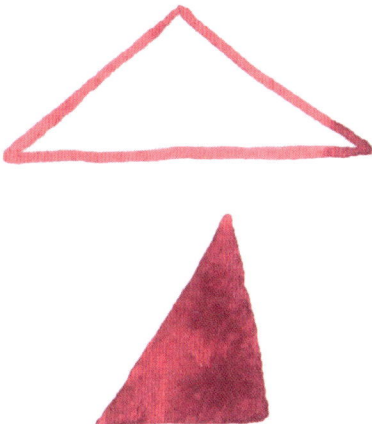

STEP TWO:

Choose a color palette

For today's piece, we're going to continue painting with an analogous color combination using warm colors. Today's colors derive from red, yellow, and orange. On the color wheel, warm colors start with the primary color yellow and go all the way to red-violet. Picture splitting the wheel in half; the top colors are considered warm, while the bottom colors are cool.

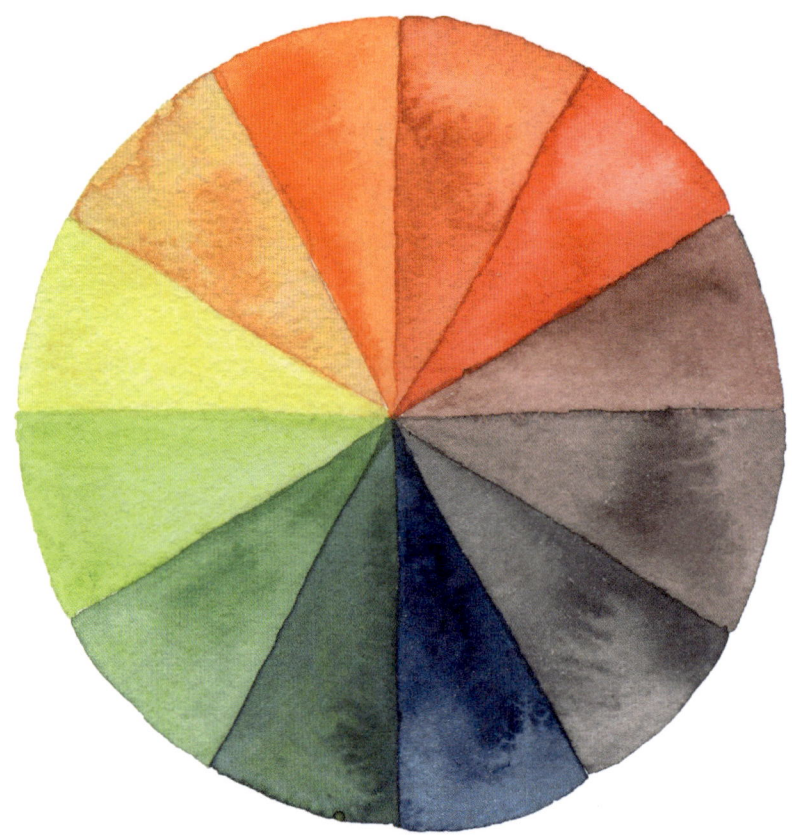

You're going to apply the same knowledge and techniques we discussed on day 2 for an analogous palette, but now with warm colors. In contrast to cool colors, warm colors are vibrant and bold. They combine the feeling of fire and excitement and can be overwhelming if used excessively. So for this piece, think of ways you can tone down the intensity by using lighter values of warm colors to create more subtlety. For the piece we're about to paint, I used an analogous color palette ranging from Winsor & Newton Opera Rose (pink) to Lemon Yellow Deep instead of Scarlet Lake (red) and yellow. This is another way to help soften the piece.

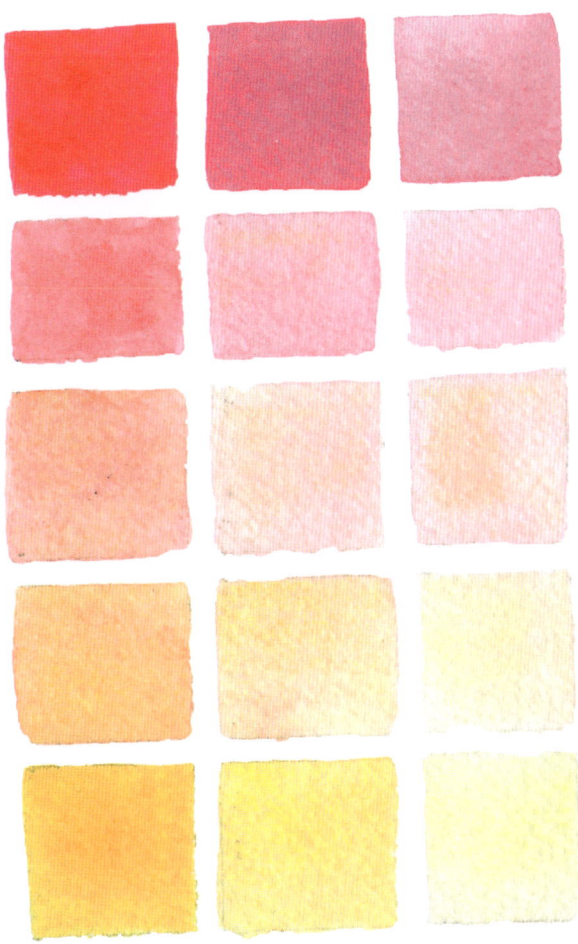

So you'll see pink, pink-orange, orange, and some yellow-orange and yellow. I have expanded the number of hues a bit; because we're using mostly subtle colors, it's a nice way to bring in more variety with lighter values. Because most of the triangles we'll be painting are on the lighter side, this makes using the WOD technique easier, as more transparent, water-diluted colors dry more quickly.

STEP THREE:
Put paint to paper

For a piece containing lots of triangles, the smaller round-tip brushes, like size 6 or 2, are best to move around the tighter corners. Don't let your ideas about color and composition get in the way of flow and expression; enjoying the process is far more rewarding than planning and methods. Stay loose, trust your gut, and play! Practice using the WOD technique to layer triangles, and build on what you've learned already with some WOW color bleeding. Alter the angles and sizes of each triangle to help create movement throughout the piece. Use this example for reference only; if you try to re-create it exactly, you'll lose sight of the real goal: developing your own muscle memory and technique.

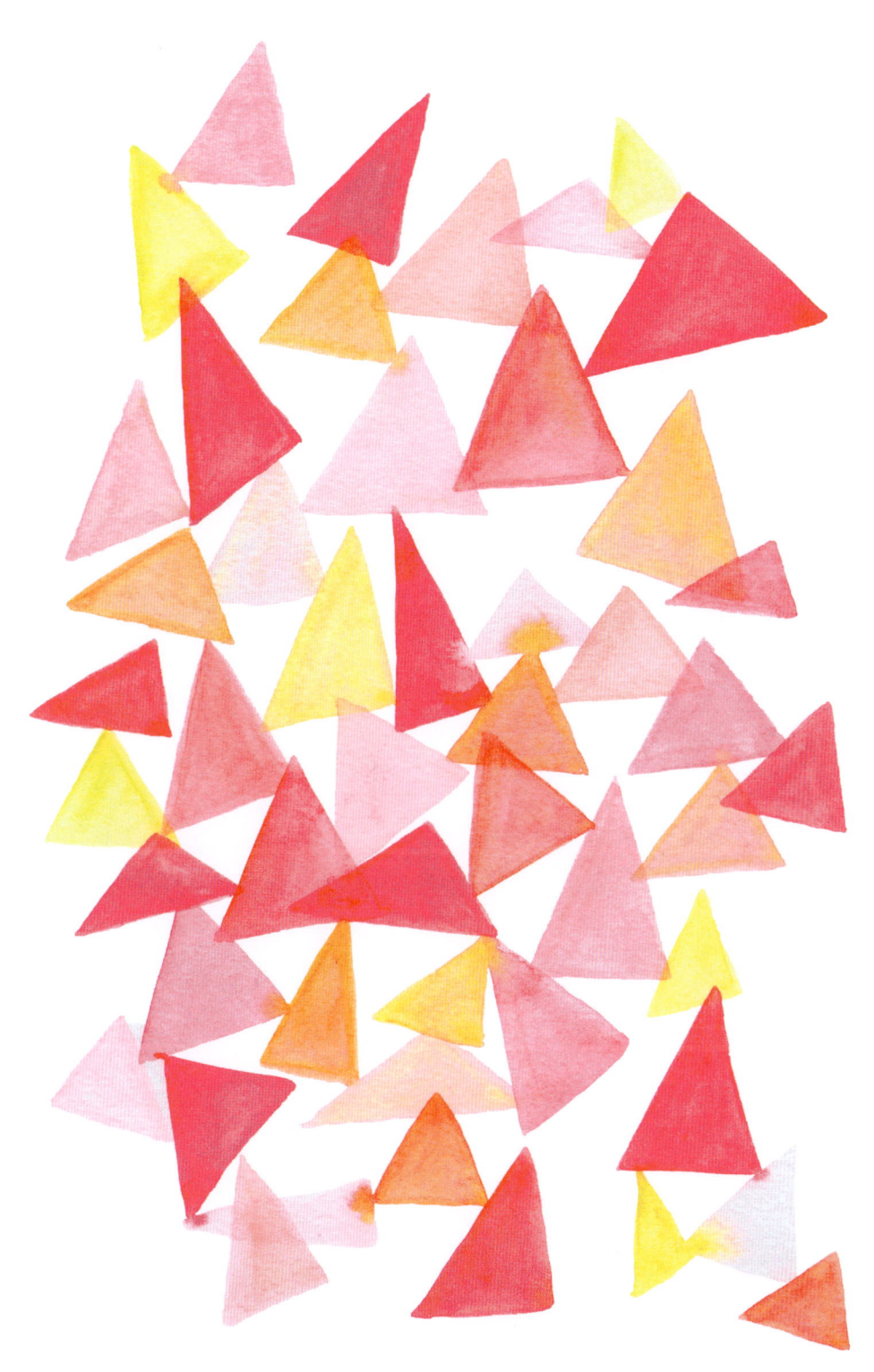

Day Four

LAYOUT

Build on previous techniques, composing a more detailed shapes piece with hexagons. Practice warm versus cool color dominance, balance, and sketching of preliminary shapes before painting.

Estimated time: 30 to 45 minutes

STEP ONE:

Sketch

First, let's discuss the basic techniques for sketching. While most abstract painting can be done freehand, pieces with more pattern and detail always look best when you take the time to sketch prior to painting, using your HB pencil to lightly lay down shapes. If your hand is feeling shaky or it's still difficult for you to create steady lines, use a ruler to create crisp triangles and hexagons for this piece. Don't worry too much about precision and making these shapes perfect—the more triangles you add, the less you'll notice any little mistakes.

Let's start by outlining hexagon shapes, sketching lightly so the pencil lines won't show through your paint later. Outline six sides for each hexagon, and vary the sizes so there's movement. Place each hexagon directly next to its neighbor with a small gap between them. The closer together the shapes are, the more detailed and complex the piece will seem.

Once you're happy with the placement of your hexagons, you can start sketching triangles or cubes within each hexagon. Draw lines from each corner of the hexagon toward the center. Make sure you leave gaps between the lines, as you will paint each triangle or shape a different color.

Do this throughout each hexagon until you're finished and ready to paint.

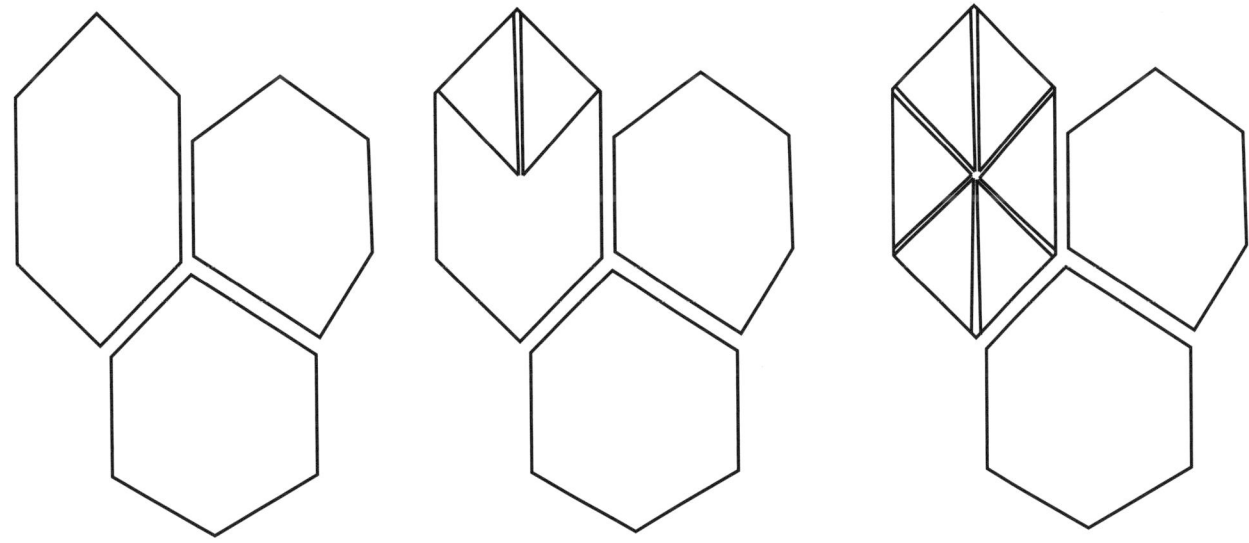

STEP TWO:

Choose a color palette

So far we've covered painting with a monochromatic palette, an analogous palette with cool colors, and an analogous palette with warm colors. Now it's time to include both warm *and* cool colors to practice how to effectively use complementary colors. Complementary colors can seem harsh and hard to look at when used in their unaltered hues. Red and green, for example, can dominate a piece and create too much strain, forcing your viewers to look away quickly. But when you use complementary colors more subtly, they can be very intriguing. There's a good reason they're called complementary colors!

Complementary colors are also known as contrasting colors. These hues lie opposite each other on the color wheel, so they are furthest away from each other in likeness. So, you're asking, how do we make these combinations more subtle? Think of blue and orange, for instance. Place a vibrant royal blue next to an equally vibrant orange, and they'll compete with each other on the intensity scale. When this happens, the contrast is more apparent. Used sparingly, this strong contrast can be effective. But for the most part, pairing a rich blue with a lighter, softer orange can help temper the competition between the two colors. The combination is still striking and powerful, but now it's less abrasive.

For the piece we're going to paint today, I've come up with a balance of highly saturated and more intense warm and cool colors; you'll see the difference compared with their lighter counterparts. I've also thrown in hints of turquoise to help intensify the cool colors, making them appear more dominant in the piece compared with the warm colors. Check out the warm and cool colors I've used—cool colors on top, warm colors below. See how they both create pop and intensity, but don't cause strain or disharmony?

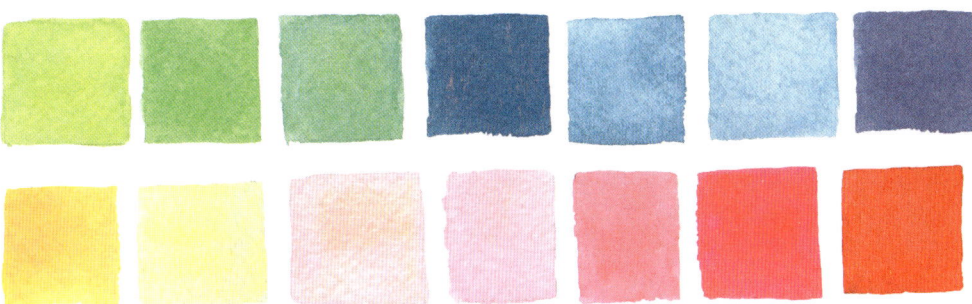

Important note: As mentioned in the introduction, I paint using two cups of water to rinse off my brushes: one for removing pigment from my brush, the other with clean water to load up the brush before grabbing a new color. Now that we're starting to paint with cool and warm colors, it's crucial that we use two cups of water and keep one clean for picking up new color. Having just one cup of water would result in using brown water to pick up paint, making all your colors muddy, because contrasting colors mixed together make brown!

STEP THREE:

Put paint to paper

Now that we've nailed down the palette for this piece, it's time to paint. For these smaller, tighter shapes I used mostly my size 2 round brush. For larger triangles I used my size 6 brush. As you can see, in this piece there's very little bleeding, as there are gaps between the triangles, so there's no pressure to paint rapidly to use the WOW technique. Just don't get too caught up in doing this "correctly." Stay loose and allow yourself to lay down color almost spontaneously. Study the colors you're using and how they complement and create balance beforehand; this will help you enjoy the flow of the process.

I start all my basic shapes pieces from the top left corner and work my way down (I am right-handed). Throughout a piece like this, I may step back from time to time and see that a shape lower down is just calling for a particular color, and I'll jump ahead and do that. But for the most part, I paint them all in order. Ask yourself periodically: Does it feel too harsh? Too subtle? Where are my areas of contrast with light and dark values? Where are my areas of break and areas of subtlety? With each new piece, you are practicing and building on what you've already learned to make it better than the last.

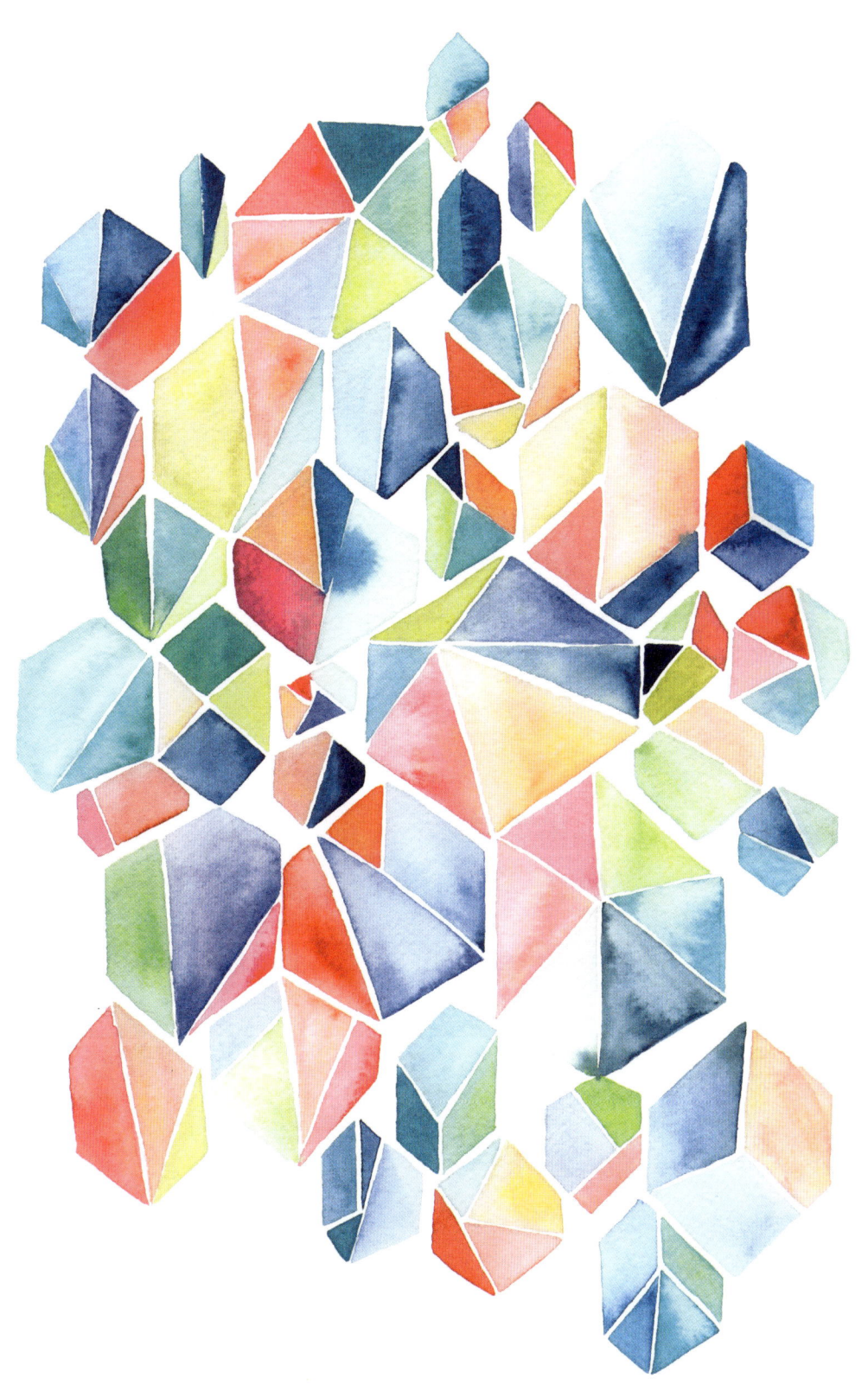

Day Five

COMPOUND STROKES

Learn the "S" curve by illustrating stems and leaves. Practice compound brush strokes, using pressure and release.

Estimated time: 30 to 40 minutes

STEP ONE:

Warm up with "C" curves

Building on how we outlined basic shapes in previous days, we're going to continue practicing using your arm to bring a fine line across the page by painting "C" and "S" curves. These two curves are foundational to anything you will sketch or paint. With a combination of these curves and basic shapes, you can break down the structure of literally anything. We'll break this down further on later days, but for now we'll focus on mastering the curves themselves.

Let's get started with a basic "C" curve for a stem. Load up your size 6 brush with a mixture of Winsor & Newton Burnt Umber and a touch of Winsor & Newton Mars Black, making it a darker shade of Burnt Umber. Apply a little bit of pressure for the base of the stem, making it like a dot. Next, trace an arc or a "C" curve from left to right across your paper, about 3 inches long.

 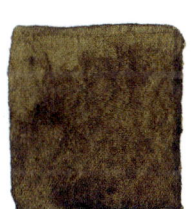 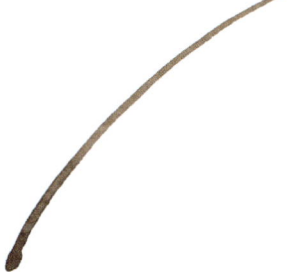

Remember from previous days how to create a thin line, with little pressure and proper brush technique. Practice this motion a few times, repeating the stroke and becoming steadier in your lines as you practice. Try "C" curves with a steeper arch, or move the highest point of the curve to the right or left. Get used to how each variation feels by repeating a few times.

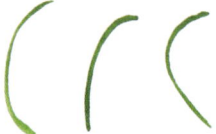

Make sure to not curve your stem back around in an "S" curve—that will make your stem look more like seaweed. Just one arch per stem.

STEP TWO:
Warm up with "S" curves

Now that we've practiced stems using "C" curves, we are going to define the "S" curve with a compound brush stroke, using two different types of strokes in one motion—in this case, a wide stroke using more pressure on the brush to fan out the hairs, and a thinner stroke with less pressure. This will make a mark that goes from really wide at the base to a thinner tip, with the outer edge of the stroke resembling an "S" curve. This compound stroke forms one half of a leaf.

To practice this, mix up a green leafy color. For the examples below, I used Winsor & Newton Sap Green. Load up your brush with paint and hold it so the handle points toward where you want your leaf point. Then place the brush tip on the paper and draw it across, starting with heavy pressure, then gradually releasing pressure as you draw it upward. Starting with pressure allows your brush to fan out, creating a wider base on the leaf. As you continue upward, releasing pressure, the leaf shape should slowly narrow to a point.

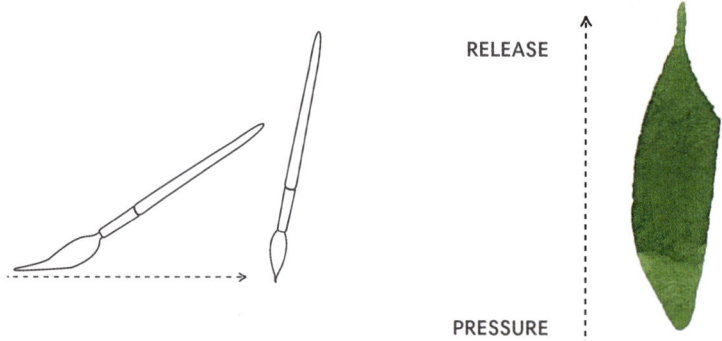

RELEASE

PRESSURE

With this compound stroke you have created an "S" curve that, when you pair it with a second compound stroke, creates a basic leaf. To complete the leaf, you'll repeat the compound stroke you just used to paint the first half of the leaf. Make sure to start and meet at the same points as you did with your first stroke, so it's an even "S" curve on both sides.

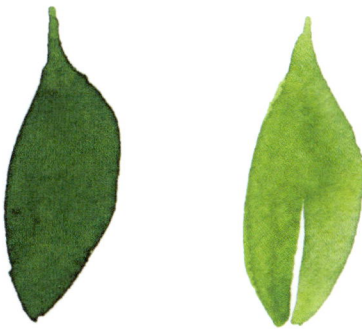

In this example, the leaf on the right has a gap between the two sides or "S" curves—I'll sometimes leave this gap in a leaf to create a natural highlight.

STEP THREE:

Use curves to paint a stem and leaves with hue and value variation

For this next step, we will combine steps one and two to create a full stem and later a wreath. To start, use your size 6 brush to paint a stem in a "C" curve, then add miniature "C" curves as stems for the leaves you will add.

In this example, I've staggered these mini "C" curves along the larger stem, going back and forth on either side. Don't make these too long, as that would make your stem look sparse once you add leaves. Once you've painted all the stems, you'll begin adding leaves.

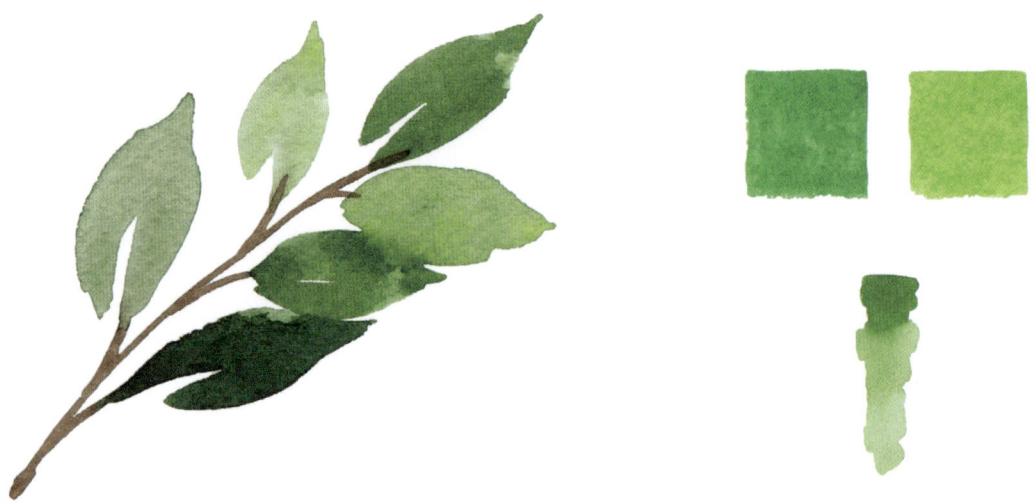

To create variety in the leaves, you'll start with the darkest value of the green hue, then add water to lighten the value as you work your way up the stem. For my colors, I've mixed up greens using Sap Green and Prussian Blue, Sap Green and Lemon Yellow Deep, and lighter values of both of these mixtures. Subtle changes in hue and value from leaf to leaf along the stem help create movement and depth of field. If all the leaves were the same hue and value of green, it would look pretty flat and boring. Have fun and practice this technique with an individual stem a few times before we jump into our final piece.

STEP FOUR:
Put paint to paper

For our final piece, we'll create a wreath by sketching a light circle as a guide, then forming the wreath stem by stem. In the example, I've incorporated only varying values and hues of green, without any brown for the stems. Follow the curve of your light circle sketch, and feel free to overlap stems and leaves.

Tip: *Alter the shade of your stems and leaves by adding Mars Black for a smokier look. The example on the left has just a touch of black; I added more to the mixture for the leaves on the right. I also used some WOW technique for explosions of color between two overlapping leaves. Isn't that a fun effect?*

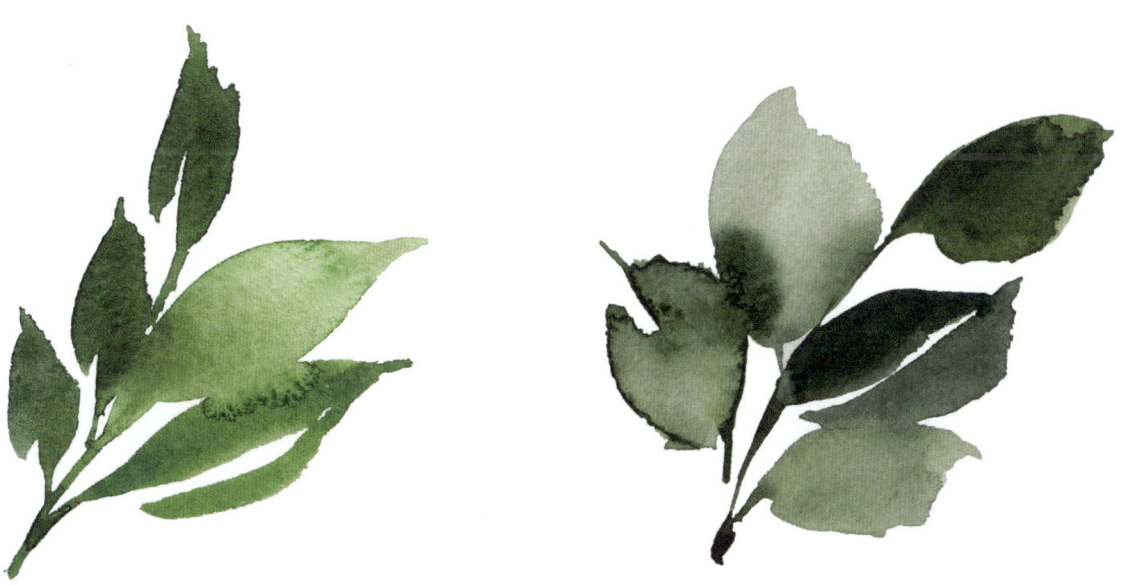

Day Six

COMPLEX CURVES

Build on previous techniques by playing with hue and value variety with different types of leaves using compound strokes.

Estimated time: 20 to 30 minutes

STEP ONE:

Choose a color palette

For this exercise we're going to get loose with our strokes. This requires painting rather quickly. When working on the faster side, I always like to mix up most of my colors beforehand. This ensures that I'm not wasting precious time mixing secondary colors while paint is drying. Today's piece will include a conglomeration of a few types of leaves including peony, thyme, sage, and eucalyptus varieties. Each leaf is broken down into its basic forms; taking this in steps is a lot less intimidating. This is a loose, more abstract style of painting as opposed to detailed and realistic, so for our colors, we'll mix up two hues per leaf that convey the essence of that particular leaf. Here are the swatches and their color formulas for you to reference and mix up before painting.

Winsor Green + Lemon Yellow Deep

Peony leaves—use more yellow to accent with a brighter hue, the darker green for shadows.

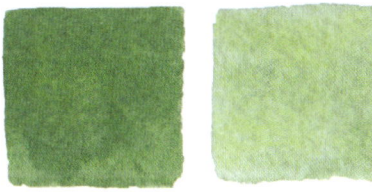

Prussian Blue + Lemon Yellow Deep

Sage leaves—lighten these mixtures with lots of water for a softer look.

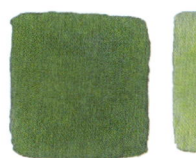  

Prussian Blue + Lemon Yellow Deep + Mars Black

Thyme leaves—same mixture as for sage, but with an added value of a deep, dark green. Add black to your color to darken.

Eucalyptus leaves—for a smokier look, use turquoise, black, and lots of water to lighten your mixture.

Phthalo Turquoise + Mars Black

STEP TWO:

Put paint to paper

If you need to warm up before diving into painting these stems and leaves, go back through yesterday's exercise for practice.

The following is a list of each leaf and its guides. In essence, each leaf is just a slight variation of the compound "S" curve we painted yesterday. Apply what you've already practiced in previous days, and don't be afraid to try something multiple times—this will help you develop muscle memory.

Two-toned peony leaves: Similar to the leaves in yesterday's exercise, these are two-sided and will start and end at the same spots. The only difference with this stroke is that you're extending each leaf to be longer. After putting in the "C" curve stems, start with a deeper Sap Green mixture for one side of the leaf, then add yellow to this mixture for a contrast on the other side.

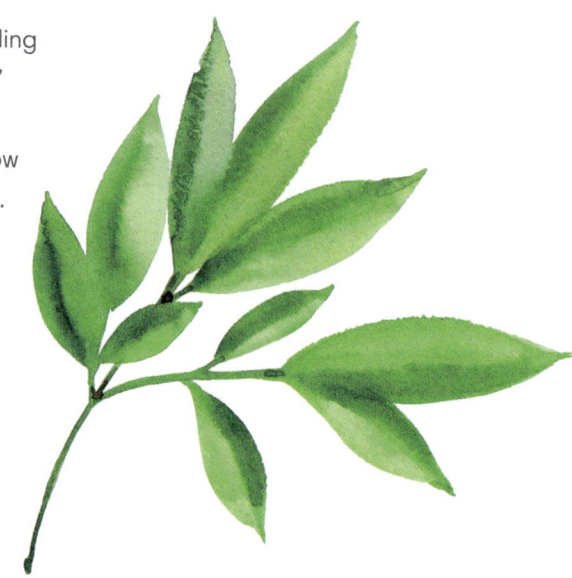

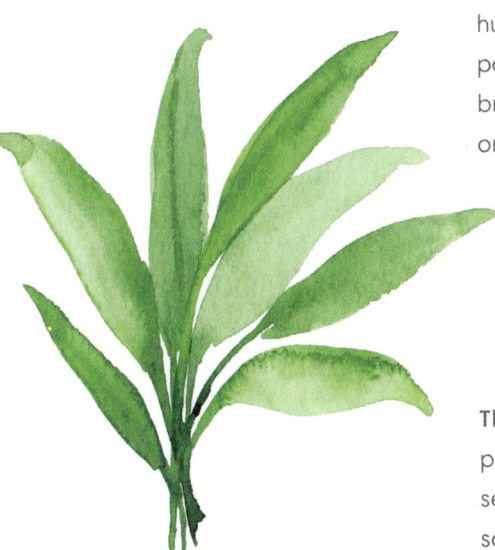

Sage leaves: Sage leaves are similar to the peony leaves, but because these herbs are more delicate, the hues are much lighter, and the leaves are rounded, not pointed. Add a bit of texture or wave as you bring your brush up the side of the leaf, so it's not a smooth "C" or "S" curve. This will show that the sage leaves ripple.

Thyme leaves: These are similar to the first leaves we practiced on day 5, with groups or clusters forming sections up the stem. Thyme leaves aren't very big, so use your size 2 brush to paint them.

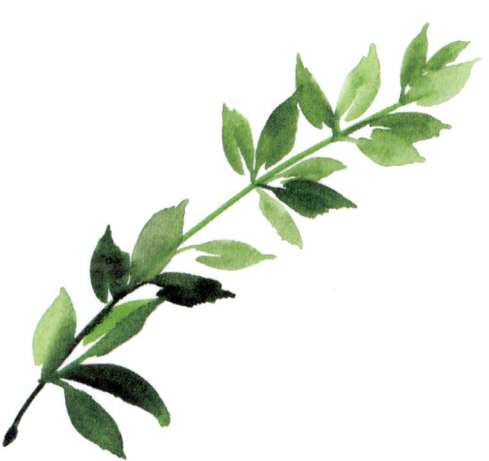

Eucalyptus leaves: For this cluster of leaves, you'll use compound strokes as in the previous exercises but wider at the middle of your leaves, making more of an oval shape. You can let the leaves overlap; because you're using the same hue throughout the stem, this won't cause muddy colors. Make sure to vary the lightness from leaf to leaf for a feeling of movement.

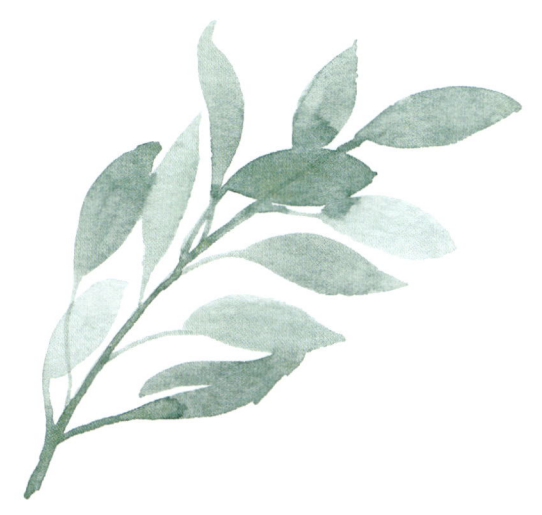

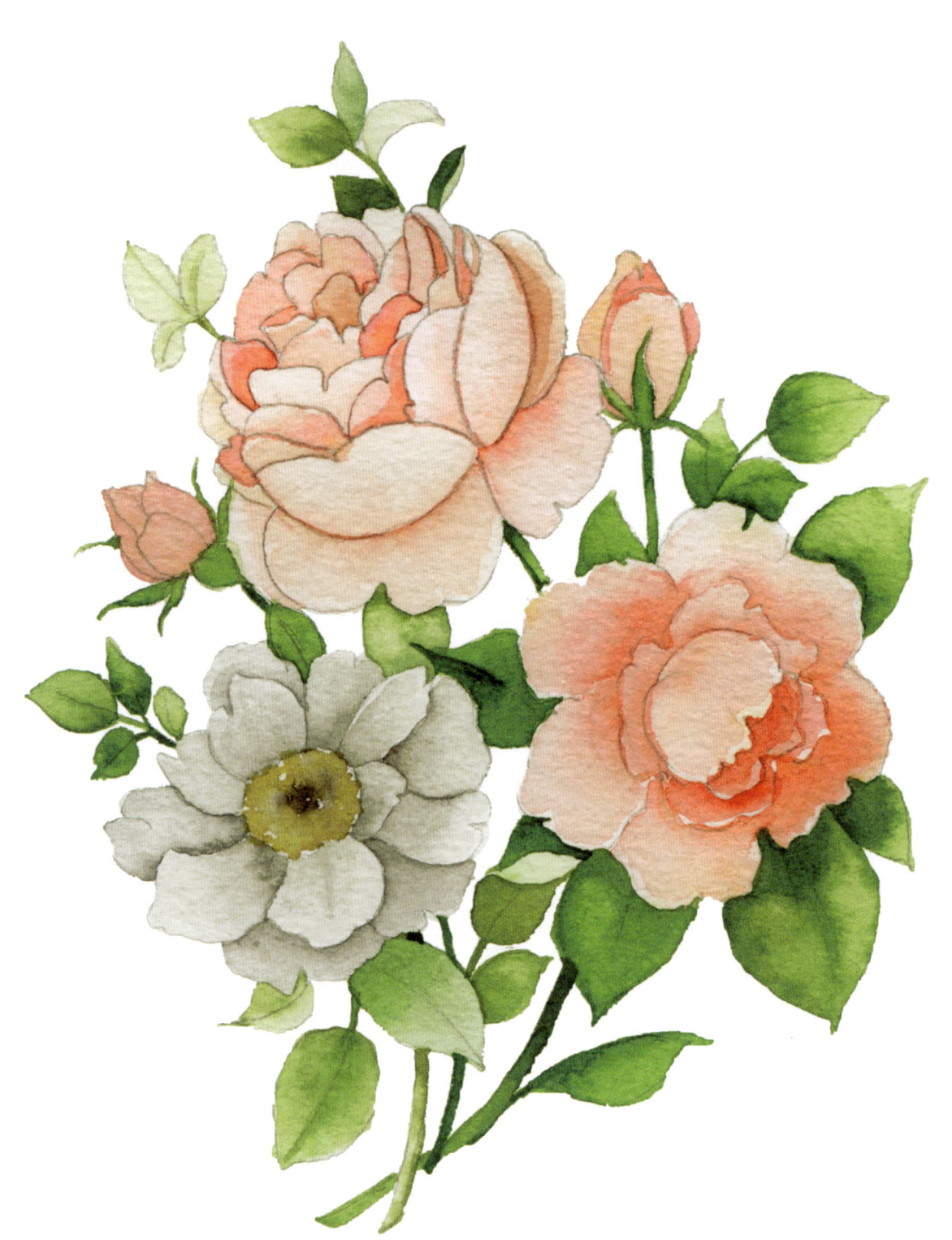

Section Two

FORM, PERSPECTIVE, AND LIGHT

Ready for the next challenge? Now that we've covered basic brush and color mixing techniques with shapes and curves, it's time to transform these basics into more dimensional forms. In this section, we'll be discussing how shading affects the form and light of an object.

Day Seven

LIGHT TO DARK LAYERING

Learn brush technique for dots and marks and how to shade a spherical form in layers.

Estimated time: 30 to 40 minutes

STEP ONE:
Warm up with marks

Today we're going to paint a basic tree. I'll show you how to bring the form of the tree forward with a basic shading technique: applying dots or marks. What do I mean by marks? Simply taking the point of your brush and lightly dabbing your paper with paint. This type of stroke will add textures representing the abundance found in nature, such as leaves in trees or berries on a stem. Now, you may be thinking, *Painting dots? Sounds easy!* But this brush technique can be tricky; it's easy to overthink it. These marks aren't planned out, but randomly placed; if done in excess, they can overwhelm and spoil a painting.

To begin, practice this stroke by itself using your size 6 brush. Point the brush downward and use only the tip to just lightly poke at the paper. Try changing the angle of your brush or paper, and see how just changing the angle of your brush alters the size and shape of the mark. Practice this a few times and get used to how this feels.

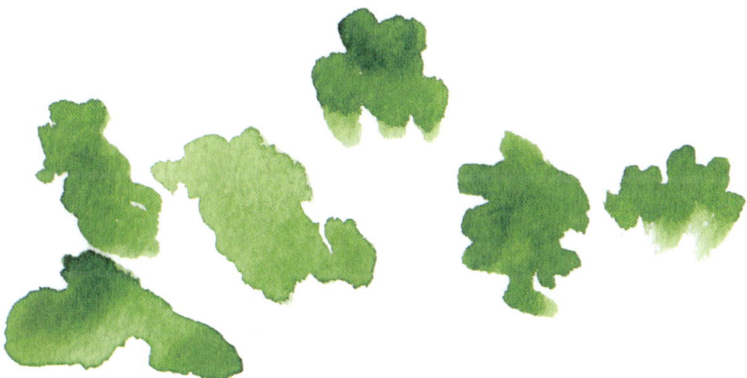

STEP TWO:
Sketch

Now it's time to build a tree from basic shapes. We're going to start with a sketch using the HB pencil. Outline the trunk first, using two "C" curves and erasing marks if necessary until you come up with a proportional tree trunk. Next, sketch the crown of the tree—the leaf area—by drawing four circles above the trunk. You can vary the placement, but this looks similar to the way most trees grow, with the largest circle on top of three smaller circles below it. See the sketches that follow for reference.

Tip: We won't need to define or sketch in shading like the final sketch on the right; you'll do that with paint in the next step. Just start with basic circles, then an outline of the crown that shows the contour of the tree. These sketches are just guides; before you begin painting, you'll erase the basic shapes (circles) sketch.

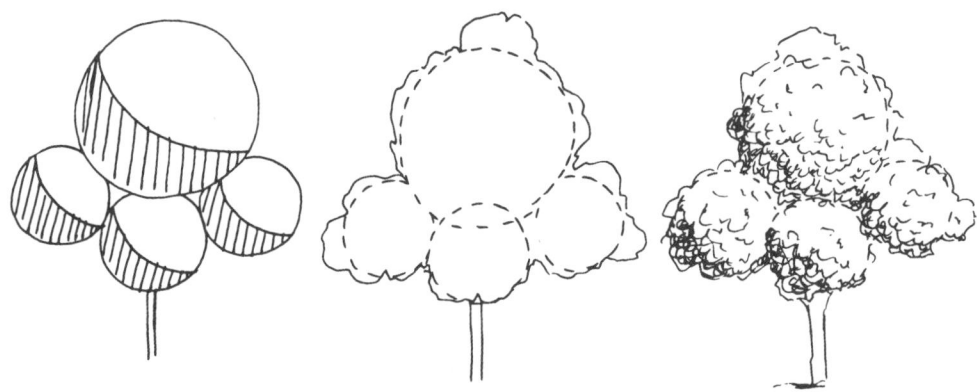

The sketch on the left is a guide to help you understand how basic shading of a sphere or circle works. The tree example on the right defines it even more realistically. The shadows will be deepest near the base of each sphere and lightest where it's closest to the light source. Do you see the difference in form between the middle sketch and the more final one on the right? By sketching and shading properly, you're essentially forming light. Always break down your subjects into their basic shapes first so you can understand how they should be shaded to create dimension.

STEP THREE:
Put paint to paper

FIRST LAYER
Once your sketch is done, it's time to paint in the base layer of the trunk. Mix up a light wash of Burnt Umber with a touch of Mars Black. Add lots of water for this first layer; then, with the belly of your size 2 brush, paint right up to the outer edges of the trunk sketch.

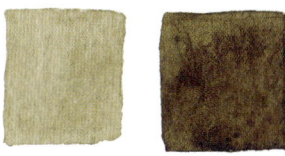

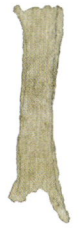

Once you've painted this first layer, quickly load up your brush with a slightly thicker, darker value of brown and lightly drag the point along the left edge of the trunk, barely touching the outer rim of your first layer, using WOW. You should see your darker value start to bleed and blend into the lighter wash. Then clean your brush, and with just water, drag the belly across the base of the trunk for ground and a slight shadow effect. If you don't like the way something in particular is blending, grab a paper towel and dab it up. Paper towels make great erasers when paint is still wet.

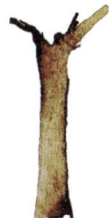

SECOND LAYER

For the leaves, we're going to paint in layers using WOD. There will be similarities to how we painted the trunk, only we'll be using spherical shading techniques. For this next step, pay attention to where each circle lines up; this will help guide your shadows. Take your size 6 or 16 brush and load it up with a light yellow-green wash. Paint in the wash using circular motions and dipping in water as you go to help move the paint along. Let this layer dry completely before adding the shadows.

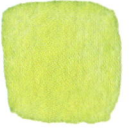  

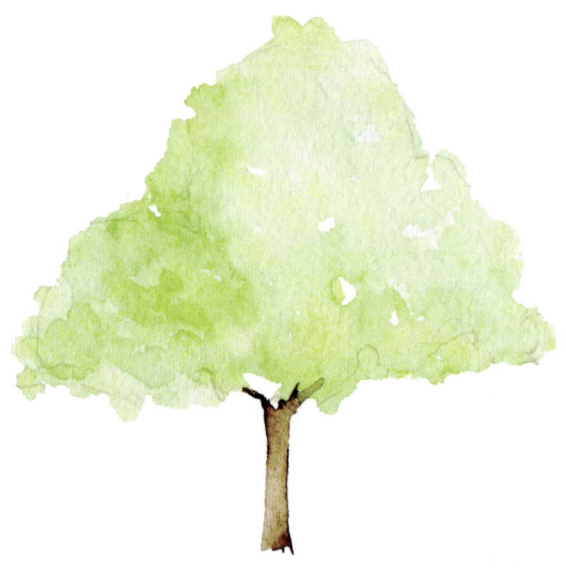

THIRD LAYER

Now that the base layer of your leaves is dry, load up your size 6 brush with a deep, thick mixture of Sap Green. With the tip, apply marks, placing your shadows in a curve along the base of each circle section, adding volume to the tree.

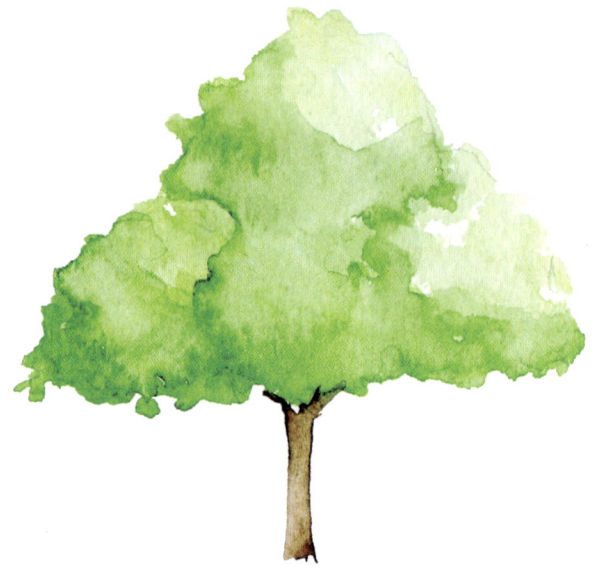

Remember the three tree sketches and how to shade a tree. These creases will be the darkest point, with a gradual transition from shadows to highlights.

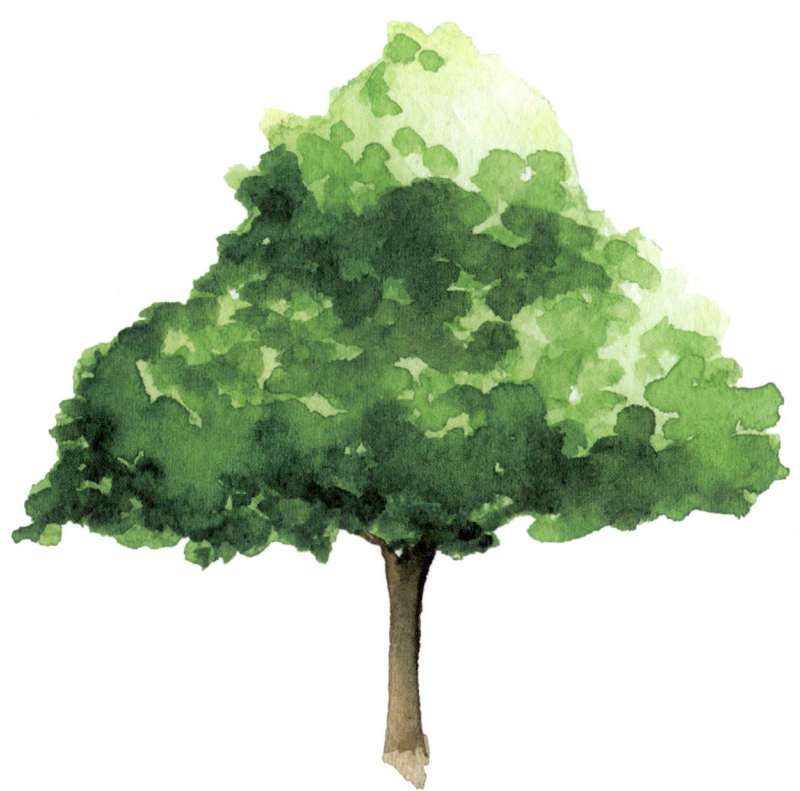

Tip: To add even more texture to your leaves, while this section is still wet, grab a paper towel and dab it around in the lighter areas, leaving the dimpled texture of the paper towel throughout the leaves.

See how the bases of these spherical shapes are emphasized with shadows and mid-tones? Make sure to not overshadow and cover up the highlights or the areas being hit by the light source, as this portion helps to show the form of the subject. We will be dissecting highlights, mid-tones, and shadows later on in this book, but today's exercise is a great practice in defining these important terms.

Day Eight

BACKGROUND AND FOREGROUND

Paint a forest to learn to evoke distance with tint, shade, and basic value variation using WOD.

Estimated Time: 45 minutes to 1 hour

STEP ONE:

Warm up

Throughout the rest of this book, I'll talk quite a bit about adding depth. Similar to what we discussed on day 5 with leaves on a stem, you want to create distance by adding darker and lighter values. For the piece we're painting today, we'll be depicting a thick forest of evergreen trees using WOD to add multiple layers of trees. But beyond just adding a bunch of trees to make the forest look dense, we need to add depth of field by placing darker trees in the foreground and lighter trees in the background. If you think about looking out to a horizon full of trees, the in-focus trees will be deeper, richer, and more detailed, while those far away will become progressively less detailed and faint in value.

Before we get into painting the full piece, let's warm up by painting a few individual evergreen trees. Start with the tip of your size 6 brush and paint a straight vertical line for the trunk, about 4 inches tall. Then flick your brush outward from either side of the trunk in shorter straight lines for branches and needles. Be loose with where you're adding these lines, flicking your brush across quickly, so these remain gestural and organic. Practice this a couple of times, and when you're comfortable, move on to the next step.

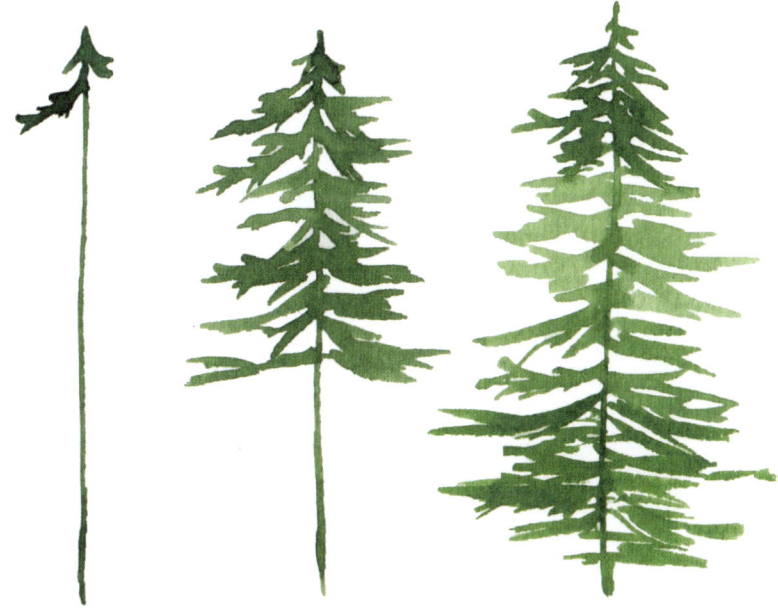

STEP TWO:

Choose a color palette

Here are a couple of variations of an evergreen tree. The first is a mixture of Phthalo Turquoise and Mars Black with water added to make it lighter; the second is Sap Green and a touch of Lemon Yellow Deep; and the third is Sap Green and Mars Black.

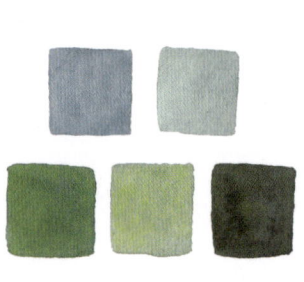 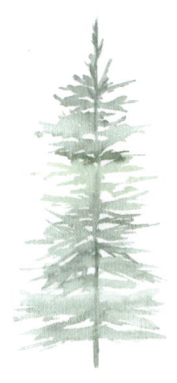 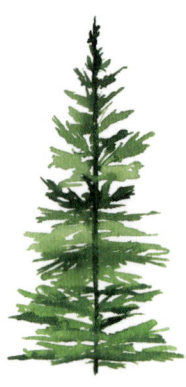 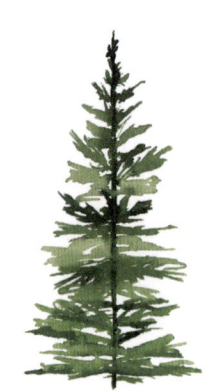

STEP THREE:

Put paint to paper

FIRST LAYER

To apply the first layer, use a very light Phthalo Turquoise and Mars Black mixture to add trees to the background. Allow these to overlap a little, and stagger their heights to appear more natural and dense.

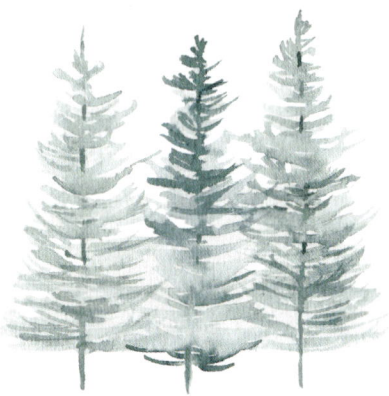

SECOND LAYER

Once the first layer of trees is dry, mix up a slightly more green and darker color to add the next row of trees. Because you're using WOD, this layer should appear closer and on top ("in front") of the first layer.

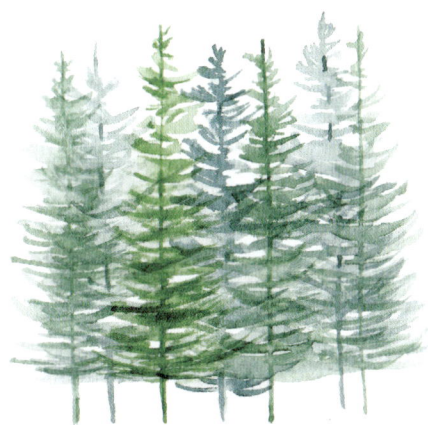

FINAL LAYER

As mentioned earlier, the trees in the foreground will be the richest, darkest hues, while those in the background will be gradually lighter and duller in color. For the final layer of trees, add a bit more green to your mixture for more dense color; then, as on the previous day, swipe the belly of your brush across the base of each trunk for gradual bleeding to create shading.

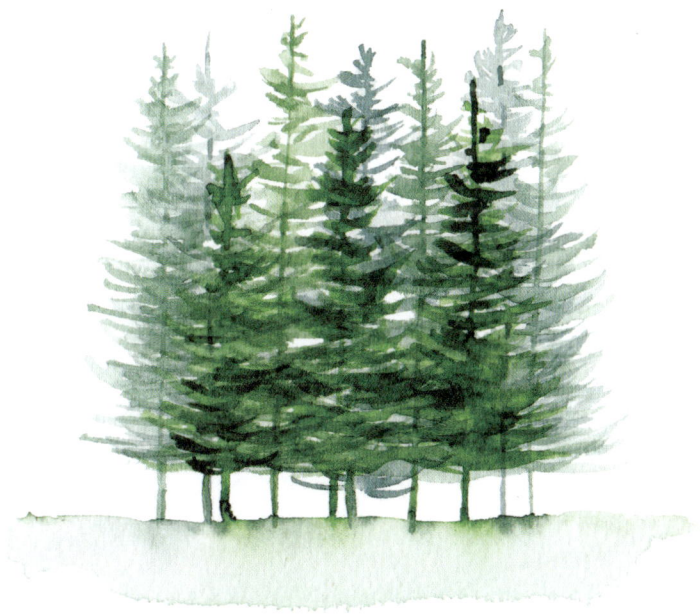

Day Nine

PATTERN

Break down form within complex botanical
elements and create patterns with layering.

Estimated time: 1 hour

STEP ONE:

Warm up

Are you ready to get wild? For today's piece, we will be creating a patterned floral painting consisting of poppies, stems, and leaves. It's going to be busy, and it's going to be so good. Don't be too intimidated by the finished piece (page 71); to simplify, we'll break down this pattern into its individual parts. We'll warm up with single flowers and leaves.

First, let's practice the flower. Use your size 6 brush to create an upside-down teardrop shape for the petals. Start with the fine point of your brush, then add pressure to create a wider upward stroke for the petal. At the top of each petal, loop back down to meet the base. Think of the head of a flower as a cone or cup shape: the outside petals are shorter than the central petals. Make sure that each petal points from the stem, so that all petals appear to be growing from one point. Vary them in height and width and even in hue or value. Practice this by following the step-by-step guide that follows.

 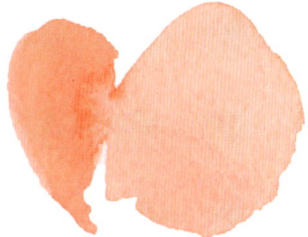 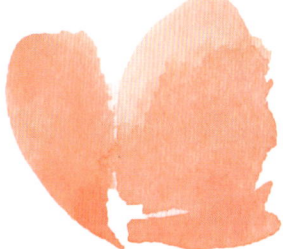

STEP TWO:
Choose a color palette

Instead of painting with traditional floral colors, we're going to continue to develop our eye for color harmonies by sticking with a two-color palette of complementary colors: blue and orange. Remember, complementary colors are hues directly across from each other on the color wheel, making them high in contrast. But when the value or hue is altered just slightly, the combination can be very powerful.

For today's piece, I mixed up a palette of blues using deep Prussian Blue, midnight blues, cobalt, and turquoise. For a more subtle orange, I used varying hues of Opera Rose and Lemon Yellow Deep. Shown here are of some of the individual pieces I used in the painting—practice these beforehand to make sure you're familiar with your mixtures.

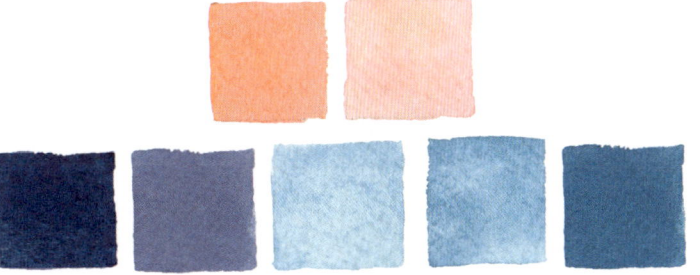

STEP THREE:

Put paint to paper

Now that you've practiced the individual pieces, let's paint the full picture. Similar to the structure and composition of days 1 through 3, I began this piece at the top left corner and gradually worked my way down the paper. You'll notice there's quite a bit of layering in this one. As I made my way down the paper, I came back to sections that appeared to be dry to add more pieces on top. The most important part when painting a piece like this is to not overthink it or give in to intimidation. Have fun! Yes, I know, having fun while painting is implied, but sometimes we need to be reminded to relax! This is practice, which is one step in further advancing your painting skills.

Remember to create movement with angles. Separate the different hues so they appear randomly down the page, applied in a zigzag fashion, making sure there's no buildup of similar hues in one section. Reference the completed piece for guidance, but make sure to create with your own flow and rhythm. It may help to picture the overall structure of this piece as if you found yourself in a field of wildflowers, plucked a handful of them, and tossed them up in the air to watch them land on your paper. That random, organic structure is what you're going for here. Color balance will help take that composition up a notch!

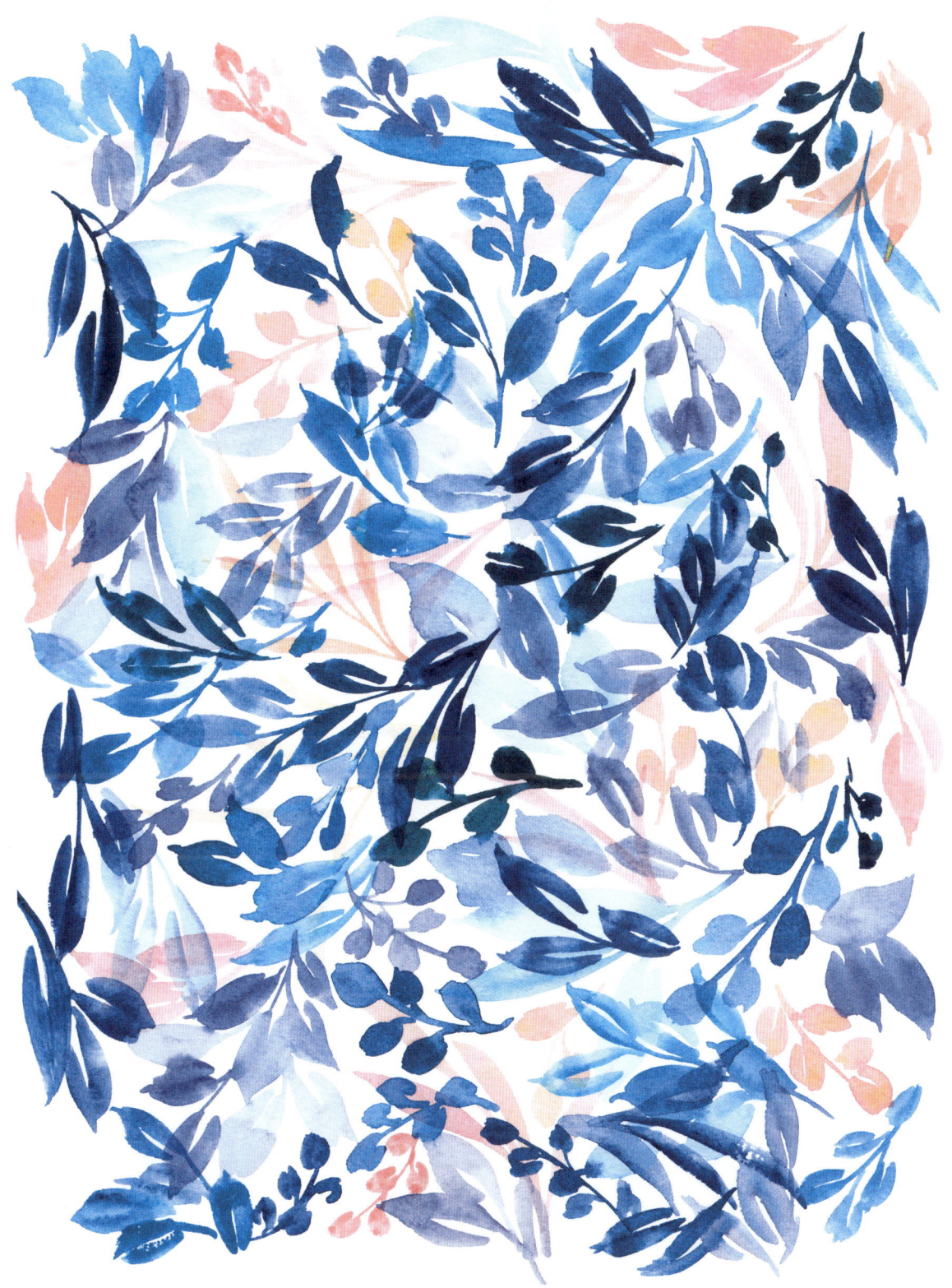

Day Ten

LIGHT SOURCE AND SHADING

Build on compound curves and shading for
a cylindrical form to paint a banana leaf.

Estimated time: 45 minutes

STEP ONE:

Sketch

Today we're going to cover basic knowledge of light source and shading techniques for a more defined form. A banana leaf is simply a combination of "S" curves and "C" curves. With your HB pencil, lightly sketch a "C" curve for the branch or main vein upward from the base to the tip of the leaf, curving it over to about 65 degrees. Just below the tip of the initial "C" curve, make an inverted "C" curve that comes two-thirds of the way down the main stem to form one side of the leaf. For the most natural look, both sides should start and meet at the same points on the leaf. Take a look at the sketch example for reference.

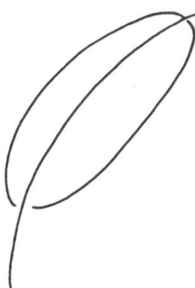

Once you have your basic curves down, add little inlets or tears in the leaf (characteristic of banana leaves), using two "C" curves. Make sure these point inward toward the center vein, not down.

Now that I have the contour sketch of a banana leaf, and I'm going to add two side-facing or folded leaves on either side. For these side-facing leaves, you're essentially sketching the first two curves of the previous leaf.

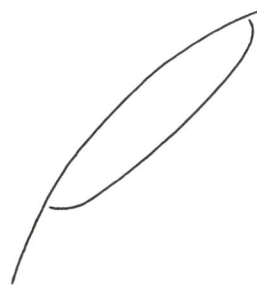
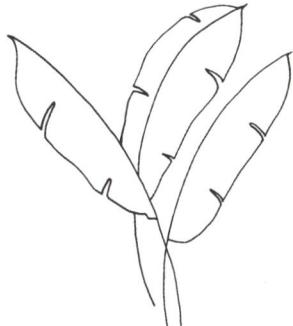

Note: When broken down, each side of a banana leaf curves like a cylinder, so shading will be very important to help accentuate this. Make sure your shadows and details aren't straight lines, but "C" curves, curving in the direction of the form. Also keep in mind where the light source is and how it is hitting the leaf. Take a look at the sketch for reference. The left side of the leaf has long, straight lines for shading and therefore makes the leaf feel more flat on that side, while on the right the short, curved lines indicate a more curled edge.

Correct shading

STEP TWO:

Put paint to paper

FIRST LAYER

To start, we're going to apply a light green wash to most of the first leaf on the far left. Load up your size 6 brush with a light mixture of Lemon Yellow Deep and Sap Green for your base layer. Paint this quickly, applying this base layer to most of the leaf, leaving the outer edge that's farthest from the light source dry to add our next layer: mid-tones.

Once this layer is done and still wet, quickly load up the same brush with a mid-tone green (same hue, just a darker value). Apply this hue with the tip of your brush to the dry edge of the leaf that will be in shadow. Let these two layers "kiss" or diffuse into one another for WOW bleeding.

Now let that particular leaf rest, and practice the same technique with the rest of your banana leaves. Make sure to be consistent with where you choose to add mid-tones. If any leaves are touching or overlapping, wait for one of those leaves to dry first. Otherwise, these two leaves will blend together and create a blob—not what you want. After adding mid-tones, darken your paint mixture again for the shadows you'll add to accentuate any overlapping and parts of the leaves in shadow.

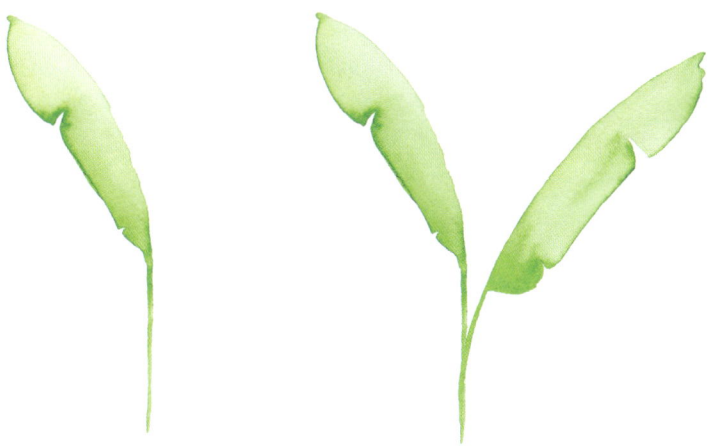

SECOND LAYER

While some of the leaves are still drying, you can go back over the dry leaves to add some basic detail. WOD technique works only when you work from light to dark; WOW is perfect for achieving a soft blend and shading bigger areas. Use the hue you have already mixed up for the previous step of shadow tones; darken it just a touch by adding black or more Sap Green. Grab your size 2 round brush and begin by outlining the outer edge of the shaded area. From there, draw out thin "C" curves from the leaf's midrib of varied lengths up the face of the leaf and from the outer rim of the leaf toward the midrib. Make sure these smaller curves parallel each other, pointing in the same direction. On an open-faced leaf, leave a section through the middle of each side of the leaf for a highlight.

Day Eleven

VARIED HUE BLENDING

Learn to blend a variety of hues using WOW, and accentuate form with details using WOD.

Estimated time: 35 to 45 minutes

STEP ONE:

Sketch

Today we're going to cover forming a spherical shape with more in-depth shaping. You may have noticed by now that sketching basic shapes first helps with proportions; this also helps guide how to add shadows to a subject—as we practiced on day 7. It can be intimidating to go straight to the brushes to paint a more detailed subject with no idea where to start. Take, for example the next piece we're going to study: the gorgeous papaya. To get a feel for the correct proportions, we need to first lightly sketch its basic shapes.

You can break down the papaya shape into a circle and an oval, connected with curves. We're going to be painting both a whole fruit and a half fruit, so turn your paper horizontally and sketch these fruits next to each other. Lightly sketch out a circle for the base of the papaya, with an oval about 2 or 3 inches directly above, as shown below.

Next, you'll fill in the contour shape or outline of the fruit by adding two "C" curves on either side of the top oval. Then extend the outline of the circle to meet the curves on top. The whole fruit will have a dip in the top to show the stem end, and in the bottom to show the blossom end.

Do this for both pieces of fruit, and for the half papaya, in the middle of the fruit pencil in a light outline shaped like an almond; that's the cavity where the seeds are clustered.

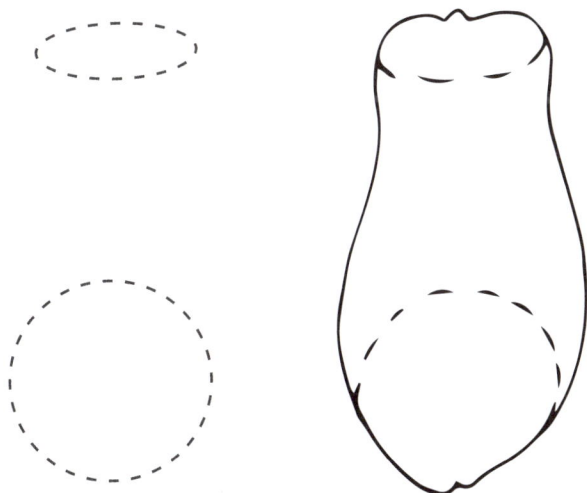

STEP TWO:

Choose a color palette

For today's piece, we'll use painting techniques similar to yesterday's, but instead of using just one hue, we're going to be painting with an analogous palette. The papaya's colorways complement each other so well: the flesh of the fruit is a gradient of orange to yellow-orange to yellow, while the skin of the fruit is another analogous combination of green, to yellow-green to yellow. The papaya really kills it in the color department!

For this piece I've used Cadmium Orange mixed with Lemon Yellow Deep for the papaya flesh. The green I used for the skin, a blend of Sap Green and Lemon Yellow Deep, will also be added to this portion of the fruit for the gradation from green to yellow.

  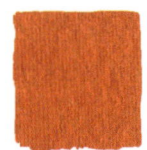  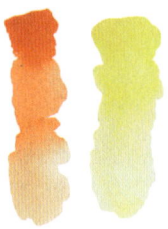

STEP THREE:

Put paint to paper

FIRST LAYER (PAPAYA HALF)

Next, we'll add a light layer to the half papaya. Load up your size 16 brush with a lighter value of Lemon Yellow Deep. Apply this yellow wash to the inner part of the half papaya, avoiding the seed section and painting quickly. Remember to keep loading up with water to keep this section wet.

While this wash layer is still wet, grab your size 6 brush, dip it in Cadmium Orange, and outline the seed section. Because the fleshy part is wet, WOW should create a gradual bleed into the yellow wash, with a hue ranging from a deep orange to a lighter yellow-orange. While this is blending, add some

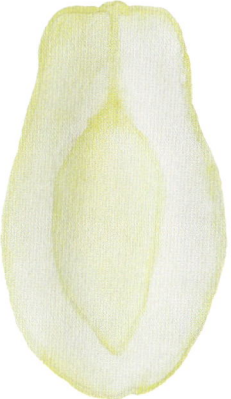

yellow on a few spots closer to the outer edge of the flesh for more blending. Try loading up your brush with just water and help the colors blend into each other more. Be careful to not add *too* much water, as it would become one big blob of yellow-orange. You'll acquire a touch for this with practice.

Now that the outline on the seed section has started to dry, with just water on your brush, swirl it along the inside of the "almond," gradually brushing against the slightly damp orange outline. We don't want the background of this seed section to be completely white; by grazing the outer rim of the almond with water, you'll create a gradual bleed of orange inside the almond.

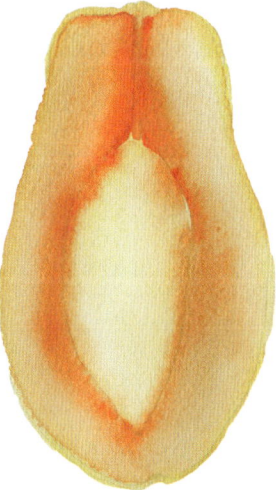

If you need to speed up the drying of the outer rim of your wash or wet portions of the fruit, use a dry paper towel to soak up the excess.

FIRST LAYER (WHOLE PAPAYA)

Before adding the last details and steps to our half piece of fruit, we're going to let that piece dry and in the meantime move on to our whole papaya. Start with a light yellow wash over most of the fruit, leaving some of the left side dry.

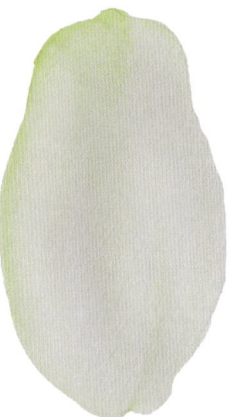

Next, load up your size 6 brush with a yellow-green and use WOW to fill in the left section and gradually add color to the lighter wash. The greener side will be the shaded area, showing the natural curve and round shape of the fruit. Try to accentuate the curve between the oval and circle portions by adding more mid-tones around the left curves of each shape. Similar to what you did with the half papaya, add only water to your brush and help these two colors transition more gradually. Next, add a slightly darker hue of yellow-green in "C" curves coming down the fruit. This will show the natural grooves in the fruit; in the final step, we'll darken these with shadows to bring them forward.

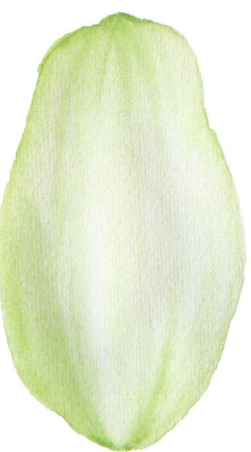

FINAL DETAILS

Once these layers dry on both pieces of fruit, we can add the final touches to both. For the small, round seeds, mix up a combination of black with a hint of red and brown—pure black is too harsh. Next, use the tip of your size 6 brush to add seeds to the cavity. I've left some of my seeds as outlines, to show a shine or natural highlight, and others filled in. Vary the size of these circles and work your way around the space until it's filled in. After this, add a thin layer around the rim of the half papaya with a light yellow, then with WOW add green on the very edge for a soft bleed. Add details to the whole fruit by outlining the greener border, using your size 2 brush with a deeper green hue. Add a darker layer to some of the "C" curves or grooves in the fruit to bring the details forward.

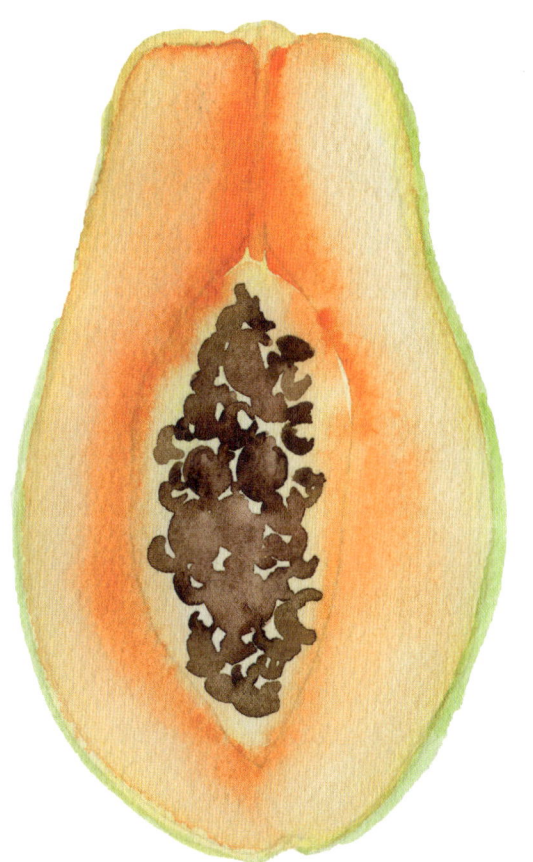

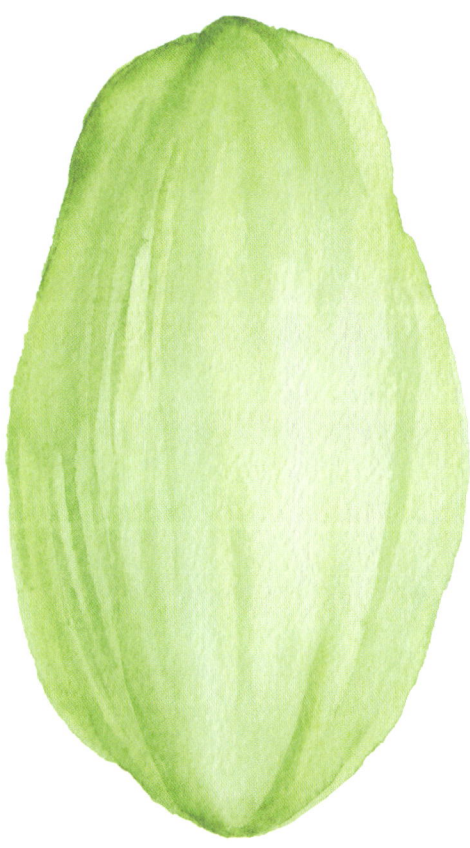

Day Twelve

CAST SHADOW

Add to basic shading techniques by painting
a potted cactus to create a cast shadow.

Estimated time: 40 to 50 minutes

STEP ONE:
Sketch

On previous days we've examined what it means to define the form of a subject with light. Up till now, we've accentuated these forms with *core shadows*—that is, those found on the object itself. Today we'll introduce the *cast shadows* made when a subject blocks light and therefore casts its shadow onto a table or surface. This helps indicate where the light is coming from and adds further dimension. Take a look at the diagram for the basics of cast and core shadows on a sphere.

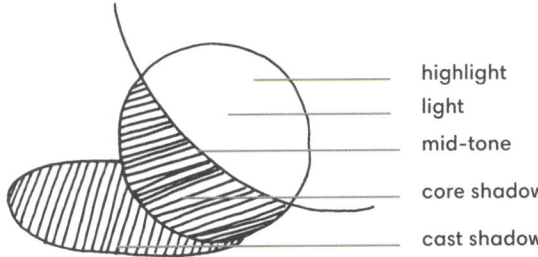

highlight
light
mid-tone
core shadow
cast shadow

To begin, lightly sketch a plant pot on your paper, 3 or 4 inches high and wide. If you don't feel confident enough to freehand this, start with a wide oval to form the top rim. Then draw a slightly smaller oval, about two inches below the first one to form the bottom of the pot. Using "C" curves and straight lines, connect these two to form the sides of the pot using straight lines. You can keep the top oval open, as parts of the mouth of the pot will still show in the finished sketch, but erase the top curve of the bottom oval, as this won't be seen. Use the illustrations on the following page for reference.

Now, to add the cactus, sketch in upside-down teardrop shapes. Vary their heights and widths, remembering to keep things interesting with an odd number. Once you feel good about the placement and structure of your cactus pads, erase the top rim of the pot where cactus would block the view.

On the top portion of one of my cactus pads, I've added a flower. Sketch out this form by starting with a cone or cup shape with an oval opening. From here, add petals within this cone shape for a flower, referring to the example on the following page.

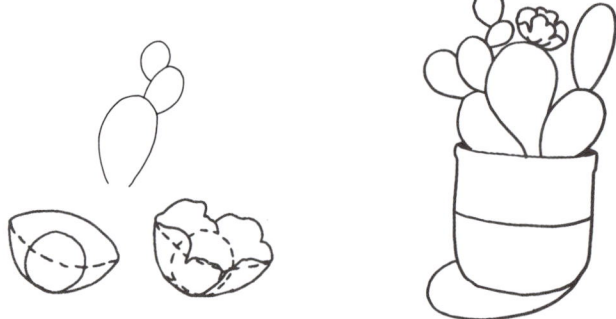

With the foundations of your sketch done, you can sketch a fun pattern or detail on your pot. This isn't totally necessary, but it's fun to perk it up, and who doesn't love a colorful, patterned pot?

STEP TWO:
Choose a color palette

By now, you should have a decent grasp of color harmonies—what works and what doesn't. For today's piece I was inspired by the patterns and colors found in a Mexican hacienda. Think bright turquoise and cobalt contrasted with bold, saturated pinks—creating balance and connection with the blue-greens and yellow-greens of the cactus.

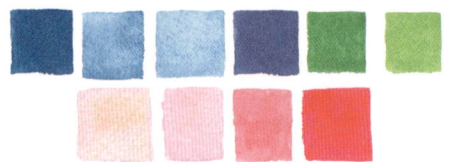

STEP THREE:
Put paint to paper

FIRST LAYER
To start the cast shadow, load up your size 6 brush and apply a light wash in a crescent moon shape, hugging the base of the pot. The brightness and angle of the light source affects how deep and dark the cast shadow

will be. The direction the light source is coming from determines the size of the cast shadow. When most people think of shadows, they think of the color black, but look around you and start noticing shadows. You'll see that most are not black! It's important to think about the surface your object is on, the color of your light source (yes, light has color), and what is being reflected from the object onto its cast shadow. To make this painting a bit more interesting, I've chosen a pink cast shadow, assuming that the surface this pot is on is also a pink hue. Using your size 2 brush, apply this same color to the cactus flower so these colors can echo each other.

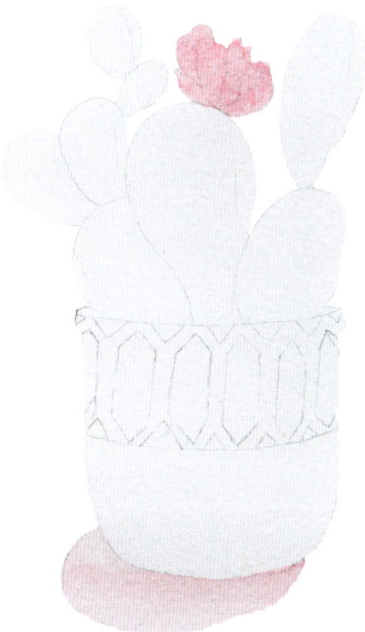

SECOND LAYER

While the first layer on your cast shadow and flower are drying, mix up a few varying hues of green for lighter first layers on your cactus. In my example, I used fuller values for the foreground parts of the cactus and lighter tones for those in the background. I mixed the blue-greens and yellow-greens using Phthalo Turquoise and Lemon Yellow Deep, along with touches of Prussian Blue and Sap Green. This coloring helps add variety and dimension. Make sure to start with the cactus near the pot rim and work your way to other ones so these pads dry before you paint the pot.

For the first layer on the pot, I used a very light mixture of Phthalo Turquoise and made sure to leave more color on the far left side, to accentuate the core shadow and cylindrical form of the pot. Next, with your size 2 brush grab a thicker version of Opera Rose and apply it to the inside of the flower. This will help accentuate the cone shape of the open flower.

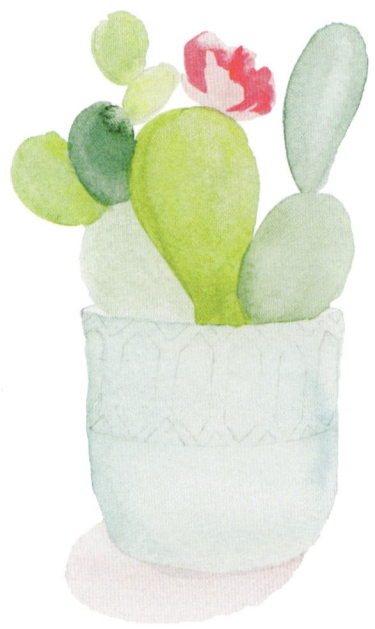

THIRD LAYER

Now that we have the base layers down, it's time to bring some elements forward by adding mid-tones and detail. First, I've applied Phthalo Turquoise in a pattern on the pot, using my size 2 brush. These shapes don't need to be absolutely perfect; a hand-painted look adds character to the pot.

Now add deeper, thicker base layer hues to the cactus for mid-tones and shadows. For the yellow-green portions, create shadows with a darker mixture of yellow-green. For the blue-green portions, use—you guessed it—a darker version of blue-green. Keep in mind what we've previously discussed about light source and where to add core shadows. Once these mid-tone and basic shadows have dried, start adding detail to the cactus and petal with finer lines. Add the spines of the cactus and emphasize the folds of the flower with fuller color and thin lines.

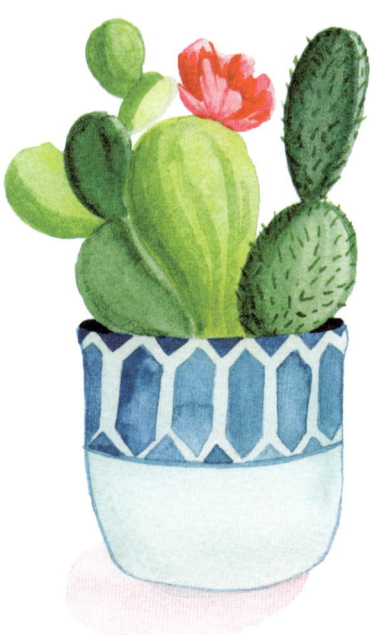

FOURTH LAYER

For our final step, finish adding detail to the cactus with these fine dash marks and put in a dark cobalt mixture for the inside of the pot that can be seen around the cactus. Then darken the cast shadow with more Opera Rose. Touch up the painting by adding any final details or smoothing out shadows.

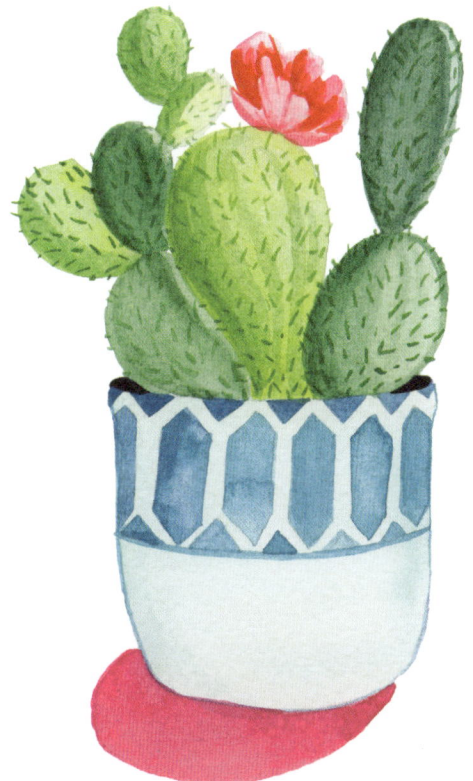

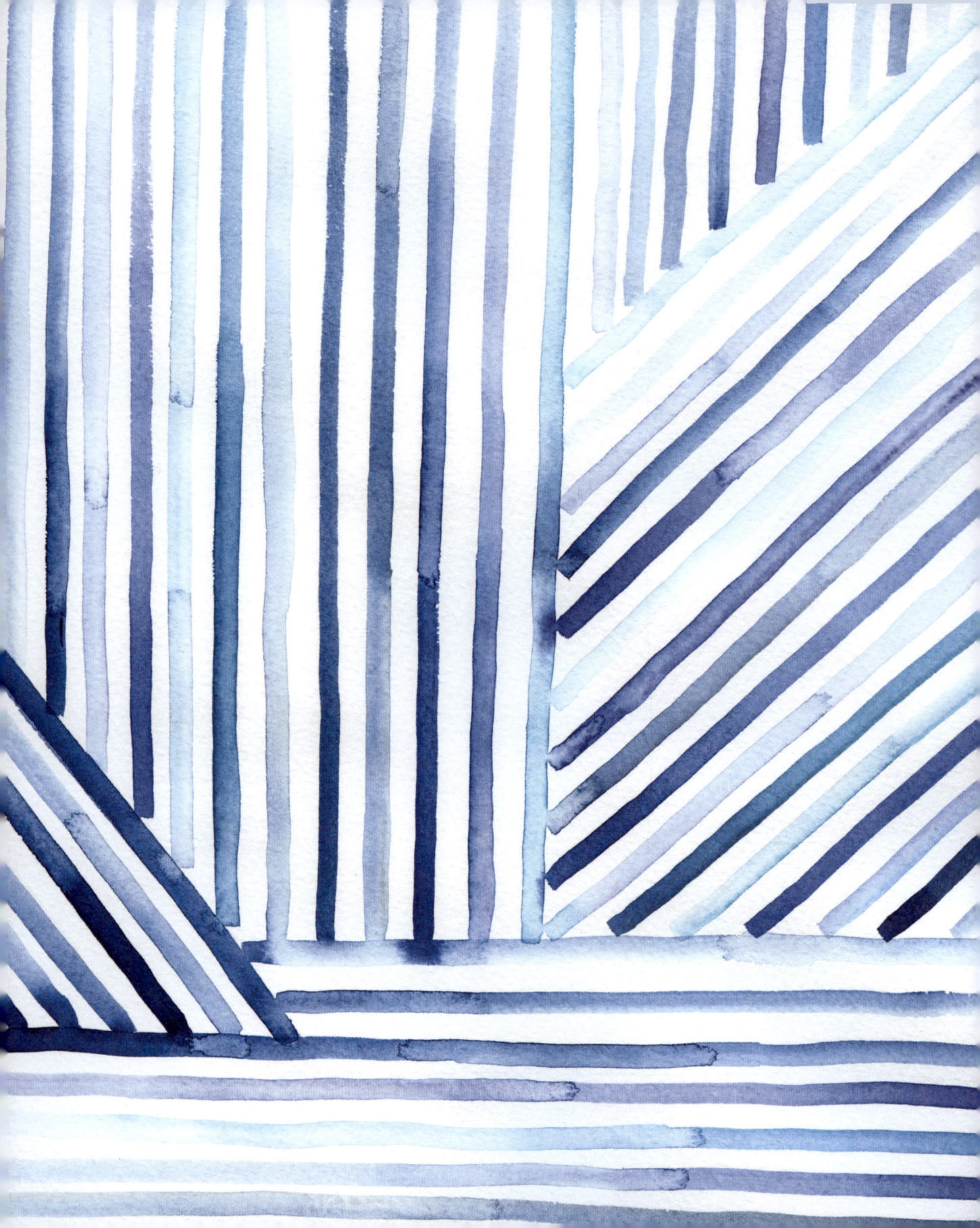

Section Three

COMPLEX SHAPES AND FORMS

Are you up for a challenge? Moving into this next section, it's important for us to use each technique we've covered thus far to influence and construct these next subjects. Some of these pieces may seem a bit difficult, but don't stress! Each day will have a guide for you to apply what you've already learned and to paint with ease. Remember, patience is what separates the developed, mature artist from the amateur artist. So allow yourself to be challenged, accept where you're at, and be proud of what you've accomplished.

Day Thirteen

ANGLES AND FOLDS

Combine basic shapes and curves for
a more detailed subject.

Estimated time: 1 hour

STEP ONE:

Sketch

The *Monstera deliciosa* is a dramatically structured plant native to tropical rainforests. The leaves on this plant give it the nickname "Swiss cheese plant," as there are usually holes in the body of the leaf. This particular leaf is a bit more complex than the leaves we painted on days 5 and 6, but let's break it down into its basic shapes and curves; you'll be painting these all over the place.

This plant has unique twists and curves, but broken down to its basic form the leaf is essentially a heart shape. Lightly sketch a heart, then grab the top point and run two "C" curves down the middle of the heart for the midrib of the leaf. From there, add smaller veins that extend from the main vein to the leaf edges. Next, erase the pencil marks at the base of each smaller vein so they appear connected and flowing out of the midrib.

After this, go back and break up each side with individual deep slits along the leaf edge. Each of these slits in the leaf is simply a thin "U" shape. Make your way down one side with roughly four or five "U" curves. When you reach the bottom, leave a section for the point of the leaf tip.

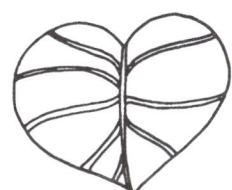

Repeat the process on the other side. These sides don't need to mirror each other—in fact, it's more realistic and interesting if they don't. After adding all these sections, add holes sporadically along the midrib of the leaf. Varying these holes creates a more natural, lifelike leaf.

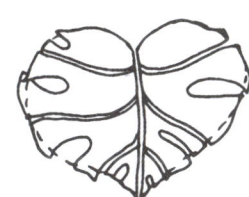

After making a wide-open leaf, we're also going to sketch a side-facing leaf. Start with a "C" curve for the main stem of the leaf. Then, for the far left side, draw an "S" curve connecting at the tip of the midrib and most of the way down. Make this curve really wide at the base of the "S" curve to show this side peeking out from behind the fold of the leaf near the tip.

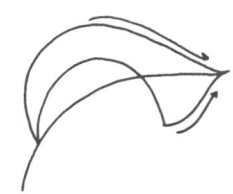

This next part may seem a bit tricky, but it's quite simple when you break it down. Add the bottom part of the folded up-leaf, which will be a "C" curve connecting the tip where the top of the fold meets the bottom of the midrib. Create the slits or holes in each leaflet by adding long "U" shapes up the side of the leaf. Apply the same technique as you did on the wide-open monstera with these sides.

STEP TWO:

Choose a color palette

Today's painting will be similar to our painting of day 10, when we illustrated a banana leaf. Mix up three main values of green so they're ready to use. A light, washy yellow-green will be our first layer; the mid-tone layer is slightly darker and richer, and the shadows will be the darkest of the three. For yellow-green I've used Lemon Yellow Deep and Sap Green, darkening these by adding more green and even a touch of Prussian Blue and black for the shadows.

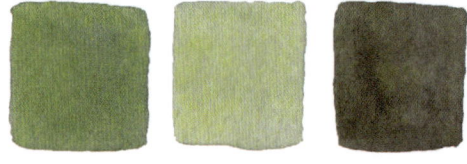

STEP THREE:

Put paint to paper

FIRST LAYERS

To complete this leaf, we will paint using the same technique we discussed on day 10. Since this leaf has more compound curves, it's going to be easiest to work around tighter portions with a size 2 brush. Because of this, we have to paint really fast—moving down one side of the leaf at a time and applying a wash, then applying mid-tones leaflet by leaflet.

To begin, apply your wash on one side of the leaf, then apply mid-tones where you feel they enhance the shape and form of the leaf. Analyze where the light is hitting your leaf, but don't overthink it. We'll discuss shading for this leaf in more detail once we get to shadows.

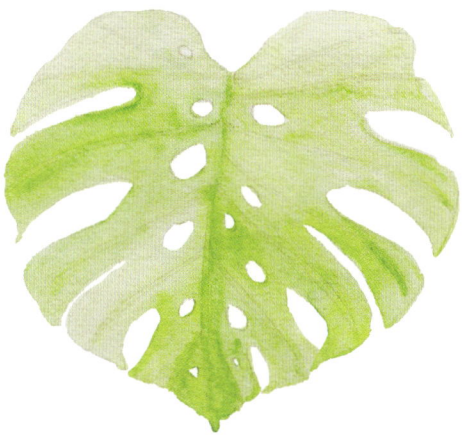

As you can see in my painting, the lighter value of yellow-green and the slightly darker value vary quite a bit on the leaf, emphasizing its veins and curves but not defining the leaf much at all. The wash also covers the entire leaf, so the veins are a pale yellow-green, not plain white. While waiting for the first side of your leaf to dry, start applying the same wash and technique to the other side. Make sure to define the middle of the leaf by adding mid-tones on either side of the midrib. This will help show more definition rather than just a mass of color.

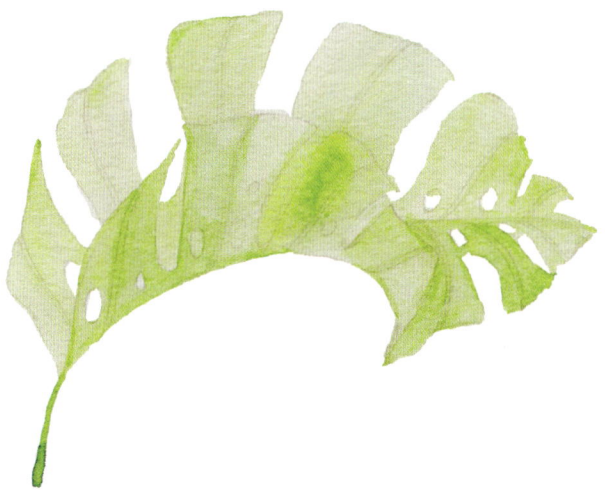

SECOND LAYER

Now that the base layer on your first leaf is mostly dry, it's time to start bringing details and shapes forward by adding shadows and richer color. Paint one leaflet at a time and outline the vein first; then, with just water on your brush, use WOW to help that outline gradually bleed into the rest of the leaflet. Apply darker shadows toward the inside, midrib, and curves that are farthest from the light source.

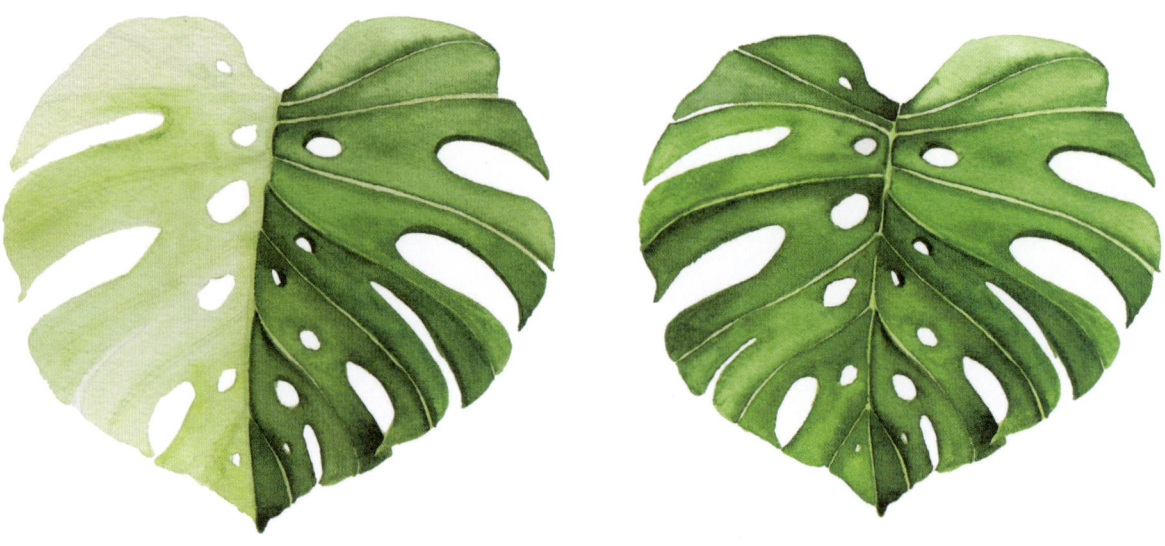

Make your way along the leaf and to the other side to repeat the process. Avoid adding any paint to smaller veins; let the base layer show through for contrast.

Now apply the same techniques to the side-facing leaf. Because the flipped-up portion of the leaf is closest to us, I've decided to make this lighter, with the inside of the leaf in shadows. With that in mind, we'll apply only mid-tone values of paint to the underside of the leaf and add shadows on the inside only. To do this, it's best to start with painting the mid-tones of the underside of the leaf and wait for this to completely dry, then paint the inside of the leaf. Apply the steps from the open monstera leaf, avoiding the veins and accentuating the curves of the leaf with mid-tones and placement of deeper color.

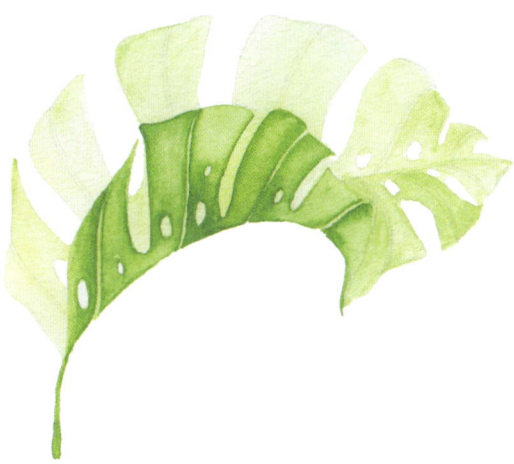

Already you can start to see the sections appear to flare away from each other, emphasizing the fold. Once this section is dry, apply the same process to the inside of the leaf, but take it a step further by applying darker values to push the fold of the leaf forward.

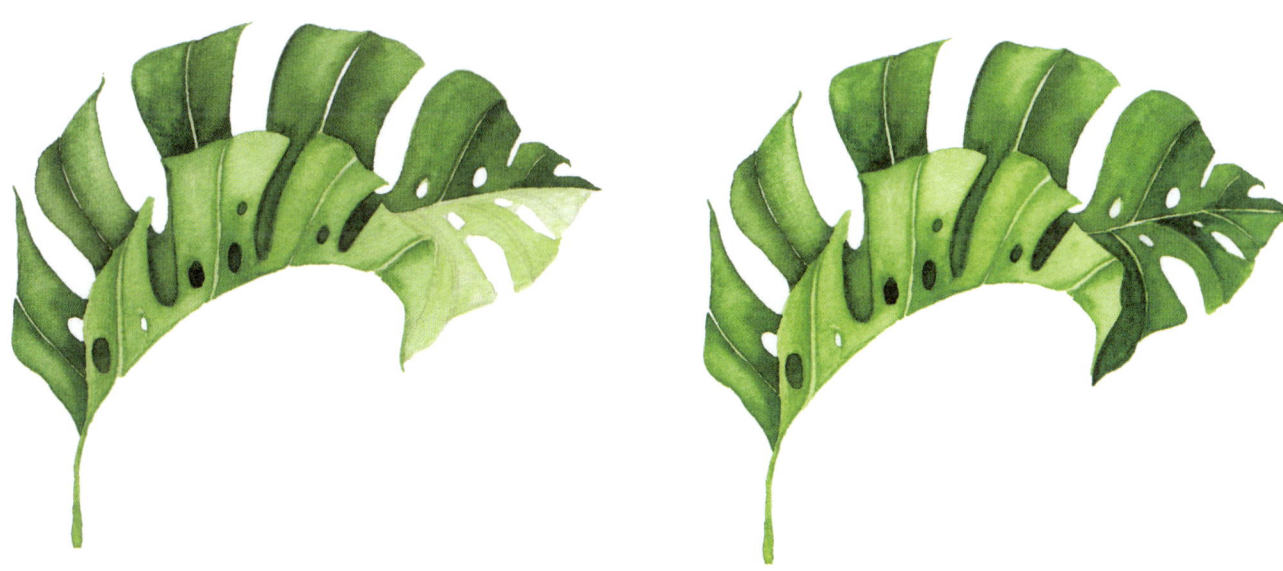

Day Fourteen

PAINTING IN SECTIONS

Learn to paint in sections for contrasting
colors to create a dragon fruit.

Estimated time: 35 to 45 minutes

STEP ONE:
Sketch

Take your pencil and lightly outline an oval. From there, start adding the curves and nuances of the dragon fruit, making sure to clearly separate the two sections of the fruit—pink for the body of the fruit and green for the leafy parts. Draw this twice: once for a half piece of fruit and another for a whole, as we did on day 11.

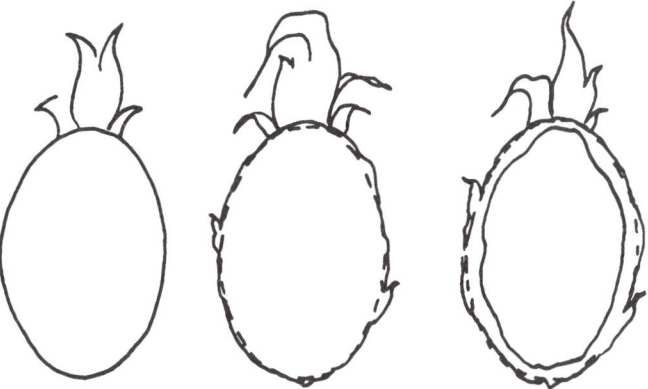

STEP TWO:
Choose a color palette

This is one of my favorite fruits to paint! The rich colors and contrast between the pink and green are so striking, it makes for a fun palette to play with. Because pink is a form of red, this color contrasts strongly with the bright green of the leaves. We aren't painting with straight-up red for the body of the fruit, so we don't have to deal with Christmas vibes, but this pink-and-green combo delivers similar contrast. These colors complement each other, and their vibrancy will grab your viewers' eyes.

We're going to be painting as we have in previous days, starting with a light wash layer, then applying mid-tones and shadows. For the body of the fruit, we'll be using Opera Rose for a striking pink color, then a more yellow-green for the leaves using Sap Green and Lemon Yellow Deep.

Remember, when choosing color for your piece—whether it's for this fruit, an abstract swatch piece, or a landscape—it is important to consider the mood. Your color palette will dramatically affect the overall feeling of your piece. Take these pieces, for example. The vibrancy and pop that Opera Rose gives in its purest form evokes a feeling of excitement and life. But as the tone becomes darker and deeper, the fruit becomes more neutral and passive.

STEP THREE:

Put paint to paper

WHOLE DRAGON FRUIT
FIRST LAYER

Load up your size 6 round-tip brush with a light wash of Opera Rose. Apply this wash over the entire body of the fruit, avoiding the leaf area and making sure it stays very wet so you'll be able to add mid-tones using WOW.

Next, load up your brush with more Opera Rose and start carefully applying it to the outer rim of the wet base—you choose which side of the fruit will carry a deeper value than the other, deciding where the light source is and emphasizing the spherical form of the fruit. While the surface is still wet, add some Scarlet Lake or even Lemon Yellow Deep in smaller areas to help break up the pink and add more dimension to the piece.

SECOND LAYER

Wait for the body to dry; then, with a very light mixture of Lemon Yellow Deep and Sap Green, carefully paint in the first layer of your leaf areas. Wait for the first green layer to mostly dry, then apply a slightly darker green in the areas that need shading.

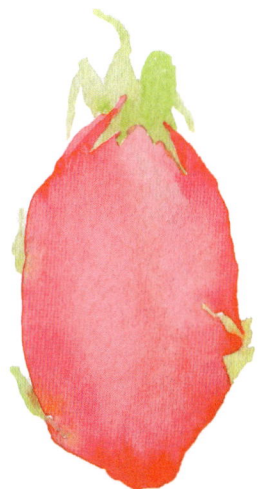 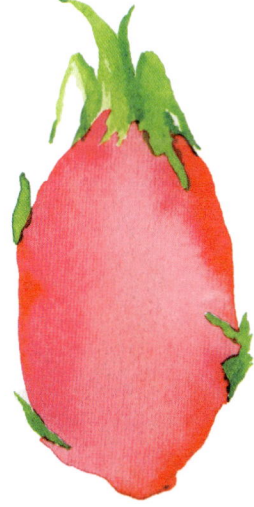

FINAL LAYER

From there, add thin "C" curve lines on the body of the fruit with a deep Opera Rose and/or Scarlet Lake to add texture and detail. Touch up any of the leaf areas to add dimension, and there you have it!

Now, in just a few more steps, we will open up the dragon fruit and paint the cut side of a half fruit.

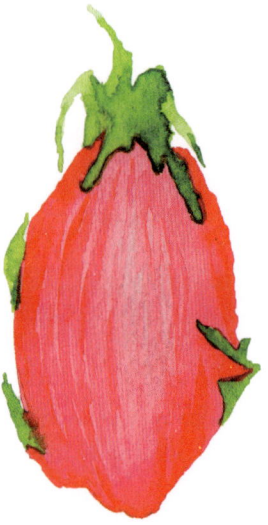

HALF DRAGON FRUIT
FIRST LAYER

Before we start painting, make sure your sketch for this portion has an inner rim to separate the pink skin from the white flesh of the fruit. From here, go through step two of the exercise, but instead of painting the entire body, you will be painting only within the lines for the outer rim. Move from a pale pink wash to a deeper pink using the WOW technique.

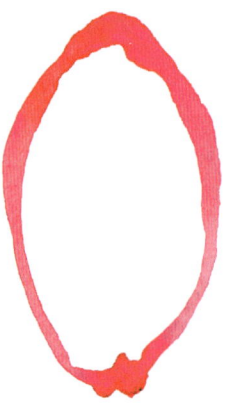

Before moving to the green section, rinse your brush off almost completely, so you still have a hint of pink, and apply a wash to the center of the fruit. If your wet brush touches the edge of the pink rim, that will introduce a unique touch of color using WOW. Allow the pink section to dry completely (about ten minutes) and apply the first layer of green. For the leaves, follow the steps from the previous exercise on the whole dragon fruit.

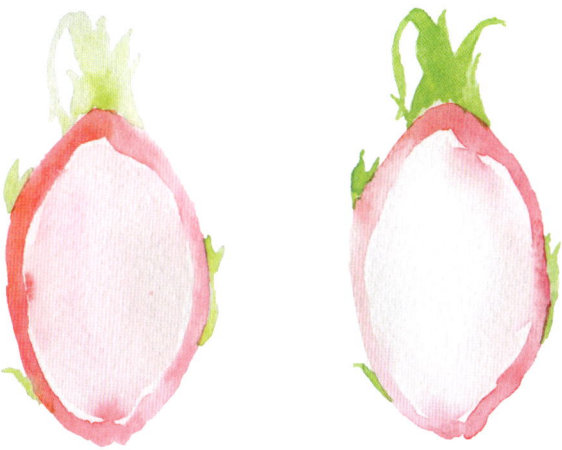

SECOND LAYER

By the time you've finished the green areas, the center of the fruit should be dry. With your size 2 or size 6 round-tip brush, use the fine point to apply black dots or seeds in the center. Vary these dots in size, lightness, and angles to make sure they're not too symmetrical.

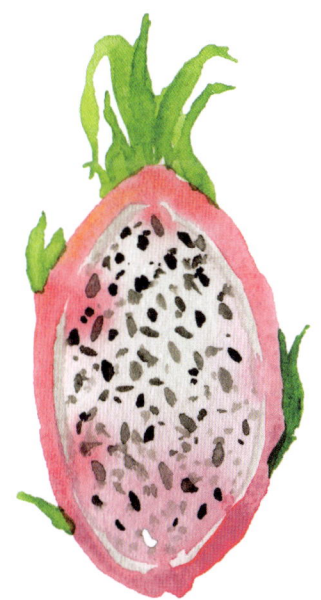

Day Fifteen

COMPLEMENTARY COLORS

Paint individual sections of a bird of paradise flower, with WOW for analogous hues and WOD for contrasting colors.

Estimated time: 1 hour

STEP ONE:

Sketch

With your pencil, lightly outline the basic curves of the bird of paradise flower. You'll start with a simple "C" curve for the overall bend of the flower. Next, add the mouth of the flower by applying another "C" curve to make a teardrop shape. Once your basic curves are established, sketch in the contour of the flower and erase your basic shape and curve guides.

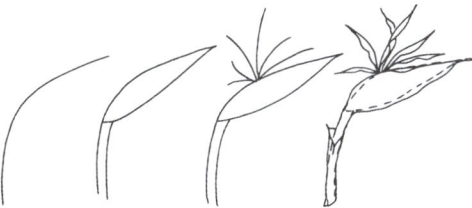

STEP TWO:

Choose a color palette

This flower contains many different hues. The stem is an analogous color area of yellow-greens and greens calling for Sap Green and Lemon Yellow Deep, like the papaya skin, while the mouth of the flower bleeds into reds and violets, turquoise, and more. The orange for the flower petals is Cadmium Orange with hints of Lemon Yellow Deep. It can be helpful to search for photos of a bird of paradise for color reference. This will help you devise a palette for yourself and know where to place each color.

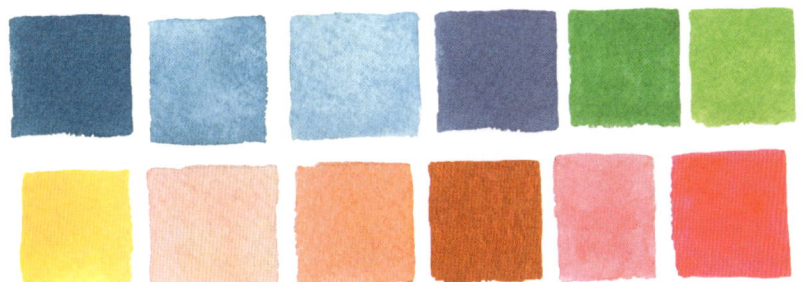

STEP THREE:

Put paint to paper

We'll start with the stem. Apply a very light wash of yellow-green, and add different mid-tones of this hue to begin showing the curve of the stem. For a soft blend, remember, you control the pigment while it's still wet. I've emphasized the curve of the stem with my mid-tones by applying the technique we learned on day 11.

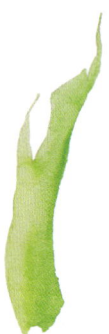

Next, we're going to paint the first layer of the crown. These forms are simply structured, like larger leaves, and will be either a yellow-orange hue or light cobalt. You can complete one of these petals in one stroke, as we did for leaves on day 5. Start with a thin line, then apply heavy pressure through the middle of the petal, then release again for a thin, pointed tip. Do this for all the orange petals, accenting shadow with mid-tones as you go, then do the same for the blue petals.

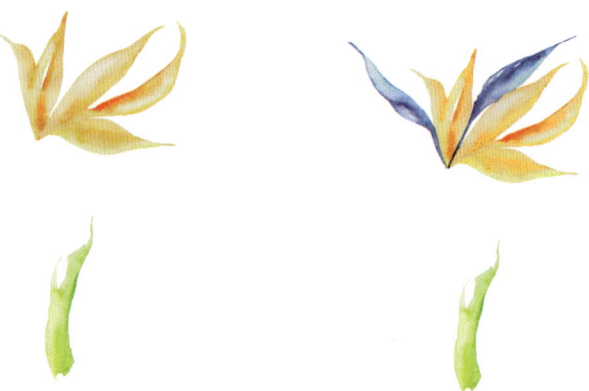

While these sections dry, a caution about complementary colors. Blending these contrasting hues is no simple task. When used correctly, the amount of contrast can be striking. It takes extra attention and care to make sure the two colors don't blend too much, which creates a muddy brown.

To start, load up your size 6 brush with a thick amount of full-strength Scarlet Lake and Opera Rose. Cover the base of the flower's beak or mouth with this color. Now wash your brush off completely, and with just water on your brush, graze the edge of what you just painted and bring in the wet paint and water toward the center of the "beak." You should see it shifting from a deep red to a light red. Now, rinse your brush off and load up with Phthalo Turquoise and Lemon Yellow Deep to fill in the middle of the beak, touching the red-pink section just slightly so the colors diffuse and blend at the edges a bit. You should see these two colors blend together to make a gradation from red, to purple, to turquoise. Add variations of color on the edges of the beak by punching in pinks and reds at the tip.

Now that most of this flower is done, see how your contrasting colors of orange and blue, red and green complement each other. If it seems overwhelming, make any needed changes at this stage before adding detail.

While that last step dries, we can move on to adding detail to the flower. With your size 2 brush, grab a darker green color and lightly brush just one outside edge of the stem, creating a look of roundness with the shadow. Add texture to the petals by incorporating wrinkles with darker lines and shadows.

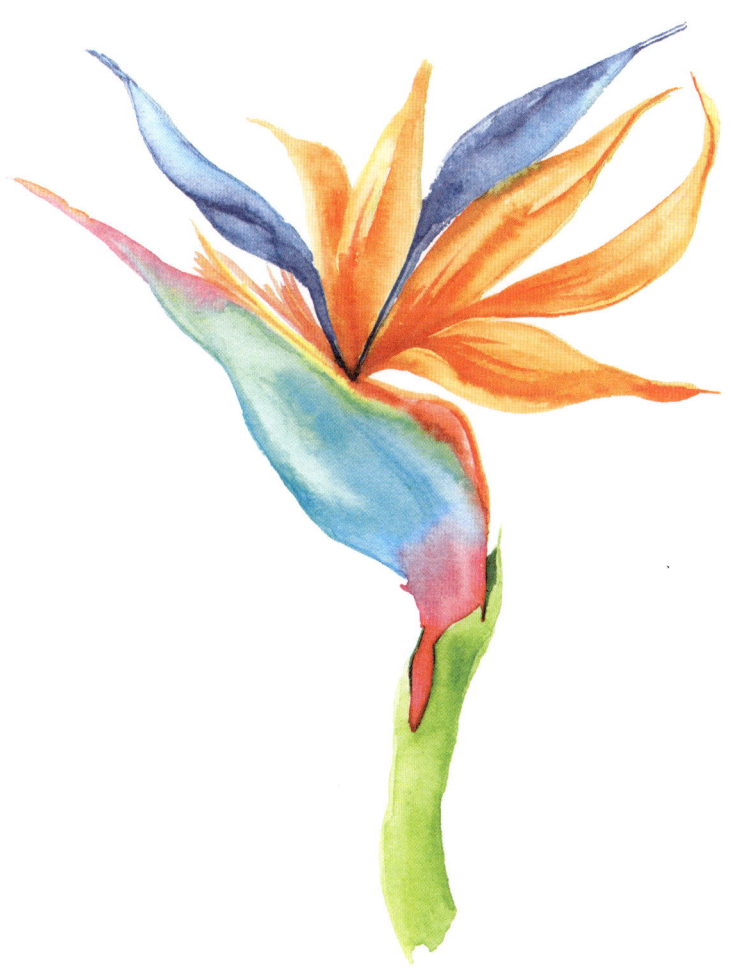

Day Sixteen

FINE LINES

Paint a cylindrical form with broad strokes, then add fine detail to practice thin lines and painting in sections.

Estimated time: 35 to 45 minutes

STEP ONE:

Sketch

We'll begin this piece by discovering what curves and shapes make up the structure of a saguaro cactus. This subject is all about mirroring curves and capturing the cylindrical shape. Start by lightly sketching three smaller circles. Each arm and section of the cactus is a cylindrical shape, so these circles will guide the form of these cylinders. With these seemingly random circles on our page, it's time to start bringing the cactus forward. Remember, the lines you're going to use when you sketch are either a "C" curve, an "S" curve, or a straight line. Don't think about sketching in the little details; we'll add those later when we paint. For now, just focus on the foundations of the subject.

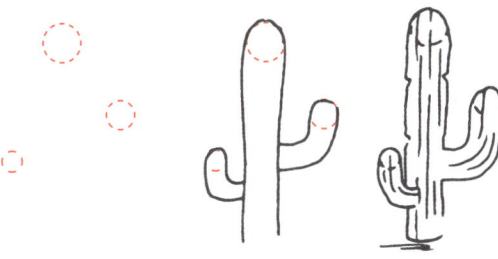

STEP TWO:

Choose a color palette

For this piece, we're going to mix up three different types of green just like we did on day 10 for banana leaves and 13 for monsteras. We'll use Sap Green and Lemon Yellow Deep, and vary the three different hues in lightness to paint highlights, mid-tones, and shadows. Sometimes these cacti have buds or flowers, so if you're feeling adventurous, we'll mix up a warm color for those as well. For the flowering parts of the cactus, think about what colors complement our green hues well. Our greens are so vibrant that a brighter complementary color will match them nicely.

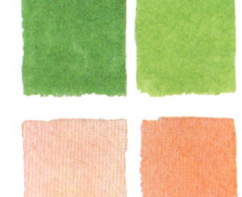

STEP THREE:
Put paint to paper

As I've noted, you'll almost always start a watercolor painting with your lightest color as the base, working toward darker colors. We will use the WOW technique for most of our highlights and mid-tones for a soft blend. So begin with a light yellow-green wash covering most of the cactus, then add mid-tone values of this color in areas that will help accentuate the cactus form. For my example piece, the light source is coming from the top right corner, so my mid-tones will be more on the left side of the cactus and on the base of each arm.

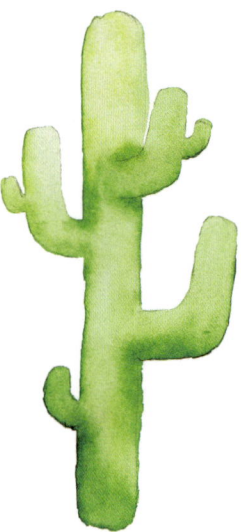

Focus on where that light would be hitting your subject. Each part of the cactus is cylindrical, so shade as if you were forming a cylinder to help the shape of the cactus pop and become more three-dimensional.

Wait for these base layers to dry, then take your size 2 brush and load it up with a darker green mixture. We'll now bring fine lines down the arms and body of the cactus, leaving just a little space between each line, to depict the ribbed surface. Use your arm to bring these strokes down and up, and if they're not perfectly steady and straight, no problem!

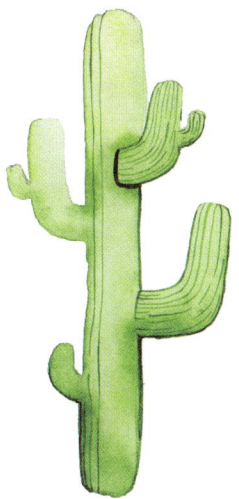

On the arms, instead of doing a straight line, make sure you curve with the arm. Maybe darken some of these shadows on the left side, and lighten them as you come closer to the light source.

Add some flowers to the tops of each arm for contrasting color and detail. Form these petals as you did with cones on days 9 and 12.

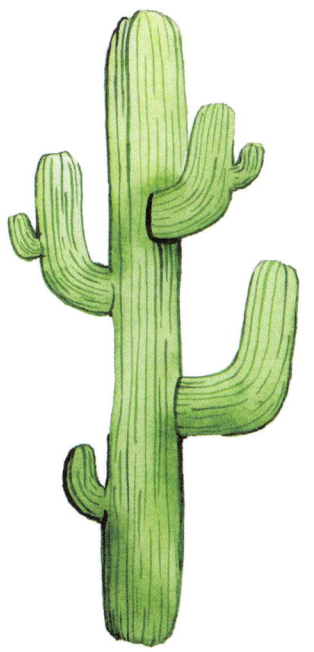

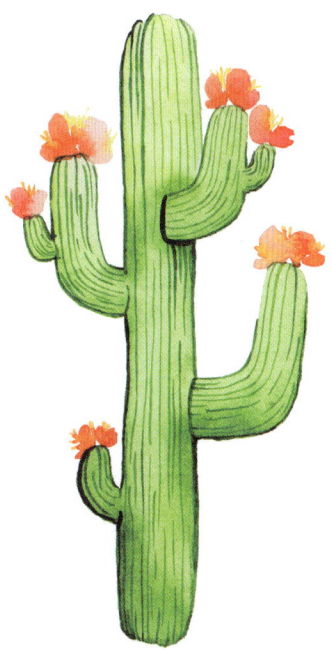

Day Seventeen

HIGHLIGHTS, MID-TONES, AND SHADOWS

Paint a more complex subject to practice alternating portions with WOW and WOD—and develop patience.

Estimated time: 1 to 1½ hours

STEP ONE:

Sketch

You have come a long way already! We've learned and practiced basic shapes and color harmonies and implemented foundational knowledge on composition, how to paint in layers, and more. For today's piece we're going to apply all that knowledge to paint something that may seem a bit intimidating at first, but I want to emphasize that we're incorporating techniques we've already learned. The key ingredient with this piece will be patience. The more detailed and realistic paintings don't require additional technique or genius talent. With practice, anyone can paint like this. I'm confident in that, and I'm confident in you.

All we'll do today is sketch a rose with basic shapes and curves and paint in layers as we've done previously. The only real difference in today's painting is that there are many more sections in a rose than in a banana leaf or cactus. A rose has many rows of petals, which can seem daunting when we aren't sure where to add each petal when initially sketching, where the light is coming from, or where to add darker color. But I'm going to break down each part of the flower and make it easy for you to grasp. We just need to look at the subject a little differently and think of each petal of the flower as its own individual painting. Let's get started!

To begin, we're going to lightly sketch a smaller circle in the center of our paper. If you think about a flower, each petal grows from one stem. All of your petals will point back to that stem and will fold out to form a cone.

The circle in the center will be your guide to how each petal forms around the flower. Picture each petal hugging the circle and pointing directly back to the base of the circle to form a cone. Lightly sketch a cone around your circle, with the base of this cone hugging the base of the circle. This will be the first row of petals surrounding the center of the flower.

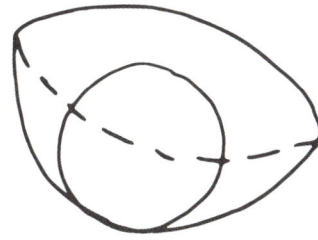

Next, add "C" curves or cone shapes for each petal. As you sketch, make sure that each side of the petal points inward and back to the circle. These curves are essentially the tops of all your petals, so proportionally they need to form a natural curve like in a flower. Sketch these "C" curves around your circle. Notice how long the curves are in the example. Take note of the spacing between rows, which will show the flat bellies of the petals; make sure this varies from petal to petal. Stagger these around each other, not just directly behind each curve, as that would start to look like parentheses. As you develop good form and width, notice that your sketch looks like a ball with curves around it. Now you can start adding detail to the petals, and it will start to look like a flower.

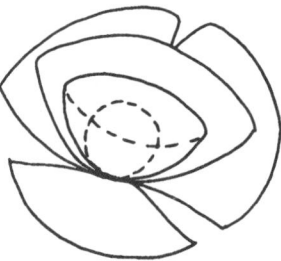

Look closely at a rose petal and notice the texture. There are grooves, little inlets, waves, and tears at the top of the petal. It's not a smooth line. To add this texture, we're going to sketch directly over these "C" curve guides with a loose, light sketch of these jagged tops, as shown in the example.

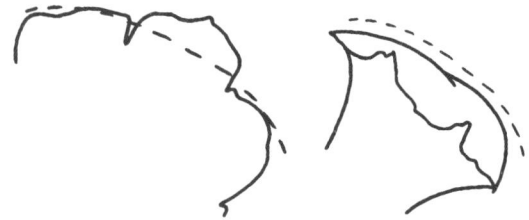

If you don't like something, erase it! Because each petal overlaps directly on top of another, these borders will be very helpful. Continue adding jagged tops and folds to all of your "C" curves. Then carefully erase the "C" curves and guides, leaving only the lighter contour sketch of the actual flower visible.

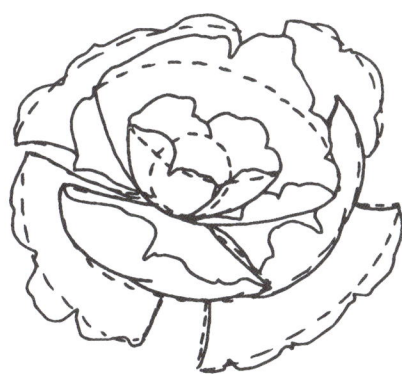

STEP TWO:
Choose a color palette

Now you can start planning your color palette. We'll be working with three main values for highlights, mid-tones, and basic shadows. For this piece, I've mixed up two different hues for mid-tones: a dusty pink using Yellow Ochre, Opera Rose, and a touch of Burnt Umber, and one with a bit more yellow. I can lighten or darken either one for highlights and shadows. Typically, a subject like this would have many different hues for shadows and highlights, but we're going to stick to these two to learn the basics of shading a multisection piece like this. The swatches below show the colors and value varieties I used for this piece.

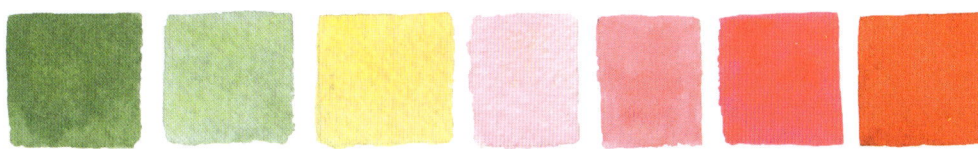

STEP THREE:

Put paint to paper

FIRST LAYER

Load up your size 6 brush with the lightest color to apply a wash across the entire rose. This will ensure that the highlights are this tint and not just blank paper, which can be too stark and unrealistic. Wash an even blend of color across the flower, and keep this layer light so you can build mid-tones and shadows later.

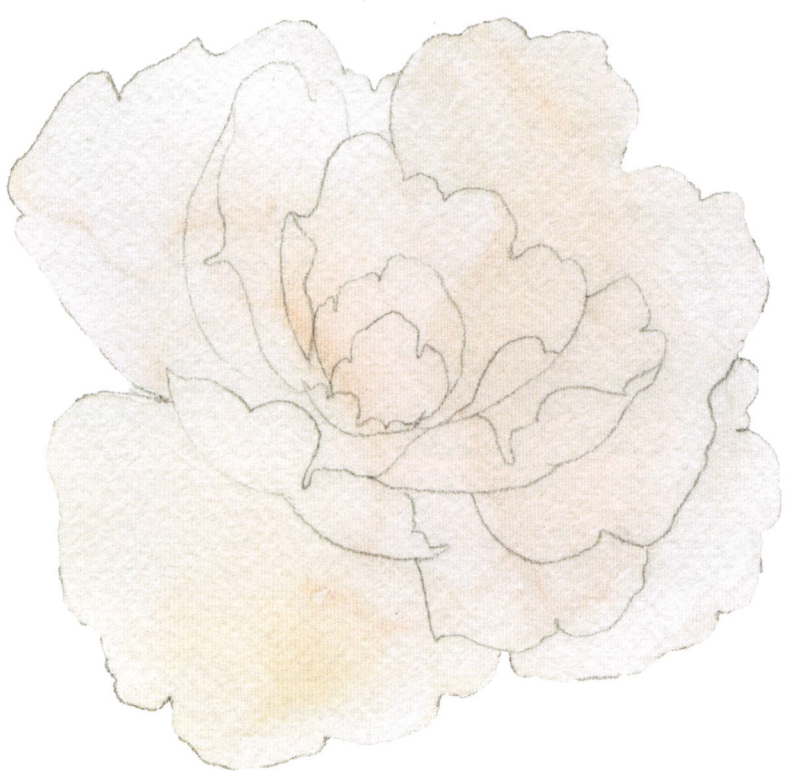

SECOND LAYER

Once this light wash is completely dry, apply thicker paint to start creating the shadow areas. I applied these darker sections with my size 2 brush. Think about the crevices of each petal: go right up to the start of the petal in front of the shadow and apply a thick, wet line of shadow color. Next, wash your brush off completely and with just water on your brush, paint a wash around the rest of the petal and just touch the edges of your wet shadow color so it bleeds into the wash. Your shadow will gradually become lighter and lighter up the wet surface of the petal for a soft bleed. Apply these steps to other petals, making sure to not paint a petal right next to one that is still wet, as these would just become one big blob. The farther the petal is from the center, the lighter your shadows will be, so make sure to apply that to your flower and add some hue and value variation between petals.

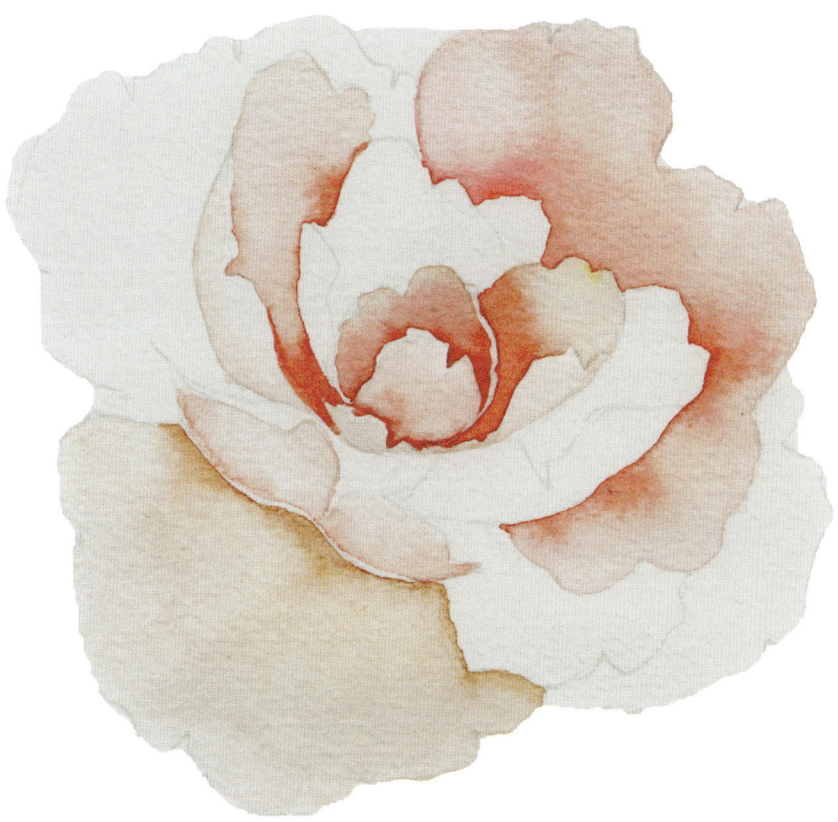

THIRD LAYER

Continue adding shadows for a natural blend from shadows to mid-tones to highlights. Remember to watch each petal as it's bleeding, and if there's too much blending going on, soak it up with a paper towel or dry brush. If there's not enough shading, help it out a bit by circling your brush around in the pigment to blend. While the paint is still wet, you control how it bleeds and blends.

Now begin adding some of your lighter petals, which will be the tops of folds or petals that are facing out, being illuminated by the light source. In the petals at the very center of the example, if you made the back side of the smallest petal the same hue as the inside, you couldn't differentiate between the inside and outside. So apply a soft mid-tone layer to the base or on the curve of these lighter sections, then use an even lighter wash to cover the rest of the section and use WOW to bleed the mid-tone and wash values. These are essentially the same steps as what we're applying to the darker petals, but with just mid-tones and a wash. You can always add darker color on top if you feel it needs more.

FINAL LAYER

Once you've painted all the petals, you can darken some of the mid-tones and shadows to make them pop. Use a slightly thicker mixture than you used for the previous layer on each specific petal and accentuate the curves and insides of the petals. The shadows help accentuate where petals end and overlap; the mid-tones help bring forward the curve of the petal and isolate the highlights.

See what we're doing? Just shading basic curves, one section at a time. Because there are so many sections, it is a bit time consuming. But when you apply a little patience with the techniques you've already learned, look at what you can accomplish!

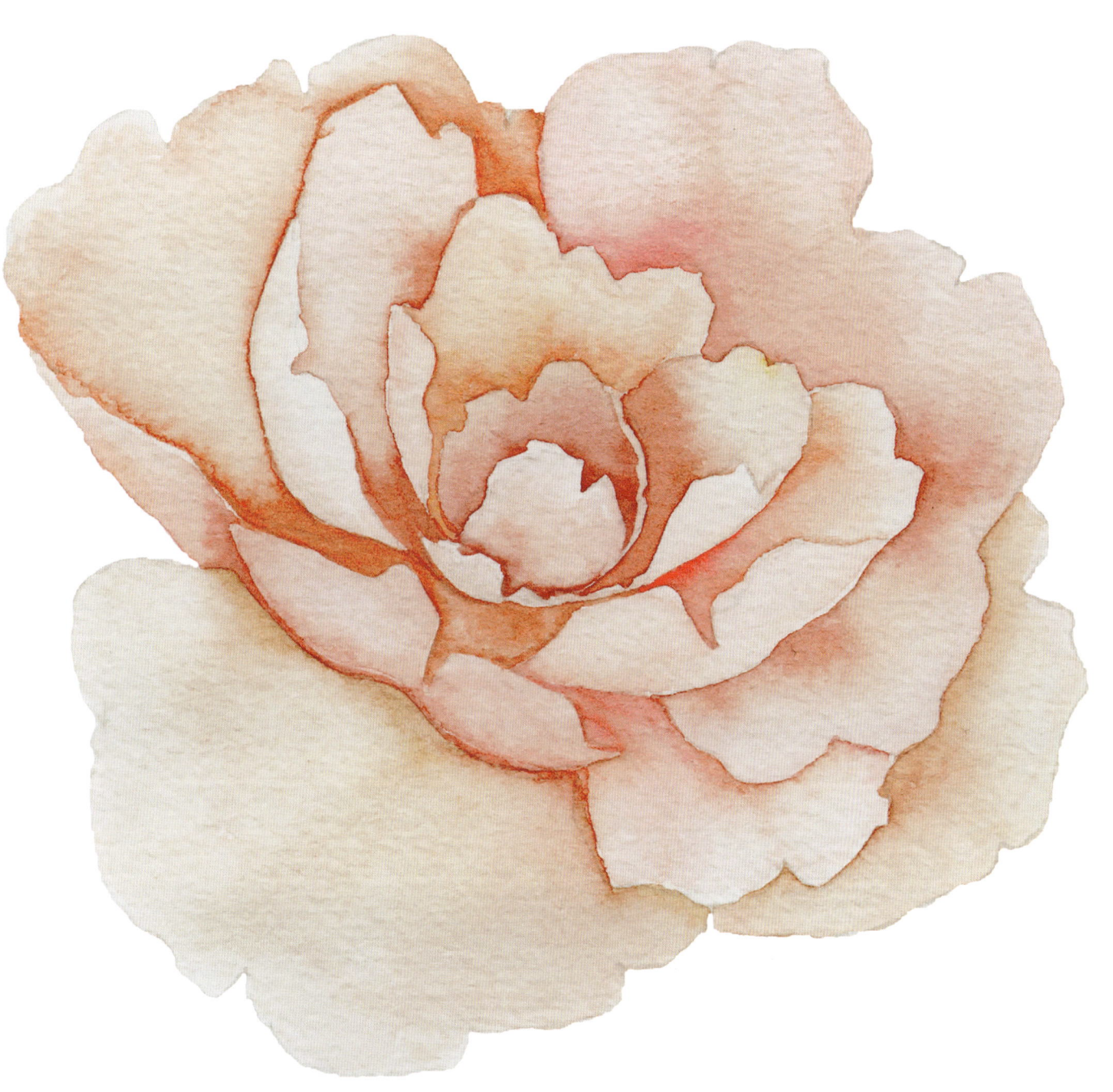

Day Eighteen

GESTURE

Combine "S" and "C" curves to analyze gesture and movement in a figure.

Estimated time: 25 to 35 minutes

STEP ONE:

Sketch

Today we paint chickens. Welcome to our first day of painting an animal in motion! With this exercise, we'll unpack a chicken in a running position and learn how to effectively paint gesture so it doesn't look stiff. This stance can be difficult to depict so the figure has flow, but with a few tips and pointers, you'll be painting lifelike running chickens. First up, we'll practice the basic curves of this stance by sketching the subject's form. This will help you understand the movement, so when it's time to start using a paintbrush you can visualize the curve of each stroke. Whether you're painting an animal, person, or group of people, gesture drawing and painting is done with rhythm, to capture the essence of a figure in motion. If you've taken a figure drawing class or even went to art school, you're probably familiar with this practice.

Start at the top of the chicken's head with a small "C" curve ending at the base of the chicken's neck. From there, this curve will meet first another small "C" curve with the ends pointing inward, then another inverted "C" curve swinging upward to the top of the tail. Bring in some varied, smaller "C" curves for the tail feathers. From here, you'll add the breast and thighs of the chicken with two "C" curves, gradually angled downward to fill in the body. Next, add a smaller "C" curve in front for the forward-striding leg in the background. Now add the leg seen in the foreground. Really extend this part so our chicken appears to be on the run. These legs are simply extensions of the thigh, so make sure to draw these out of the base of the thigh's "C" curves. Repeat this drawing a few times and maybe vary the position slightly for practice. The sketch on the left contains some spheres to show the gaps and proportions between curves.

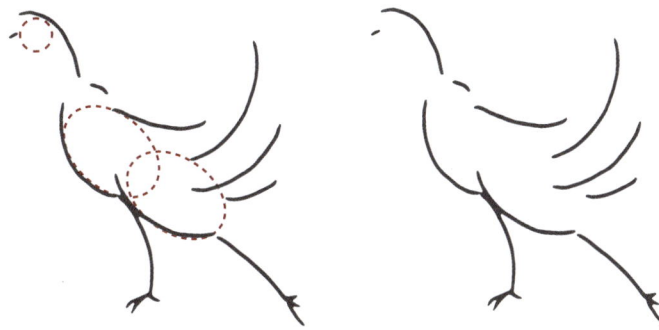

STEP TWO:

Choose a color palette

Once you've practiced this stance with sketches, you can start mixing up hues to use for following the same steps with paint. We won't be adding much detail, but illustrating using pressure and release on our round-tip brushes, forming each section of the chicken by following along its curve. You'll definitely want to add varying hues and values throughout sections so that it's not all one flat color, but for this exercise we won't be concentrating on detail with highlights, mid-tones, and shadows. Mix up some browns in varying hues and values: darker browns with Mars Black and Burnt Umber for thinner feathery details, and lighter browns to help emphasize the chicken's form and curves. For our final piece, we'll add a rooster, using the same steps, so mix up deep reds and deeper browns, black, or maybe even blues, for his large tail feathers, comb, and wattle.

STEP THREE:

Put paint to paper

Now that we've gone over the basic forms and curves of this figure, we'll apply that practice to painting these feathery friends. Just like the gesture sketches, we're going to stroke our way through painting the chicken by following the curves. Apply pressure to fan out your brush so it fills in areas like the neck and body with a single stroke or curve, then add darker color for depth and feather texture.

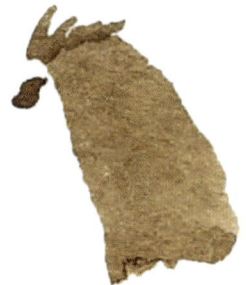

Use your size 6 brush for covering a wider area on the chicken and your size 2 to bring in the smaller details like the tiny curve of the beak, feather detail, and so on.

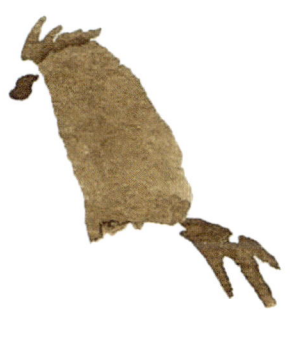

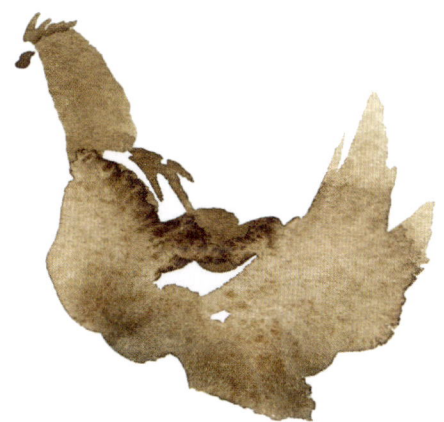

Lighten up as you work your way across the chicken so the tail feathers are much lighter than the rest of the body, creating depth. Go back and add darker color to areas like the back and feather details below the neck. With the fine point of your size 2 brush, carefully outline the curves of the legs and tiny "C" curves on the feet. These details really bring this figure to life.

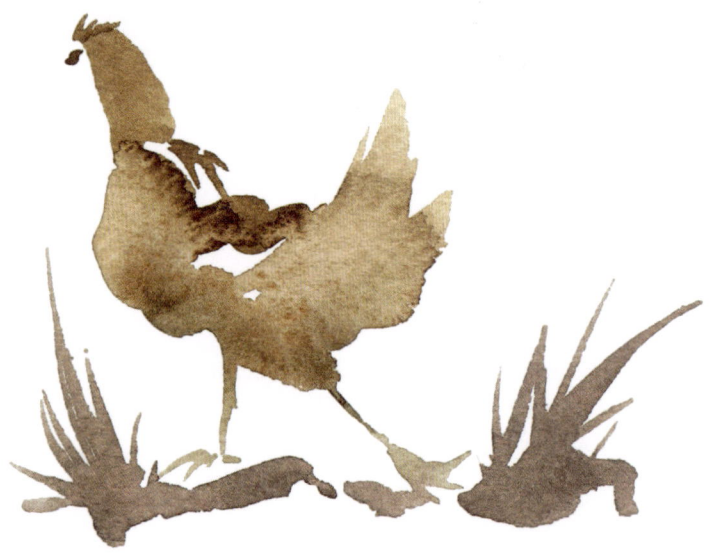

Add some grass with a couple of basic strokes and marks just below the feet to situate the chicken in its world.

For the rooster, you'll apply the same exact steps, but with a bit more flair and length. Make his neck longer and extend those tail feathers with the tip of your size 2 brush. For texture on the feathers, use a mostly dry brush with thick pigment, and as you bring these curved strokes up and over, you'll see the texture of the paper push through the paint. Just below the rooster's beak, add a deep red circle for the wattle and three tiered strokes up top for the comb.

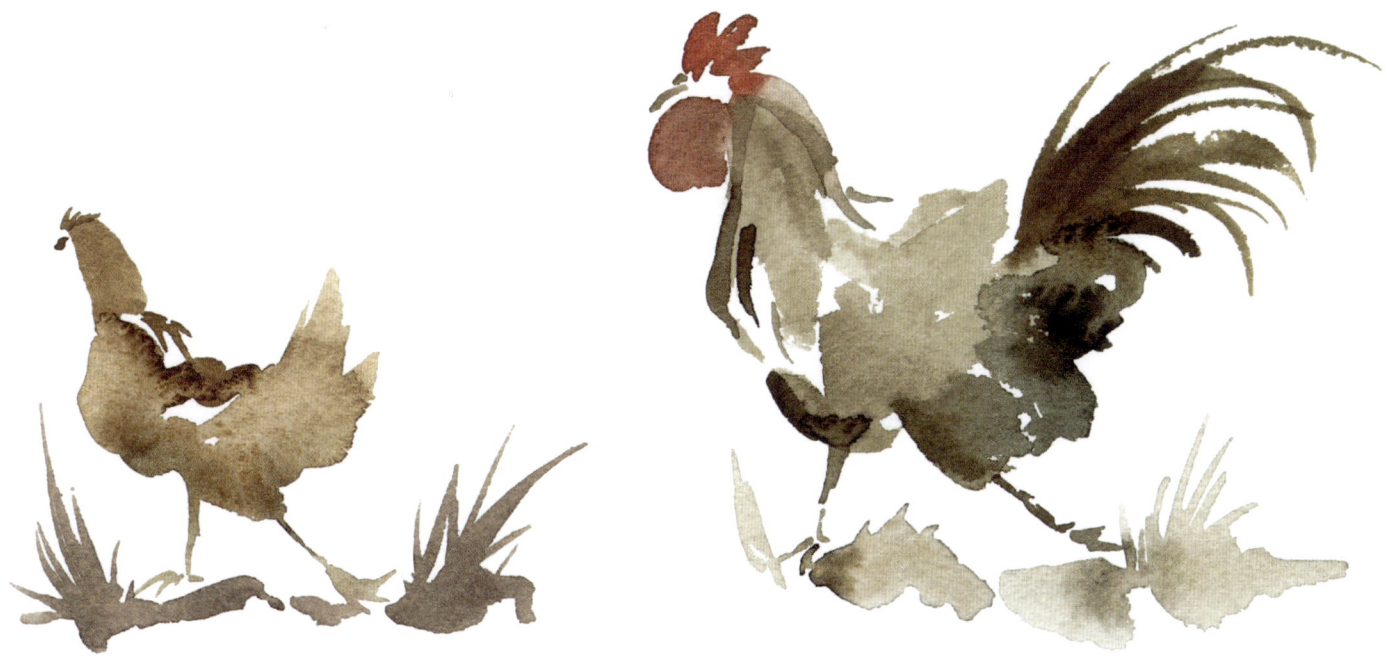

Isn't this fun? Quick, free gestural strokes like this can really bring your paintings alive. You don't need to always paint something in great detail for a beautiful painting, and practicing this approach will help you look at subjects differently. Breaking down your subjects' stances and limbs into curves will help you later on when you paint figures with greater detail.

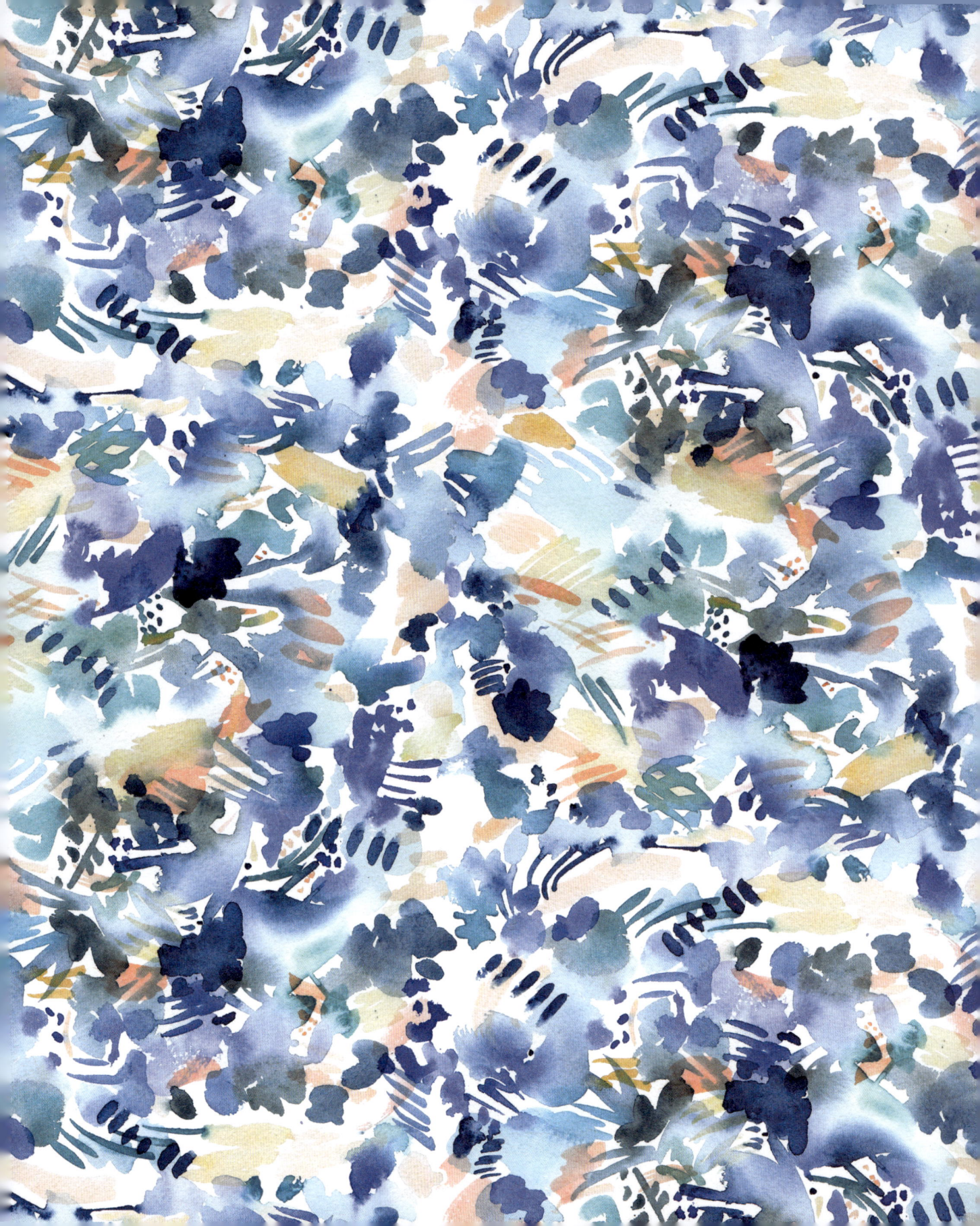

Section Four

VALUE, VOLUME, AND DEPTH

In our next section together, we'll be taking complex forms and figures even further, defining more complicated stances, the value scale, and more. Everything we've learned so far is starting to come together as we form each painting, and I'm excited for you to continue to learn and apply these practices with the following subjects. As we meet the challenge of increasingly complex paintings, with practice, we're getting better each day!

Day Nineteen

MOVEMENT

Build on previous techniques with curves and movement by painting the gesture of a bird in flight.

Estimated time: 45 minutes to 1 hour

STEP ONE:

Sketch

A bird in flight? You bet! It's going to be gorgeous. The way a hummingbird's wings spread when it hovers in mid-air lends itself beautifully to watercolor. A bird in this flight stance is defined by the "C" curve of its back. Start with a smaller circle for the bird's head; just below that, sketch a wider oval that will help curve the back and form the belly; then trace the left side of these shapes for a sweeping "C" curve from the top of the bird's head all the way down to the tail feathers. Referring to the rest of the sketch guides, add more "C" and "S" curves. Note that the wings are essentially two "C" curves for the top of the wing and a shallow "S" curve for the base. Lightly sketch in feather details as guides.

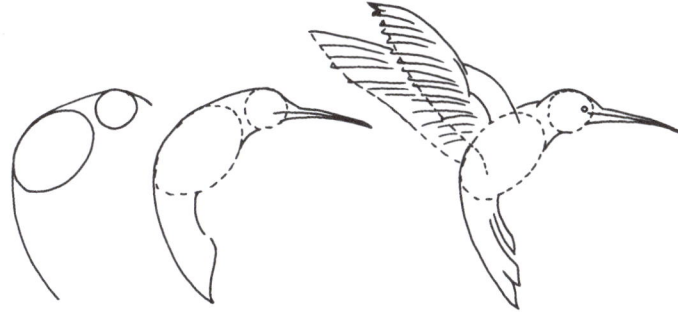

The hummingbird's rapid, blurred wing beats can be seen only in photographs—or paintings like these. If you're up for a little extra credit, take a look at how other captured moments in hummingbird flight are formed from basic curves and shapes, and practice these.

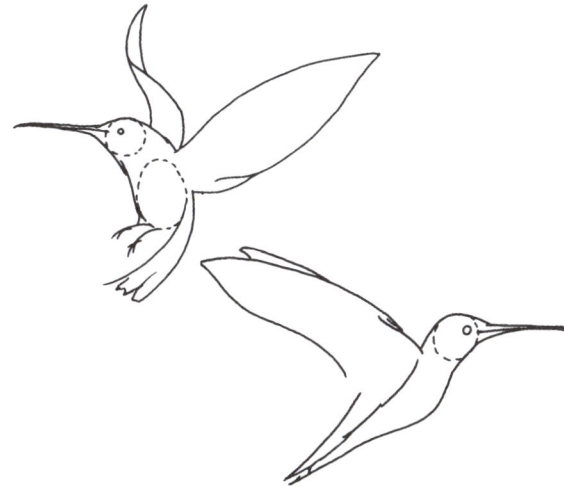

STEP TWO:
Choose a color palette

Many different hummingbird species are found throughout the Western Hemisphere. Some of the animal kingdom's most beautiful and striking color combinations are found on these tiny birds. For today's colors, I've used combinations of blues and yellows to contrast with the oranges, pinks, and vibrant greens found in the flowers this bird will be hovering next to. We'll use lots of turquoise for the curve of the bird and its tail feathers, and on the feathers closer to the wing and tail tips, I've added some deep Prussian Blue.

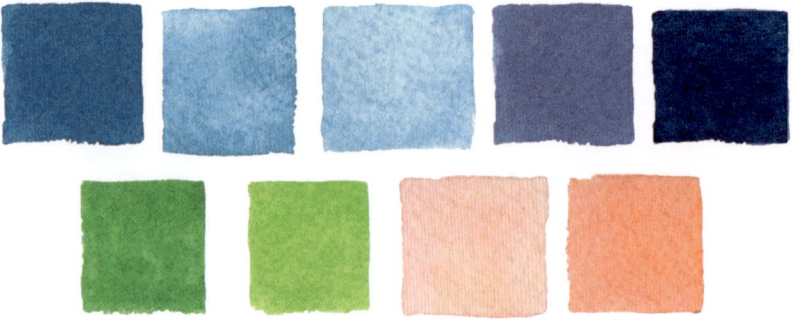

STEP THREE:
Put paint to paper

Today's painting will require depth in hue and blending with WOW. To start, load up your size 6 brush with a light wash of Phthalo Turquoise and apply this along the head and body of the bird, avoiding the beak and back wing area for now. Next, load up your size 2 brush with a thicker amount of turquoise and add the tail feathers, touching the edge of the wash so that these feathers bleed into it. Do the same thing for the wing, then add Prussian Blue at the ends of the wing for definition. Apply some yellow accents to highlight the curve of the belly and just below the wing. Play with where you add color and see how it bleeds and adds shape and form.

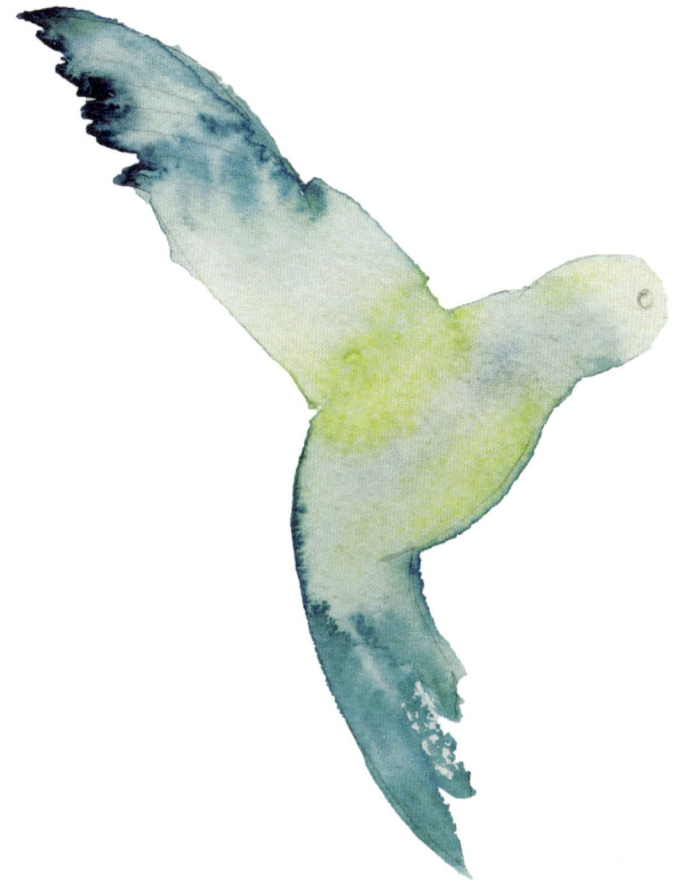

Let the watercolor bleed and move fluidly between sections, while still controlling where certain colors sit and how they explode into one another. Keep this part very loose to create texture.

While the body and front wing area dries, we're going to add some florals. Because this bird is in a perfect arch for feasting on some nectar, we're going to arch a flower directly under its beak. Apply what we practiced on our days of painting stems, leaves, and florals, starting with base layers for now; we'll come back and add detail later.

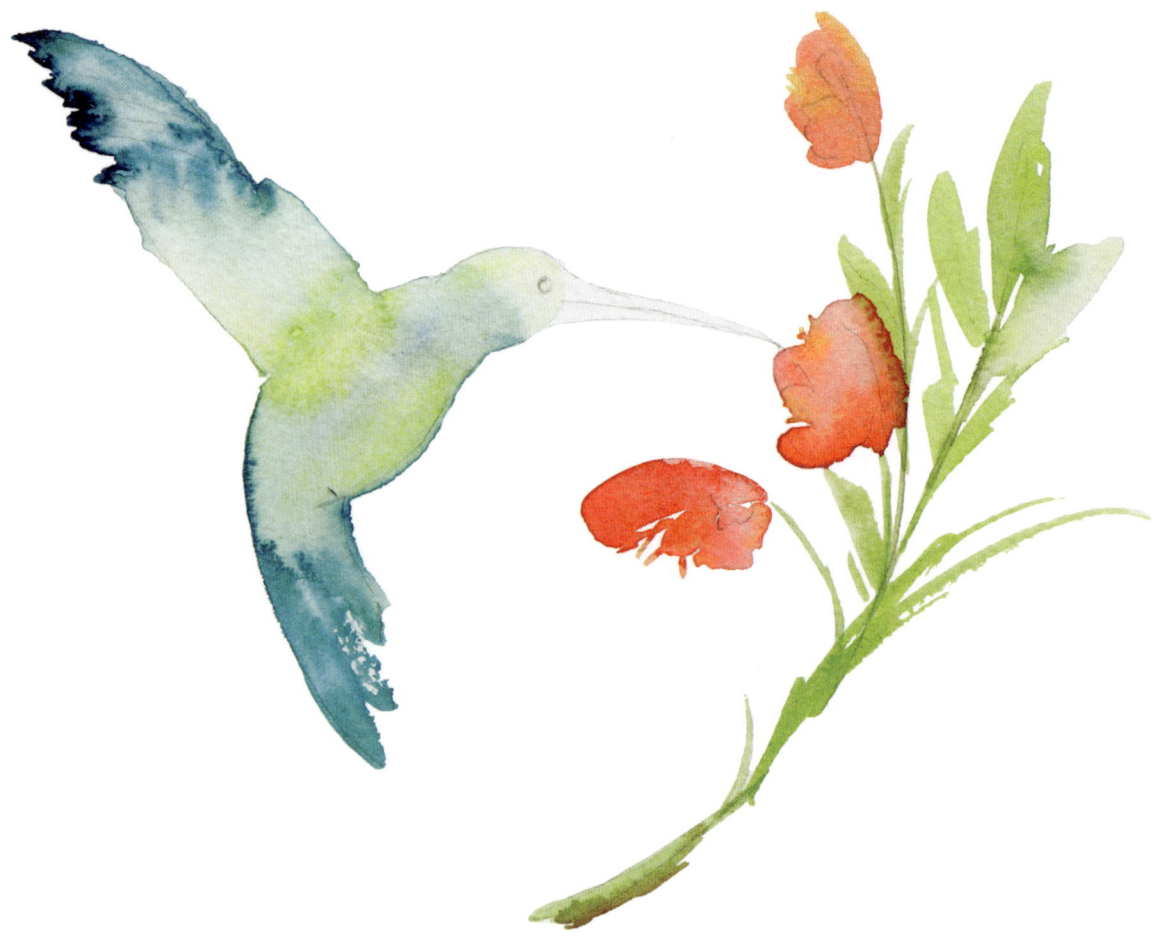

Once you've finished adding the flowers, the body of the bird should be dry and ready for detail. For the eye, make a very dark, thick mixture of Burnt Umber and Mars Black. With the tip of your size 2 brush, paint a circle, leaving a tiny dot of exposed paper in the center for a highlight. Use this same thicker color to darken the beak as well.

Next, mix up shadow colors for the feathers. For the tail feathers, add a touch of cobalt to make a deeper, richer turquoise; for the wing, combine Phthalo Turquoise and Prussian Blue. You will use these to bring the wing, and later on the body, forward with very thin curves, painting from the ends of each feather toward the body. Begin lightly, then stop to see the effect and decide whether it needs more.

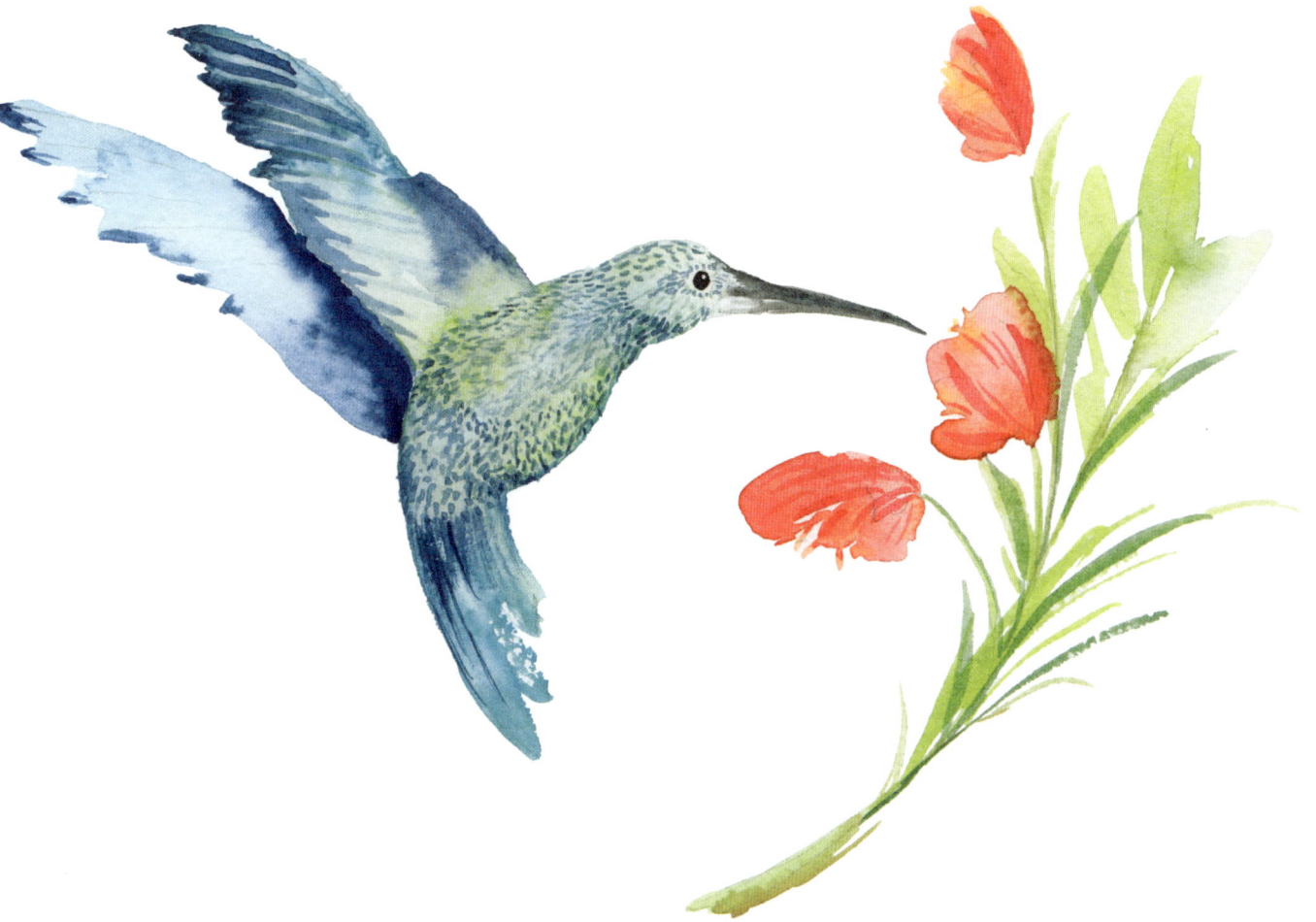

Before making the finishing touches to the hummingbird, add some detail to the flowers to bring them forward. Next, finish the bird with tiny "C" curves along the body and neck for feather detail. As a final touch, add the second wing. This will be seen as behind the wing we already painted; make it lighter to create distance. Apply a wash first, then darker shadows toward the base of the wing, right up against the body and front wing, to separate those sections.

Trust your gut and don't be afraid of messing up! That's how we learn and get better.

Day Twenty

VALUES

Learn how to pick out values using the value scale for each hue to paint a rose.

Estimated time: 1 to 1½ hours

STEP ONE:
Sketch

Are you ready to take this journey to the next level? Today we're going to paint a rosebud in greater detail than we did on day 17, using the value scale that I explained in the intro to pick out color values. Typically, when I'm painting something more realistically, I'll print two photographs of my subject for reference: one in full color, so I know what hues/colors I'll be using, and the other in black and white. Often, when looking at the color photograph, it can be overwhelming to know how to appropriately shade the subject. Usually you can pick out only a couple of values; say, lighter pink and darker pink. But when painting with just two or three values, your painting will look more flat and dull than when you use the full gamut of values found in a real-life subject.

So when you want to paint something more realistically, try this: reference the black-and-white photo for shading and value help, hold your value scale up to the photo to pick out those values and their placements, and then look at the color photo for color reference. If you'd like to print out photos to refer to, try searching on "pink rosebud" in Pinterest or Google Images for photos. That's my personal process for getting started; I hope you'll find it helpful.

Now we'll break this subject down into basic shapes. To start, form the base of the bud by lightly sketching a circle in the middle of your paper. Then, starting below the base of this circle, draw a "C" curve up through the middle and above. This curve will help position the center of the flower, where the stem meets it and where each petal arises.

At the top of this "C" curve, add a small oval for the top of the flower.

Next, starting at the base of your circle sketch, place "S" curves around the base and sides of the circle for the outer petal area. Vary the height on both sides so they're not even.

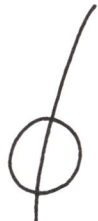 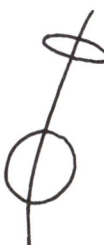 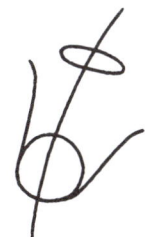

At the top of these "S" curves, lightly sketch an oval to close this off, making a cone shape. Then add sides from the top smaller oval down to the oval you just sketched for the inside row of petals. This should create two cones or cup forms, the smaller one nested inside the larger.

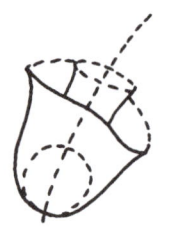

Next, as we covered on day 17, creating folds and curves in petals, we'll lightly sketch in petals and folds, making the flower more realistic. Start with either a "C" or an "S" curve to indicate the flow of the petal, then go back over this to give it more detail and petal shape, referring to my example sketch for guidance as needed. Remember that the edge of each petal arises from this original circle and curves back to it.

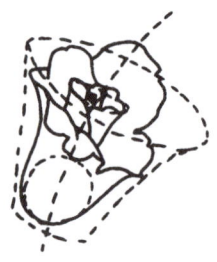

Make final adjustments to your sketch and erase any marks and guides you don't need.

STEP TWO:

Choose a color palette

For this piece, we'll use mostly a mixture of Opera Rose and Scarlet Lake for the petals, and varying mixtures of Sap Green and Lemon Yellow Deep for the stem and sepals—the narrow leafy green points that enclose the base of the bud. Instead of mixing up these hues in separate wells in my palette, I've just gone back and forth between pink and red and green and yellow and lightened these hues by washing off my brush in water. The lightness of the value you want will determine how much pigment you'll rinse off your brush.

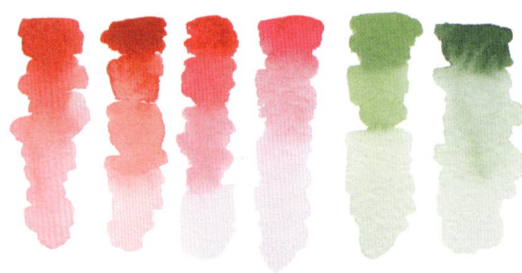

The swatch samples show the colors I mixed up for this painting. Test your mixtures on a piece of paper first to make sure you like the hues, then gradually add water to each swatch to see its value range. Sampling these colors and values beforehand will help you determine where certain values should go in the flower.

For the pinks, the hues range from a full-strength Scarlet Lake to Scarlet Lake and Opera Rose, Scarlet Lake and a little more Opera Rose, then full-strength Opera Rose. For the greens, the first hue is Sap Green and Lemon Yellow Deep; the second is the same but with less yellow for shadows.

STEP THREE:
Put paint to paper

If you are nervous at this point, think of each petal and section of this rose as its own separate painting, just as we did on day 17. This style of painting will take longer than what we covered in the beginning of this book, but knowing what you've learned already and applying that to this painting will help you tremendously. Remember, the basic shapes we used in the sketch should inform all the strokes we apply, especially how we shade this subject.

With your size 6 brush, apply a small blob (technical term, right?) at the base of the main circle of your rosebud. Then rinse your brush off completely and blot excess water onto your paper towel before going back to the paper. Wash from the top of that petal down toward the top of the circle, curving around its sides and avoiding the center. Touch the darker value (or blob) of paint so it grazes that area and bleeds into the wash. Continue to add water and outline the base of the bud, filling in as you go and getting lighter with each application. You're accentuating the curve of this circle with a gradation of deeper red-pink at the base, then around the sides and lighter throughout. The addition of water and lightening between each layer of shading shows the in-depth use of the value scale. Revisit day 7, when we discussed how to shade a circle; this will help you place the shadows and highlights.

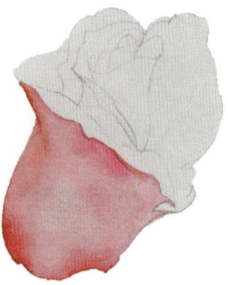

Because the top of this section is underneath the outward curve of a petal, add darker values to that top edge, underneath that curve, to emphasize shadow.

Next, paint the remaining petals, adding the darkest value toward the base or crease of each petal, then with just water on your brush, apply a thinner stroke right up against the shadow for WOW. Keep washing your brush off between strokes and grazing it against the wet edge of where you just painted to allow the gradation from shadow to highlight to become lighter more dramatically. Remember to skip sections that are touching wet petals.

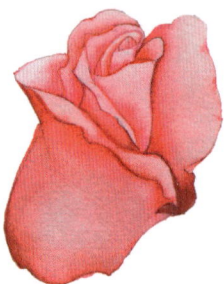

Keep your light source in mind as you shade each individual petal.

Once you've finished painting all the petals, we'll move on to the sepals and the stem. Here we will apply the WOW technique with values of greens. Our mid-tones will be varying values of the Sap Green and Lemon Yellow Deep mixture and Sap Green by itself. To start, apply a full-strength base layer of Lemon Yellow Deep on all the sepals and stem. Once this dries, use the same technique as for the petals but with green. The darkest portion of the sepals and stem should be closest to the base of the flower. Accentuate the curves of each sepal with shadows and apply washes for an even blend throughout the sepals and stem with WOW. If the deeper color spreads too far and makes the whole section one color, then use a dry brush or paper towel to blot it.

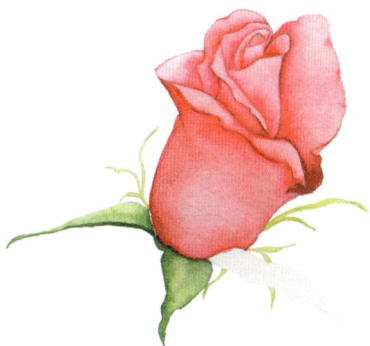

Avoid overlapping any green onto the pink-red sections. Red and green are complementary colors, so any overlap will only cause darkening and create black.

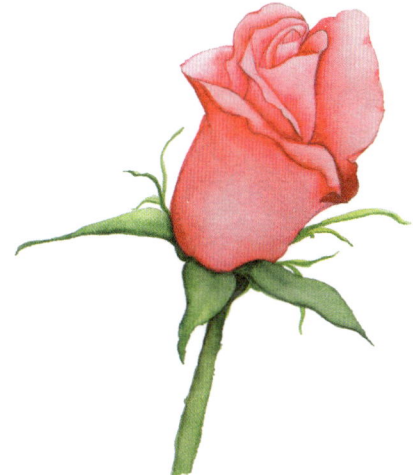

Once all your sections are dry, reevaluate the piece and touch up any areas that need cleaner edges or more blending. This is also a time to wash over any colors that may not have mixed very well.

Just like anything you do for the first time, each new subject you paint brings new challenges. Keep focused on what you've learned and keep at it. Having fun while you paint is the most important part. Each time you paint something it will look better than the last. You've got this!

Day Twenty-One

SUBJECT IN A LANDSCAPE

Build on previous techniques to create a subject in a landscape. Paint a toucan using curves, following form, and painting in sections.

Estimated time: 45 minutes to 1 hour

STEP ONE:

Sketch

Today we will paint a toucan on a branch simply by—you guessed it—breaking it down into basic shapes. Use the following steps as a guide as you work through your toucan sketch. Remember to be loose and follow the natural curves of the shapes.

First, use your pencil to lightly outline the shapes of the head and the body with two spheres: a circle for the head, then a wider oval directly below for the body.

Next, connect these shapes with curves on either side and down through the tail. Use a more dramatic "C" curve for the left side of the body to give it a big belly (our toucan is facing left).

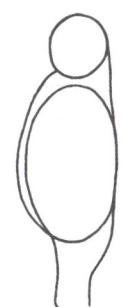

Now define the rest of the toucan by sketching a "C" curve for the top of the big beak, connected to two straight lines for the middle and bottom. Toucans also have a black teardrop-shaped section at the tip of the beak, so make sure to sketch that. Next, add a circle for the eye, which is directly behind the midline of the beak (between the two mandibles—the bird equivalent of jaws). Section off a triangular shape around the eye—this part is typically a different color than the rest of the feathers—and add varying sections for where the wing feathers overlap some of the body and tail feathers.

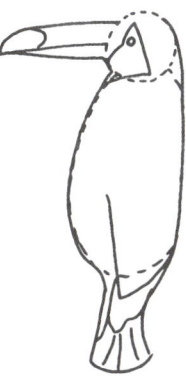

STEP TWO:
Choose a color palette

For mixing up your colors for this piece, it may be helpful to find a photo of a toucan to reference. There are many different species with different color combos; in my painting, I've used a combination of blacks, yellows, oranges, and blues. The most important hue in this piece is the black of the feathers. Most people expect to use pure black to paint the feather section, but this would look flat. Instead, you want to depict the way light is reflected by the shiny black feathers. Typically, when light hits black it is reflected back with a glimmer of blue. You can create this effect by adding a touch of Prussian Blue to a mixture of Mars Black.

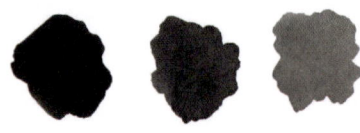 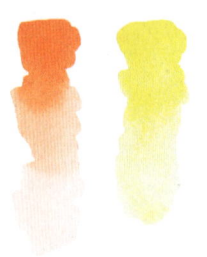 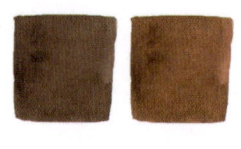

STEP THREE:
Put paint to paper

FIRST LAYER

Now that you have your sketch down, analyze the specific subject you're painting and plan which sections to paint first and what technique you'll incorporate (whether mostly WOW technique, WOD layers, or both). For this toucan, I've made the beak a natural diffused blend between yellow and orange hues, avoiding the areas sectioned off for black—we'll come back to those.

To get started, load up your size 6 brush with a light wash of Lemon Yellow Deep. Apply this wash all around the beak, except for the teardrop area, and leave a small gap down the middle of the beak where the two mandibles meet. Next, grab a good amount of Cadmium Orange on your size 2 brush, dab it on your paper towel a couple of times to get rid of excess water, and carefully draw the midline of the beak. Allow the orange to graze the yellow wash so it softly bleeds into the yellow. Because your brush isn't very wet at this point, its blending won't take over the entire beak. You want a soft gradation, so be sparing and try to keep the orange from completely taking over the yellow.

Next, mix up a light, blue-black wash for the base layer of the feathers. Load up your size 6 brush with this mixture and apply it to the entire body section, avoiding the portion at the base of the beak, the eye area, and the white portion just above the tail feathers.

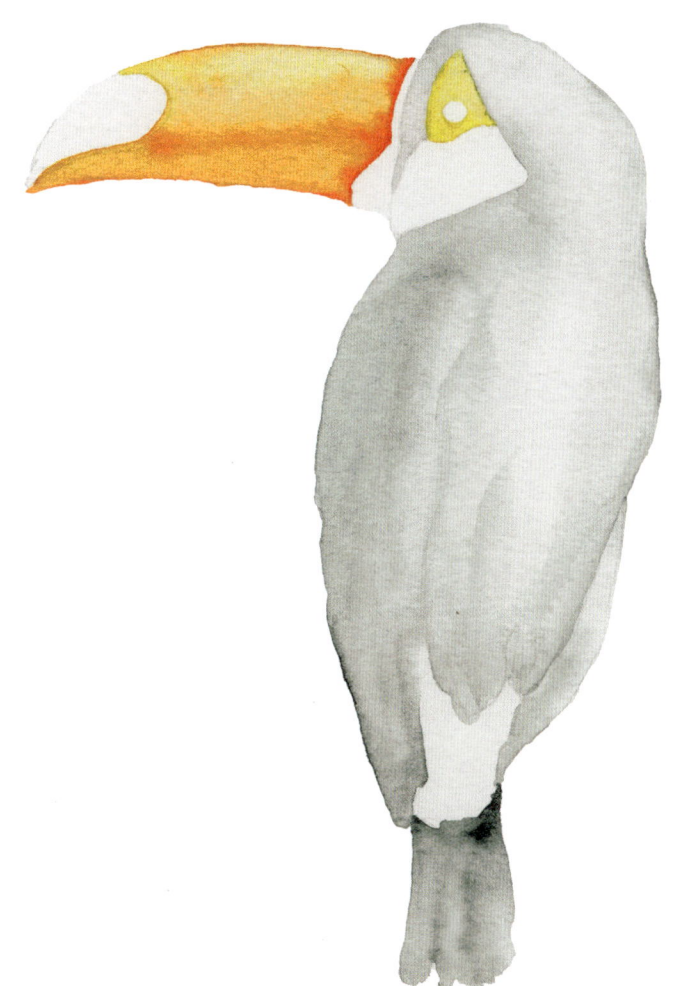

SECOND LAYER

For this next step, it's important that the base layer on these feathers is still wet, so the water and pigment can do its thing with WOW. Quickly load up your brush with a slightly darker version of your Prussian Blue-Mars Black mixture. Use the tip of your size 6 brush to add mid-tones and shadows to the base of the toucan's feathers. We can always go back after this layer and bring out further detail by painting WOD. Add this deeper color at the top of the tail feathers to enhance this section beneath the white feather section. Drag it along with the tip of your brush in curves and lines to start emphasizing the feathers. Have a paper towel handy so if anything blends too much you can blot it up before it dries. At this point, focus on accentuating the form and curve of the bird, locating the light source, and where to place most of your mid-tones.

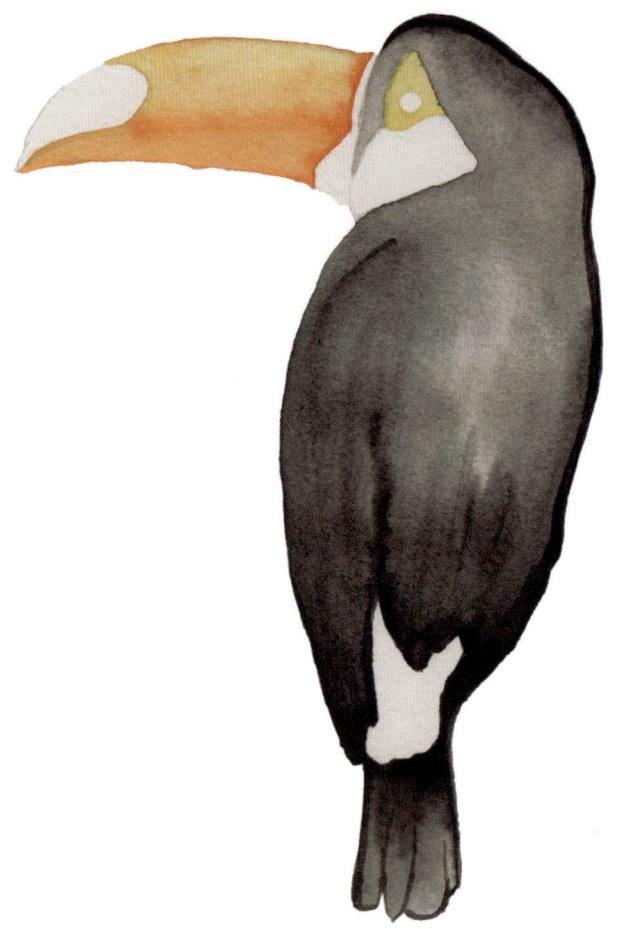

THIRD LAYER

For this next step, if you haven't already sketched the branch your toucan is perched on, simply add lines extending from each side of the bird, leaving a "C" curve gap for the back claw of its foot—from this perspective, we can see just one of the toucan's feet curving around the branch. Now let's paint our first layer of the branch with a light mixture of Burnt Umber and Mars Black. This can be more subtle; I've incorporated some WOW technique for minimal shading with mid-tones. Try to avoid the claw/foot area; you will paint this later.

While the branch dries, use the tip of your size 2 brush to add shadows and detail to the body feathers. As we've learned previously, the lower shadows, farthest from the light source, are really tight clusters and gradually become more sparse as you work your way up the subject toward the light source. Think back to days 7 and 19, when we shaded a tree and added feather detail to a hummingbird. You'll shade the curved form of the toucan's back with similar practices.

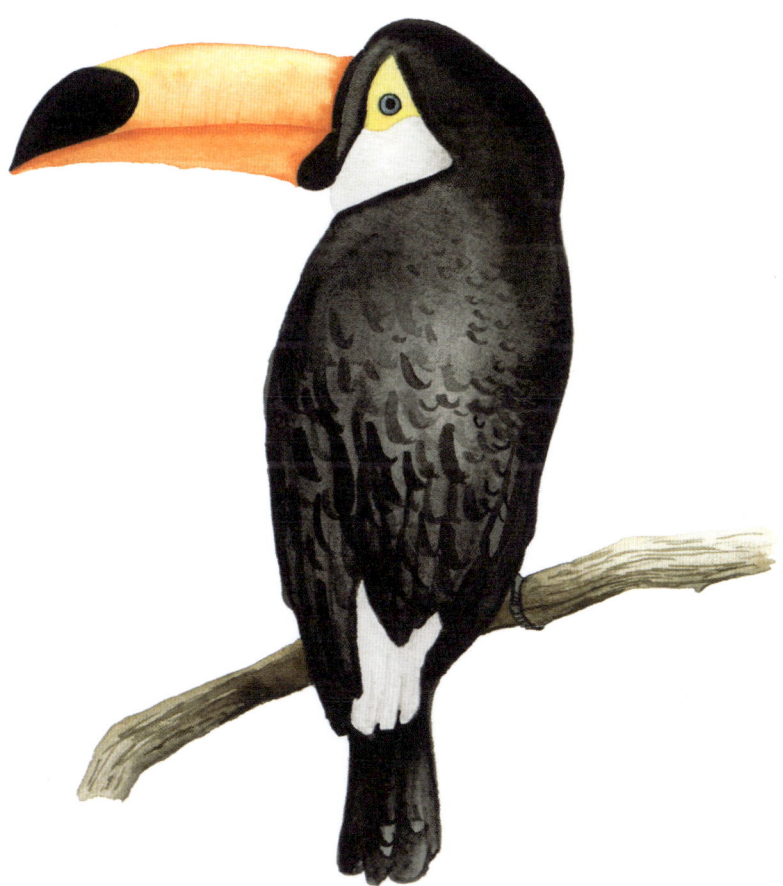

FOURTH LAYER

Once this section has definition, with convincing feathers, move on to the small section of white feathers directly above the tail. With a very light blue-gray mixture of Prussian Blue, Mars Black, and water, pull a few feathery curves forward to show depth in this section. Follow this with the section around the eye. Then paint in the triangle area beneath the eye with a yellow hue. Next, fill in the black teardrop tip of the beak. Once the yellow eye area is dry, add the black section at the base of the beak, connecting it to the rest of the toucan's black head.

While these layers dry, move down to the branch and bring out the texture with a mixture of Mars Black and Burnt Umber to make a very deep shade. Using your size 2 brush, bring the tip across the branch in sparse, broken strokes, depicting the rough texture of the bark.

Next, add a Prussian Blue wash to the claw of the toucan and add shadow and small details with Mars Black, using your size 2 brush for this tiny area. Once you feel this section is finished, assess each part of the toucan, adding detail where needed. Finally, paint the eye: a black circle with blue skin around it. With your size 2 brush, paint the black circle for the eyeball. Once this is dry, finish the eye with a blue wash around the rim, and voilà! The details help this guy stand out, and this practice will help when we start painting full, detailed landscapes with multiple figures and sections.

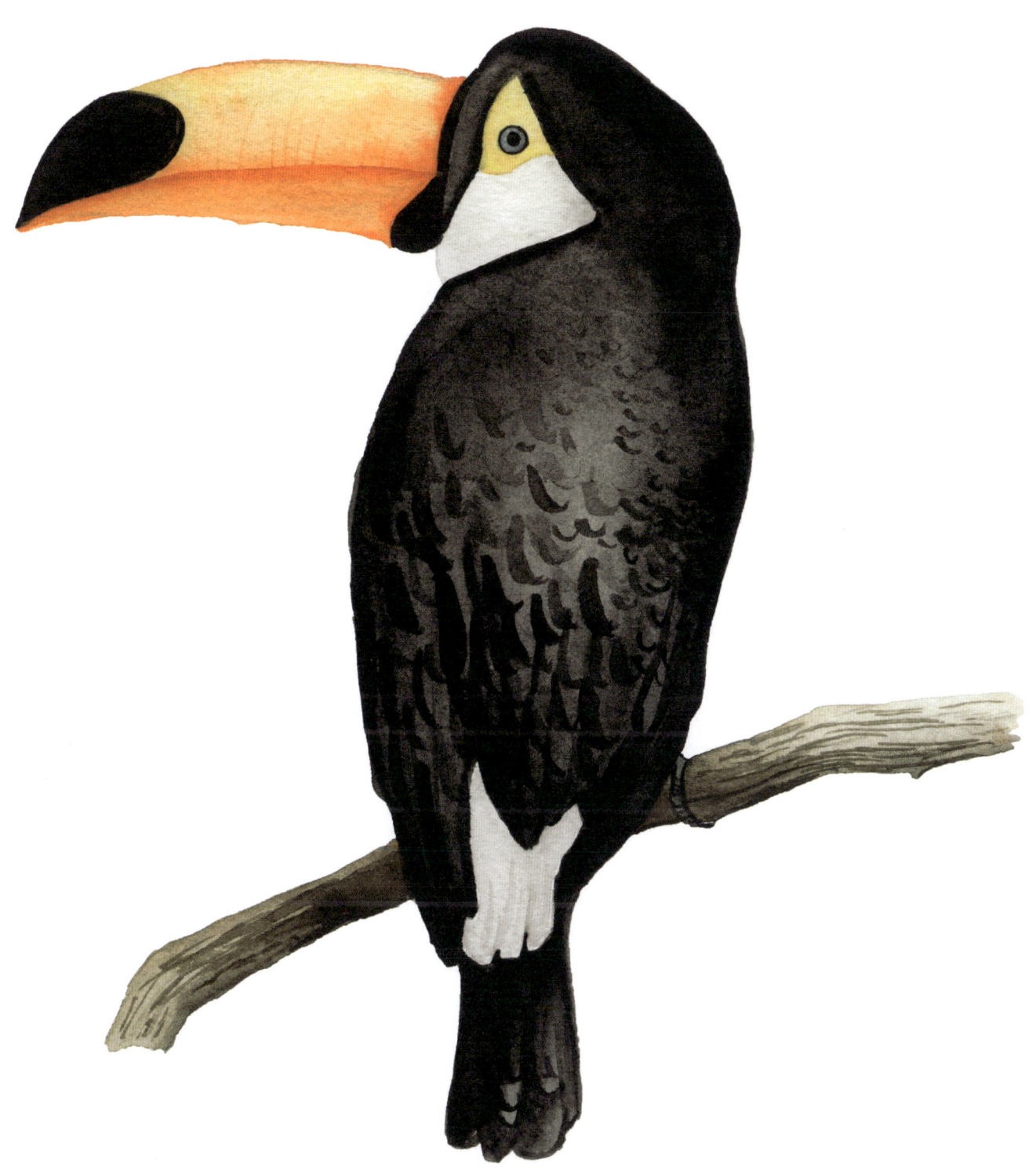

Day Twenty-Two

ATMOSPHERIC PERSPECTIVE

Use WOD technique to practice depth of field and atmospheric perspective by painting a desert landscape.

Estimated time: 45 minutes to 1 hour

STEP ONE:

Sketch

For today's piece, we'll mainly use the WOD technique for a desert landscape. An important part of sketching a piece like this is the placement of the horizon line. This can have a dramatic effect on the composition of the entire piece. A horizon line placed in the upper two-thirds of the composition highlights the foreground, placing those subjects in focus and accentuating the depth of field. A horizon line placed on the lower two-thirds of the paper gives it a more expansive look, with the big sky covering most of the piece and evoking the loneliness and emptiness of the landscape. Because we're practicing showing depth of field and perspective on a landscape, we're going to place our horizon line just above center, in the top two-thirds, so we can create a more detailed, focused foreground.

To begin this sketch, lightly place two "C" curves to indicate the horizon. Next, pencil in a few mountain ranges just above these. These mountain sketches are composed of mostly "C" curves and straight lines angling up and down, creating small nooks and crannies to show rocky details. Flat-topped mountains indicate mesas—iconic features of the deserts in Arizona, New Mexico, and Mexico.

Next, we're going to sketch foreground features. You can apply your previous practice on the saguaro cactus to add these as smaller details on the distant horizon line and larger, more sharply focused cacti in the foreground.

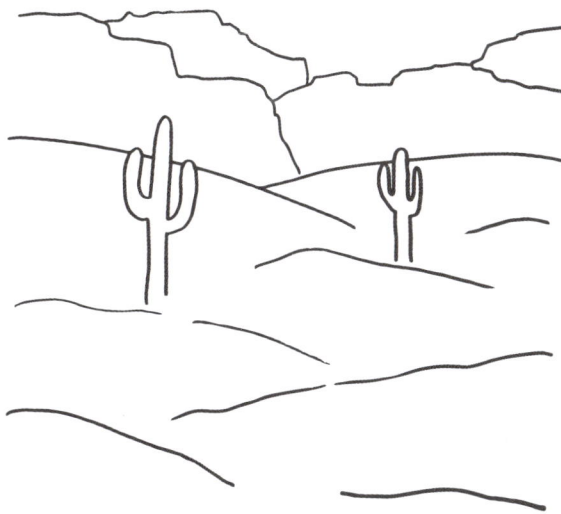

STEP TWO:
Choose a color palette

We're painting today's desert as a daytime landscape. We'll paint with neutral browns and gray tones, using Yellow Ochre, Burnt Umber, Mars Black, and some greens for the foreground details. For the mountain ranges and sky, we'll use varying values of blue and black and some Ultramarine Violet mixed with Burnt Umber and Yellow Ochre. The items in the foreground will be richer in detail and more vibrant, while subjects that are farther away become lighter and more blue-gray. This technique—creating depth of field by lightening and adding blue to more distant parts of a composition—is called *aerial perspective*.

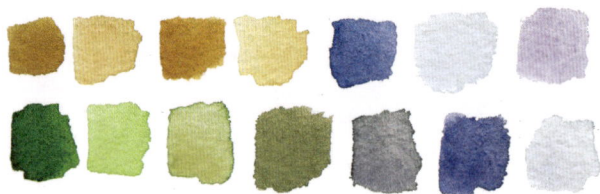

STEP THREE:
Put paint to paper

Ready to paint? Get out your size 16 brush and follow along with these layering steps.

FIRST LAYER
If you're not painting on a block of paper with all four sides glued down in the pad, make sure you have artist's tape to secure all sides of your paper. This will keep it from buckling while it's really wet, which can create pools of pigment and water. Once this is done, cover the entire surface of your paper in a very light wash of Cobalt Blue, starting from the top of the sky downward. This lighter layer will encompass the sky and multiple mountains. Add touches of Ultramarine Violet for variation in the sky, and kind of scoop back and forth, making some areas of the sky lighter than

others, to show the effect of clouds. Bring this wash down to meet the horizon line, getting lighter as you make your way down. You should still be able to see your sketch underneath this light layer, so later you can darken the mountain sections to bring them forward from the sky. While washing across your paper, make sure there are no pools of water collecting—this would take a very long time to dry and would usually leave a darker section of paint just in that area. Blot this with a paper towel or a dry brush.

While this area is drying, load up your brush with a light mixture of Yellow Ochre and Burnt Umber to lay down a wash for the bottom portion or the desert floor. Add darker hues to show where bumps and hills will go, letting these diffuse into the wash to show as shadows later on.

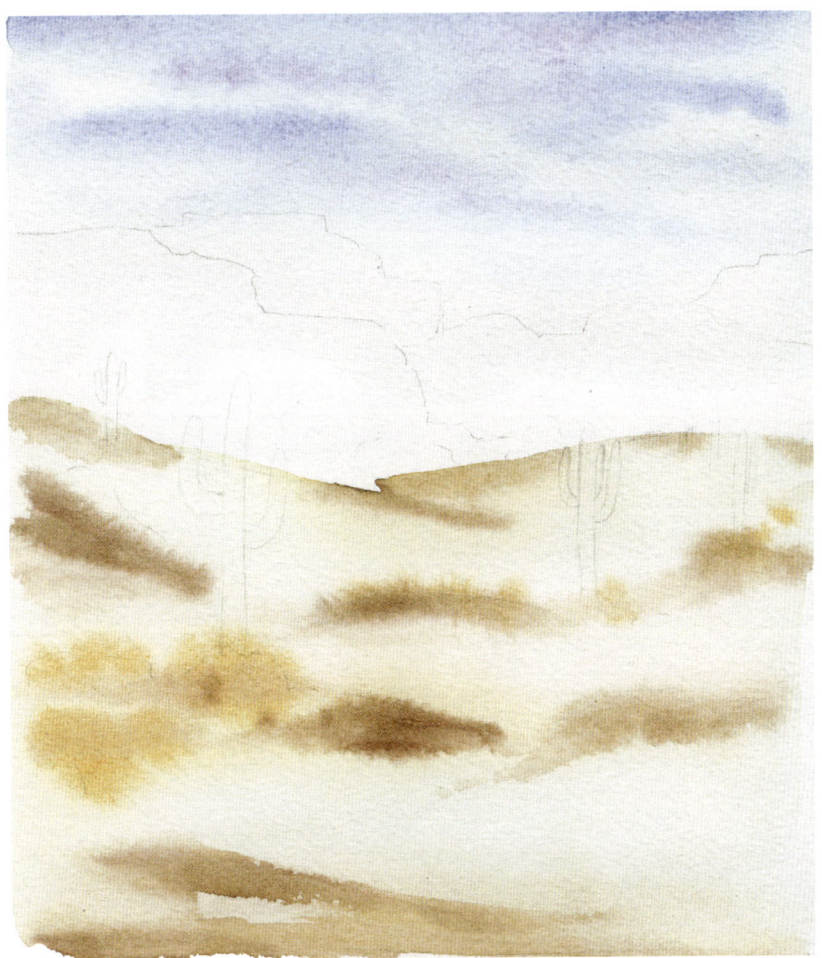

SECOND LAYER

Next, we'll lay down a light mixture of Ultramarine Violet and a touch of black, applying hints of Yellow Ochre to bring forward that color in the first mountain range. While the first mountain is drying, mix up a mid-tone value of Sap Green to add texture to the tops of hills, then wash these down to blend into the desert floor.

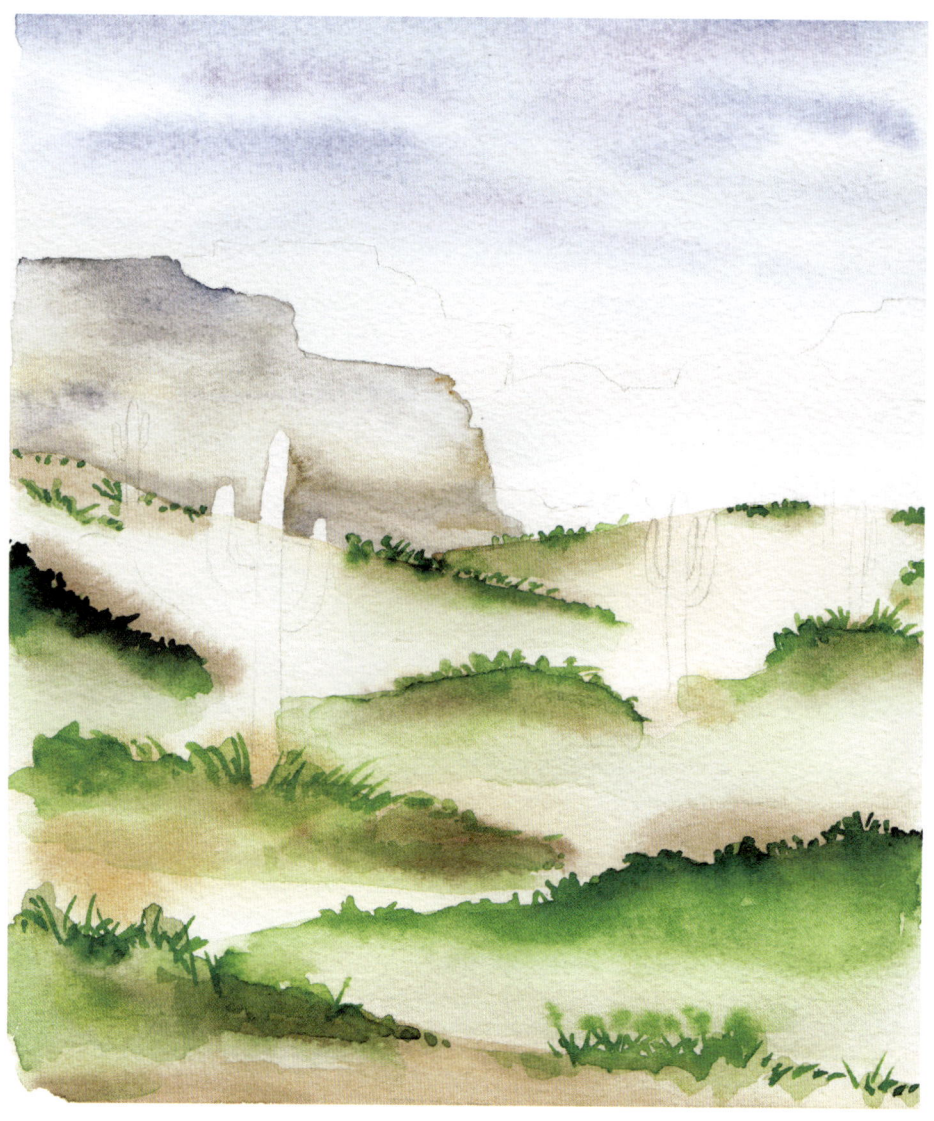

While these hills dry, test out your first mountain range to make sure it's dry, then add the second mountain. Make the mixture for this one slightly more blue-gray, but still carrying hints of Burnt Umber and Yellow Ochre. Let this dry, then start filling in the saguaro cacti. For now, paint only the ones on the left side, avoiding the wet mountain on the right. To show atmospheric perspective and distance, remember that subjects in the foreground should appear larger and more full in color and detail.

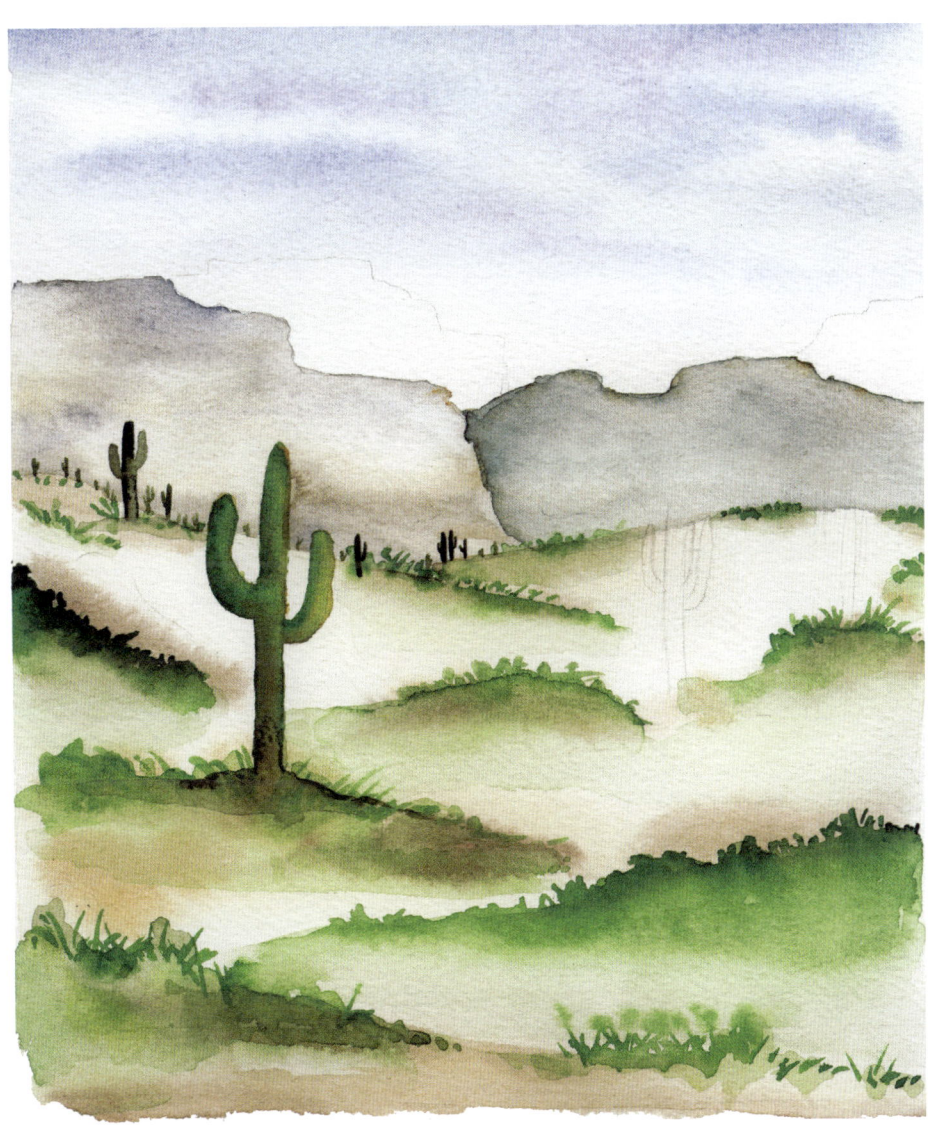

FINAL LAYER

Now we'll add the last two mountains and final details of the foreground. For the remaining mountains, add a touch more gray to the mixture and make sure they're defined against the sky. Paint in the remaining cacti along the horizon line and on the right side, making sure to use WOW for a soft blend between colors and any shadows if necessary. Add deep green strokes and texture to the nearest hill, to underscore the closeness, and make any final marks to the piece.

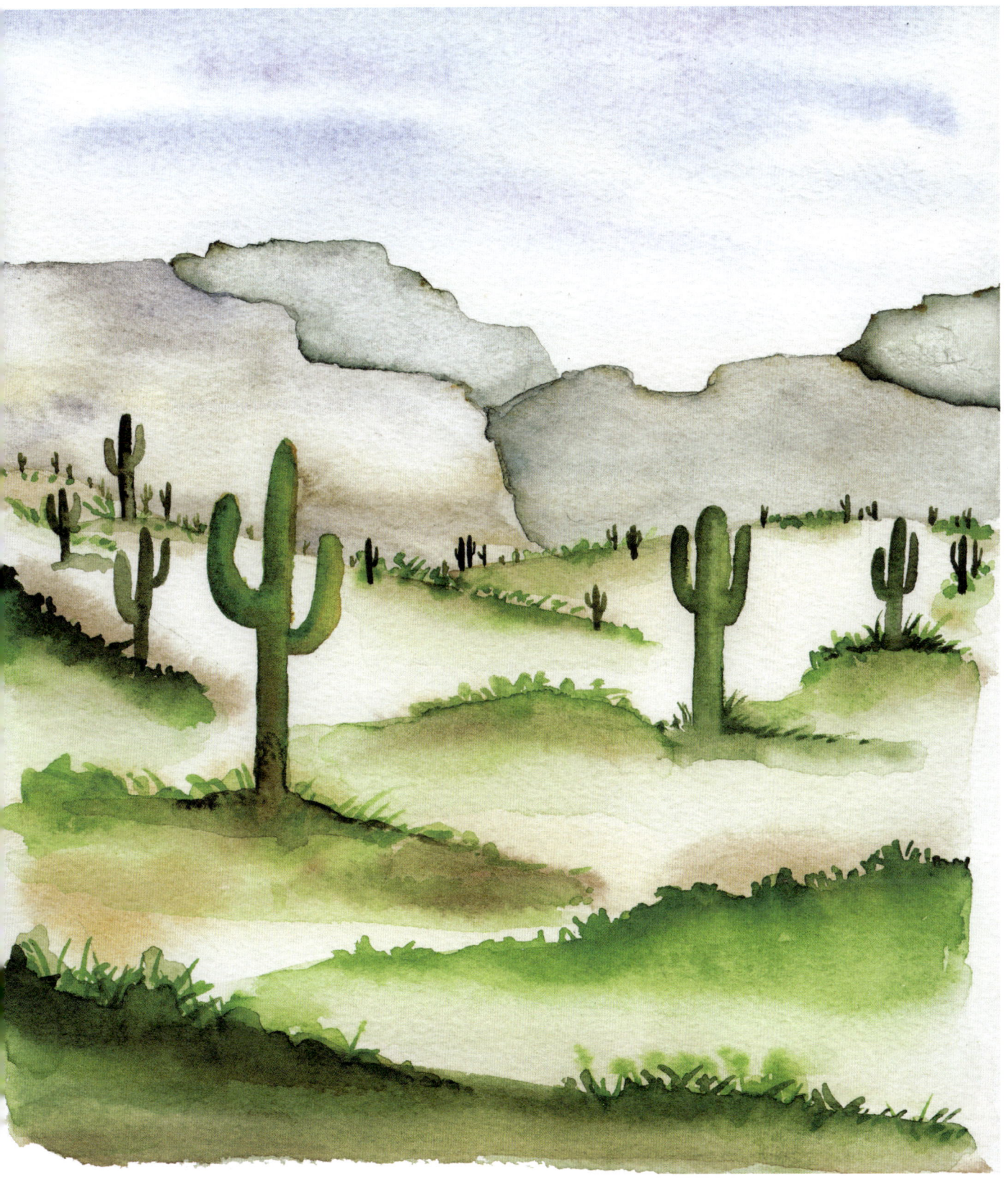

Day Twenty-Three

GRAYSCALE VALUE

Paint a more complex subject with multiple WOW sections to show varying values and grayscale.

Estimated time: 45 minutes to 1 hour

STEP ONE:
Sketch

We've painted chickens based on curves and strokes; we've painted a toucan and a hummingbird from basic shapes; and today we're going to construct an elephant out of basic shapes and curves, incorporating our shading knowledge using WOW and the value scale. This subject is a bit more complex than the previous animals because of the number of sections and the proportions of each limb. We'll be accentuating creases and shadows with darker values and using WOW for a smooth gradient between dark and light values and WOD for layering. Have your value scale card handy to reference.

To get started, follow along with the step-by-step sketch for your own elephant. Needless to say, an elephant is not a flat surface. Think of the trunk and the knees more like cylinders. These wrinkles will be little "C" curves to show the roundness of these sections.

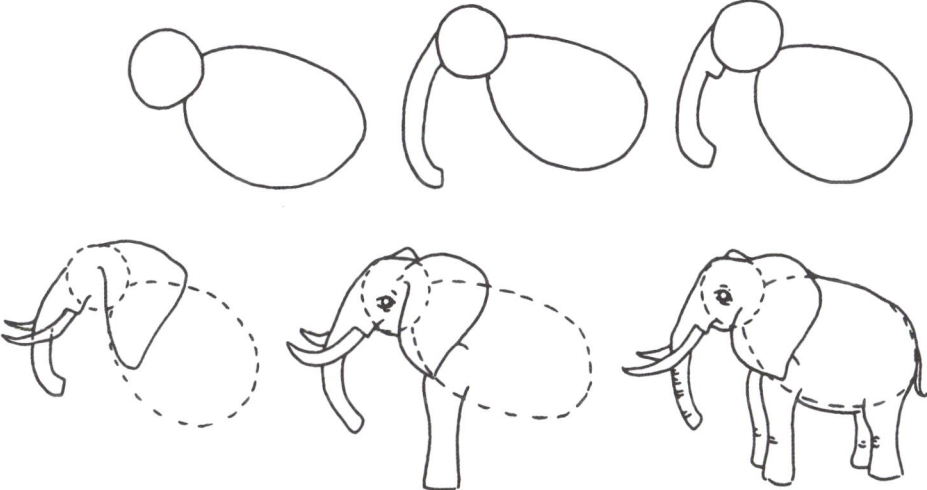

Apply what you have learned about sketching basic curves and shapes for these steps. (From the large ears, you can see this is an African elephant.) When you're ready to paint, remember to first erase the shapes and guides and leave only your contour drawing.

STEP TWO:

Choose a color palette

When you picture an elephant, what color do you imagine? Gray! Yes, most of this animal is gray, but there's so much more to this color than what's on the surface. There's warm gray and cool gray and everything in between. Warm gray is achieved by adding—you guessed it—a warm color, while cool gray is made by adding a blue tone. When painting our elephant, we'll be using a thick mixture of black with a touch of red or brown for a warm gray. This will be our shadow color, and as on day 20, we'll use this color with WOW to wash through the rest of the section while accentuating the shape with strokes. If I feel it needs to go even darker, I may accent some of the details and shadows with Mars Black by itself. For the grass, I've used varying hues of green and yellow-green, mixing Lemon Yellow Deep and Sap Green.

STEP THREE:

Put paint to paper

To get started, think about how to shade each section: Is any portion being overlapped or hidden from the light source? What is the base shape of this section, and how should you accentuate its highlights? Make sure to emphasize these portions, and your subject will really pop out from the paper. Let's begin, shall we?

FIRST LAYER

Apply a thin wet line of your darkest gray value where the ear and torso meet and down the front leg. Lighten your pigment slightly in water and brush this deeper value for WOW blending. Continue to lighten and gently brush, forming the oval shape of the stomach/torso and gradually filling in this area. As always, if there's too much water collecting in these areas, blot it with a paper towel or a dry brush. Grab more of your shadow color and apply it to the tail to darken it, and maybe reapply next to the ear if it needs more shadow.

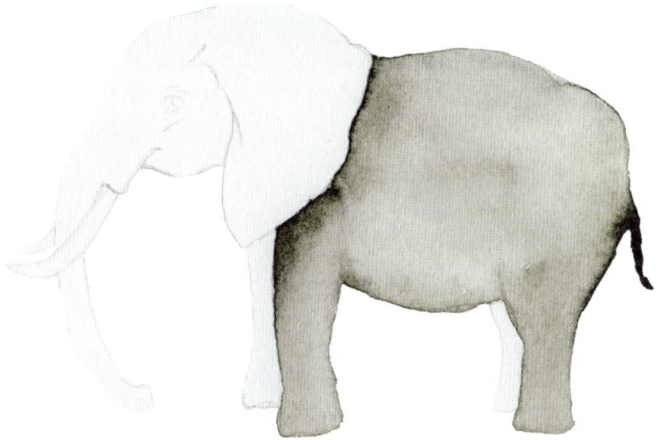

SECOND LAYER

While this is drying, hold off on painting the ear section—these two sections would bleed into each other, making a blob. Move on to the lower part of the elephant's trunk, just underneath the tusk. Apply the same WOW technique with this section. While the first layers on the side body and lower trunk dry, take your size 2 brush and load it up with Mars Black for the eyeball. Carefully outline the rim of the eye with the point of your brush, then fill in the iris. This part needs to completely dry before we can apply the wash layer to the head, so we'll come back to it.

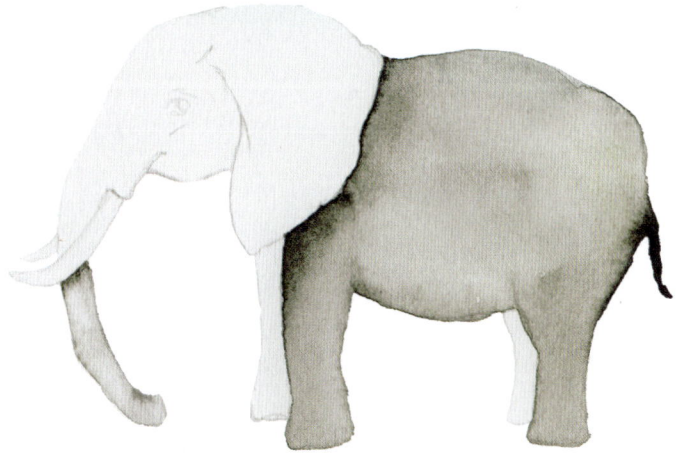

THIRD LAYER

Once the side body and lower trunk are completely dry, we'll apply the same steps we used on those pieces for the legs in the background. Add even darker values to the back legs to push them behind and in shadow. While these parts dry, mix up a slightly darker hue for your deepest shadows and details. Load up your size 2 brush with this color and add wrinkle details to the trunk. This part of the elephant has a cylindrical shape, so adding fine lines as "C" curves, as we learned on day 10, is crucial. Add even more accurate shading by painting "C" curves on both sides of the trunk. Add this shadow color to the body as well with a few wrinkle lines on the leathery body and knees.

While some of your shadows dry in other sections, paint the elephant's head with a lighter gray wash and emphasize any creases or areas that require shading by applying deeper values for WOW blending.

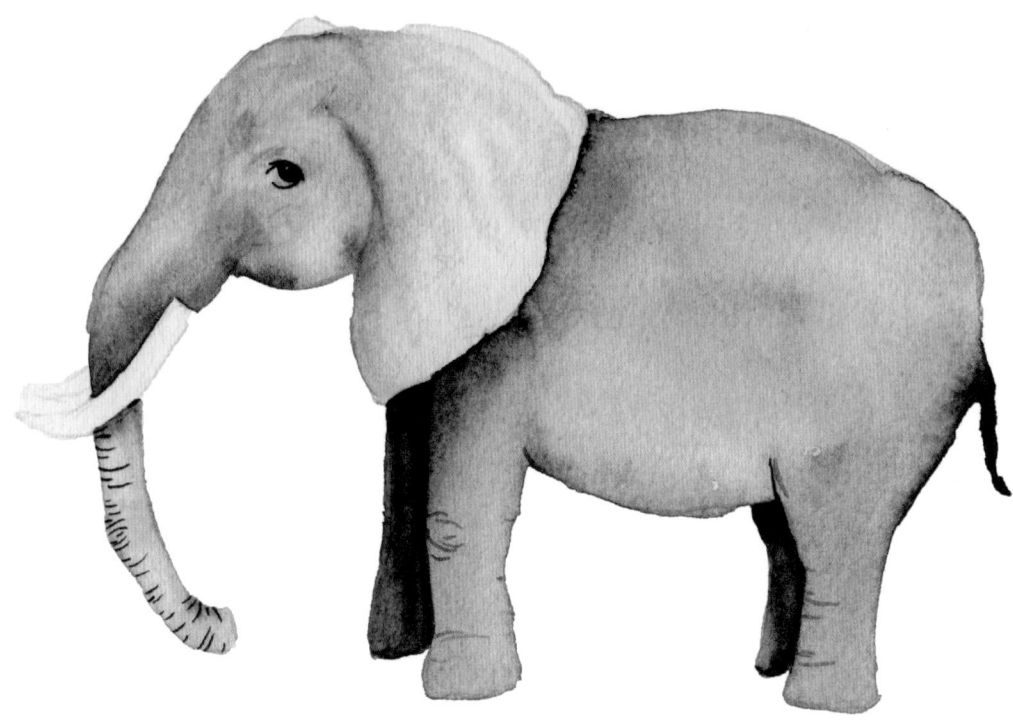

FINAL LAYER

Now let's add the final details to this subject. Use your shadow color to add a tuft at the end of the elephant's tail, more wrinkles on the trunk, and shading in areas that help bring out the elephant's bone structure. Pay attention to the eye area—accentuate the cheek and other points around the face and head. Be very delicate and don't overdo these shadow details. When you're done with the elephant, add some grass by using the tip of your size 2 brush, flicking up in "C" curves around the elephant's feet. Lighten up the green for the background blades.

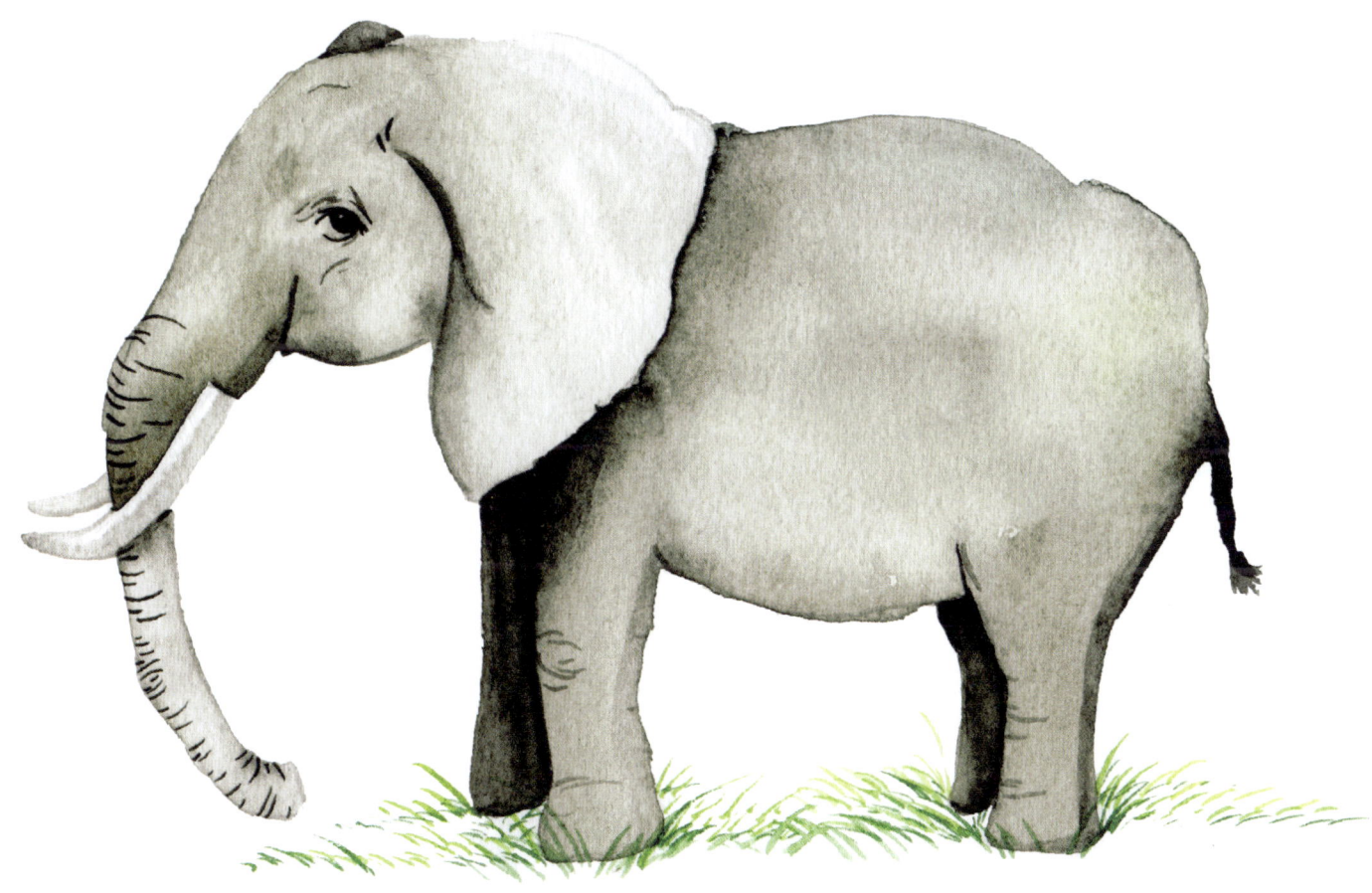

Day Twenty-Four

VOLUME

Paint cylindrical subjects to practice accentuating shape with a shading technique to show volume.

Estimated time: 1 to 1½ hours

STEP ONE:
Sketch

When it comes to creating volume in a painting, it's crucial to think about space and how each subject appears within that space. This affects how each form is shaded, how it curves, and where the shadows overlap other objects to create depth. Today we'll focus on making an object really pop off the page and away from the background. We will be using a different technique and method of shading than we have previously discussed. But first, let's talk about our sketch.

Today's piece will be an overgrown jungle with towering trees. These trees will extend beyond the top and bottom of the painting, forcing your viewers to use their imaginations, creating in their own minds the expansive scene beyond what's on the paper.

When starting your sketch, lightly pencil in a tree trunk on the left side, about a half-inch wide—this tree will be the closest in the foreground and therefore the widest. Fill in the rest of the paper with tree trunks, spacing them about 1 inch apart, making them thinner than the first and varying in width and structure as they would appear in nature.

Next, you'll add details to the piece that can help enhance depth, so lightly pencil in vines extending from the top of the page to about one-third of the way down, making them thinner than the trunks so they

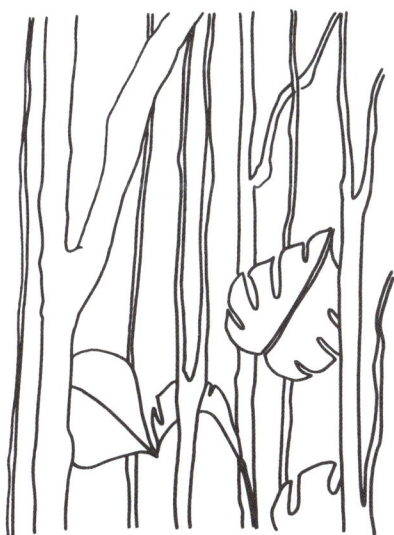

appear farther away. Apply what you've learned so far with composition and let yourself freely sketch—don't worry too much about what it should look like; just practice making marks on the paper. If you're not happy with something, erase it and keep going. Finally, add some monstera or banana leaves behind the trunks, creating varying points of interest.

STEP TWO:
Choose a color palette

To create three-dimensional depth in a painting, it's really important to use color and value for constructing form, as we've discussed before. You want this piece to feel like the jungle extends far into the background and the vine-draped trees are so tall that the canopy towers over the viewer. To achieve this effect, we're going to use three values of a Burnt Umber and Yellow Ochre mixture for shading the trunk, and an even darker shade for the details and curves of the trunk. We'll apply these colors to accentuate the trunks' cylindrical forms and create high contrast between shadow and highlight.

We'll also use ranges of hues between yellow-green and blue, using Phthalo Turquoise and Lemon Yellow Deep for our two main hues. This will create a bright background for equal contrast against the bright white on the trunks that will be showing through. We'll later add varying shades of green for the monstera leaves, and finally the complementary colors violet and yellow for added leaf detail. Instead of using traditional purple, which combines blue and red, we'll mix up a purple using Opera Rose and Prussian Blue. Get ready for a fun and very loud piece!

STEP THREE:

Put paint to paper

FIRST LAYER

Once you've mixed up your main hues, begin by painting a very light turquoise wash with your size 6 brush in your background sections, avoiding the tree trunks. If some of the corners and crevices in these sections are too tight for the size 6 brush, use your size 2. Vary each background section slightly in hue by adding a little more yellow to the turquoise mixture for one, more turquoise for another, and so on. Work your way from one side to the other, going from one background section to the next.

Once these sections are finished, wash your brush off completely and load up your size 6 brush with the lightest value of your trunk mixture using Burnt Umber and a touch of Yellow Ochre. For this piece, there will be no gradual blending between shadows, mid-tones, and highlights— just layers using WOD. So use the belly of your brush, and bring this shadow down the trunk, varying your stroke width frequently as you go, to show grooves and bumps in the trunk. Apply this to only one side of each trunk, accenting the curved form of the tree. Use your size 2 brush to do this on the thinner trunks.

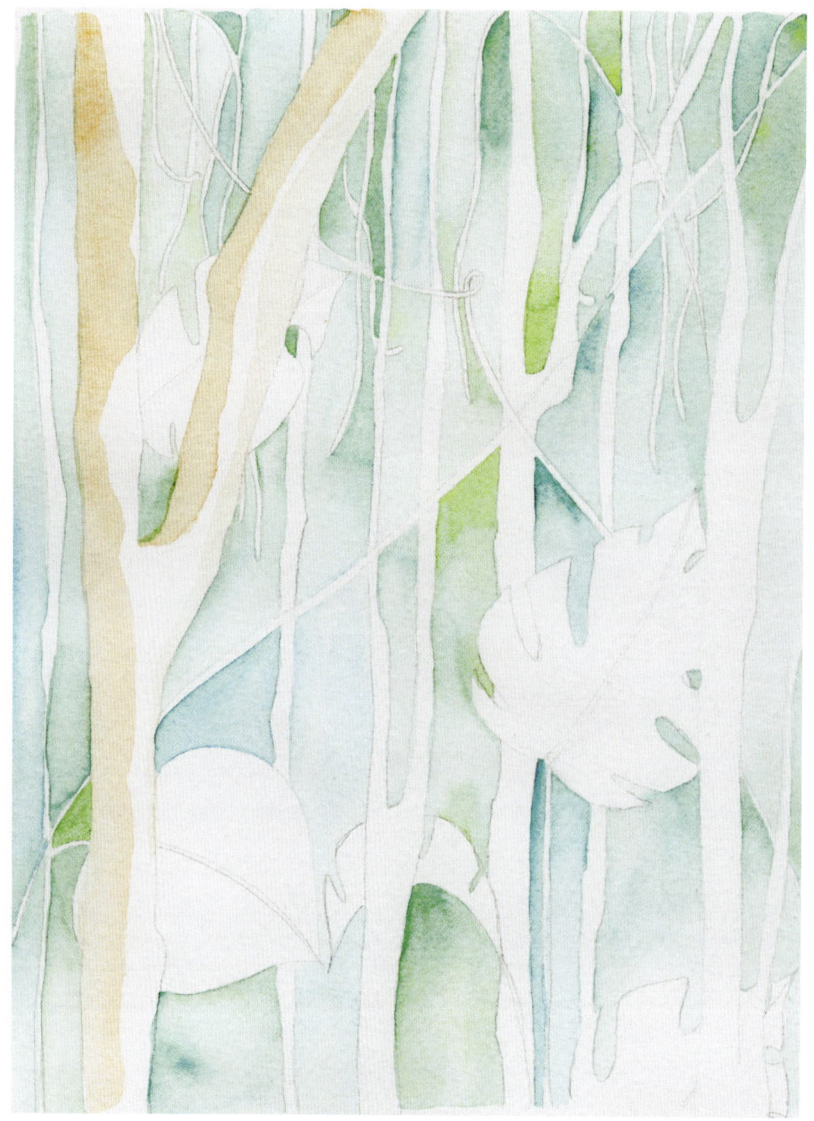

SECOND LAYER

Once you've worked your way across each trunk with your first mid-tone layer, load up your brush with more paint for a darker value mid-tone. Make sure the base mid-tone layer is dry, then layer on top, overlapping most of it, but letting some of the base layer mid-tone show through.

Once that's dry, add an even darker shadow layer on some of the wider trunks to show even more volume and form. You should be able to see three layers of shadows across the trunk, with bare white paper still showing on the right side of all the trunks for a highlight. If we were to paint these trunks in one solid color, they'd appear flat and two-dimensional. The depth of these layers helps us round out the trunks and make them pop.

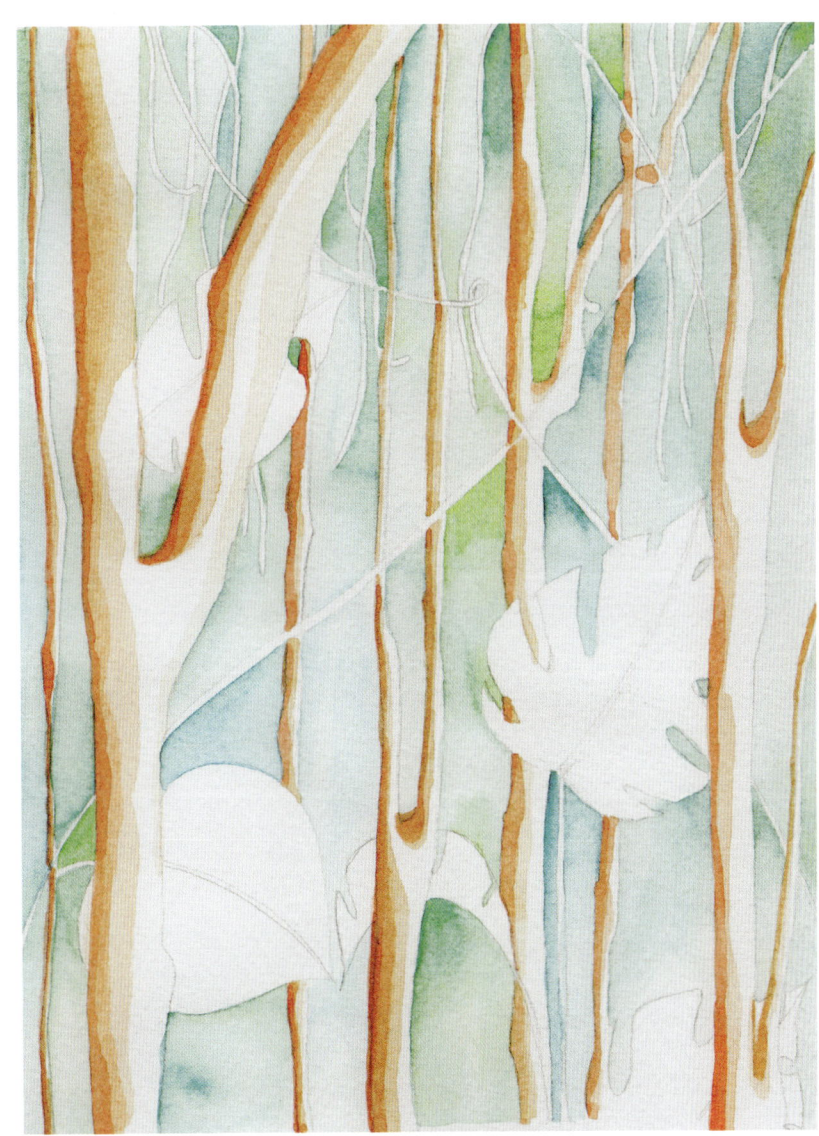

THIRD LAYER

Once those layers are dry, go back over each trunk with your darkest Burnt Umber mixture and use your size 2 brush to drag thinner horizontal creases or lines across the trunk, working your way up each trunk and curving around the form. These lines curving around the sides of the trunk help add volume by indicating they continue around the trunk and out of view. Vary the values of these details to create a realistic look.

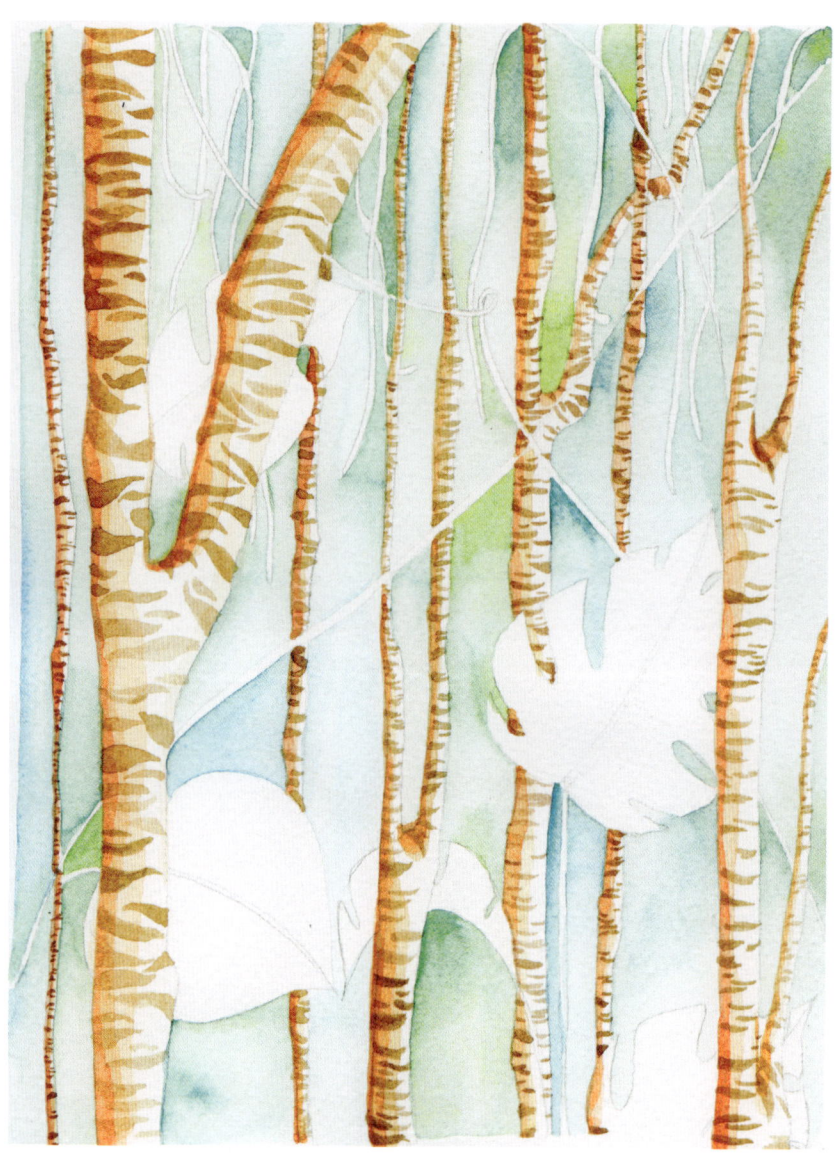

FOURTH LAYER

Once you've completed the bark detail, start adding the rest of the subjects by applying a yellow-green base layer to the monstera leaves and vines with a thick mixture of Winsor Green and Sap Green. Create a story in the piece by overlapping some of these vines around the trunks, showing how they grow in the space.

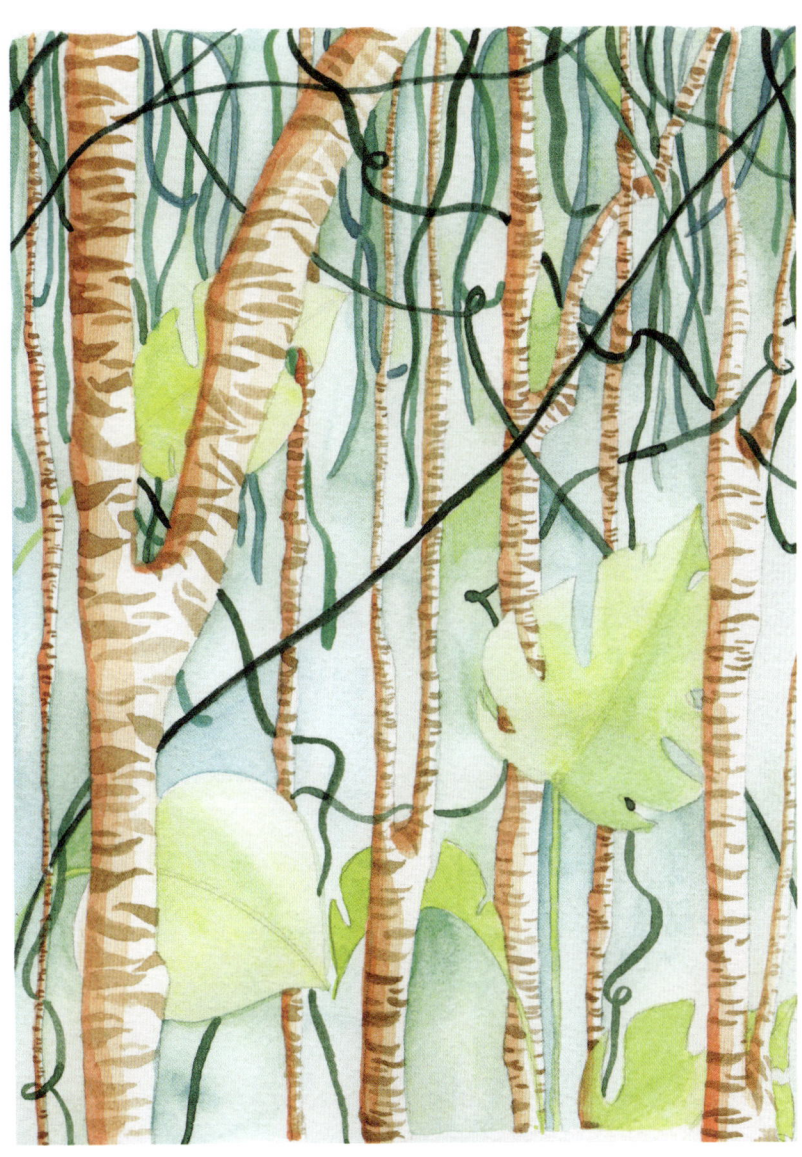

FINAL LAYER

Lastly, add some stems and leaves in varying values of your purple mixture and yellow-green mixture for added depth and contrast. In my example painting, these pieces take up the bottom two-thirds of the composition. As I've said, this helps expand the scene by forcing the viewer to picture what's beyond the edges of the painting. Add these randomly and freely.

Finally, accentuate shadows and detail on the monstera leaves, bringing these details into the foreground for added depth of field. Once you're done with this, step back and look over every area to see what needs to be added or developed upon. See how some trunks appear to be farther away and some closer? Even with the density and number of elements in the piece, we're still managing to create the sense of a wide, expansive space.

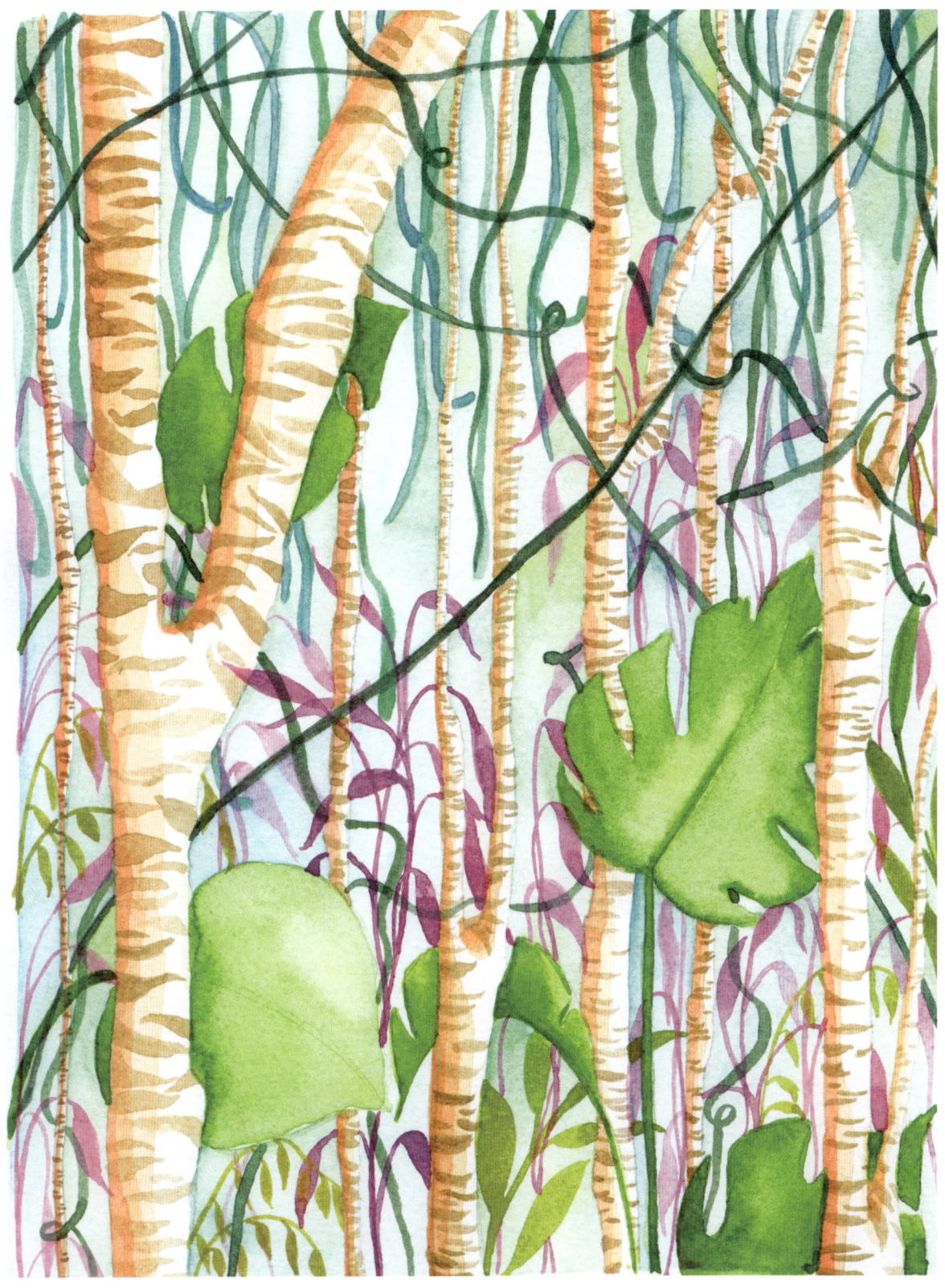

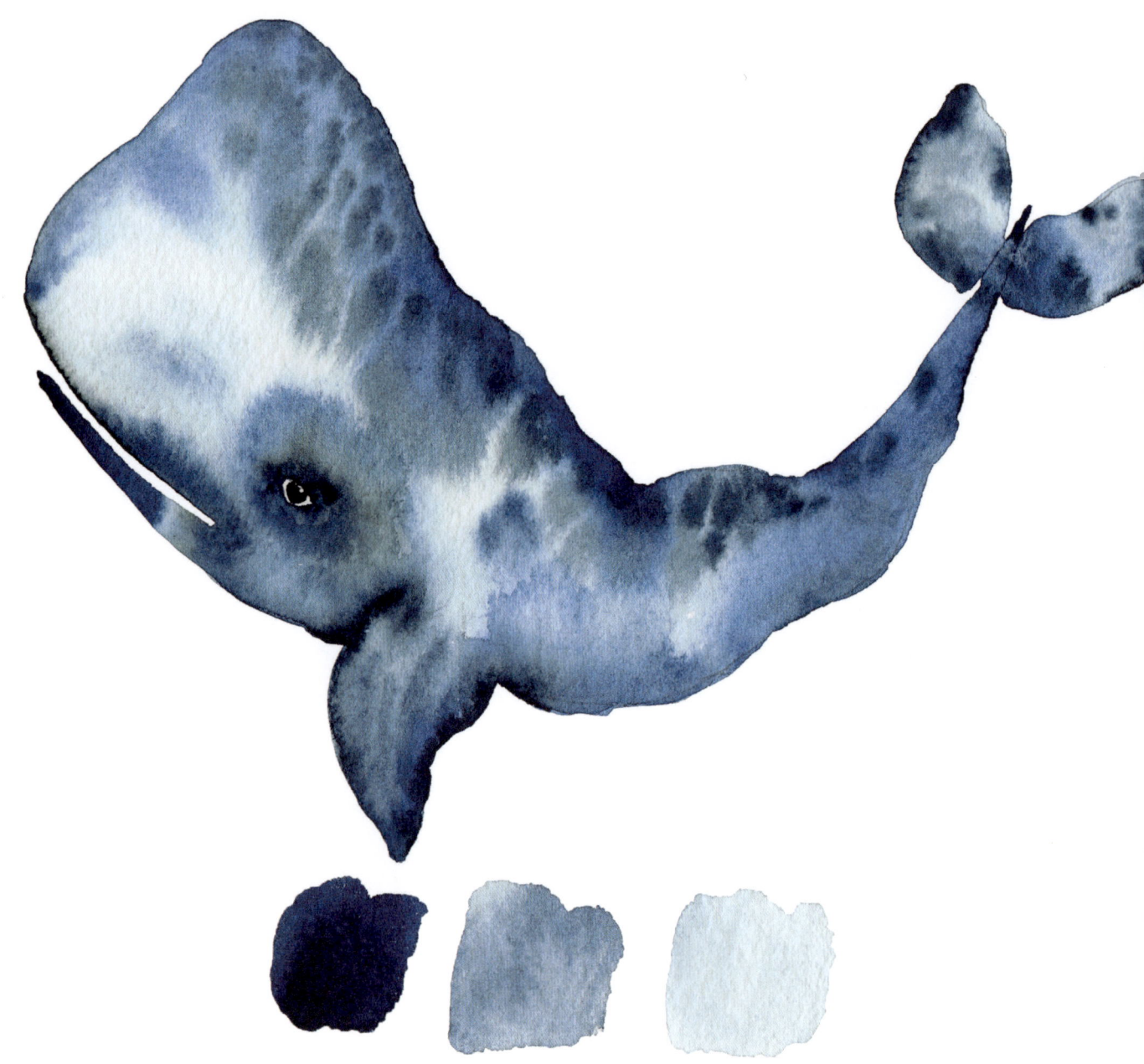

Section Five

APPLICATION

Wow! You've made it to the final section. By now you should feel comfortable with choosing an effective color palette, sketching from basic shapes, and painting and shading techniques using WOW and WOD. Painting every day is transformative when you take those important steps and challenge yourself with each piece. Constantly growing and trying out new things helps you develop muscle memory and discover your own voice and style in your painting.

Day Twenty-Five

WIDE LANDSCAPE: DESERT

Further develop aerial perspective and detail in a landscape with multiple sections by painting by a wide landscape.

Estimated time: 1 hour

STEP ONE:
Sketch

Today's piece is a wide-angle desert landscape. As in the overall structure of this course, we're kicking off the final section with an elemental landscape piece, slightly simpler than the three that follow. This piece serves as an introduction; we will build from there, adding complexity until we reach our final piece. So, let's get started, shall we?

Remembering back to day 22, we'll start with penciling in our horizon line. This point on a landscape establishes perspective; for this particular piece we will be placing it in the lower two-thirds to feature the gorgeous, expansive sunset sky found in the desert.

Start by lightly drawing the horizon line. Next, add smaller mountain ranges off in the distance, above the horizon line. Don't bring these up too high; we want the sky to be the main focus. While adding these rocks and mountains, include smaller saguaro cacti in the background, varying in size to show their placement in the scene. Continue to lightly sketch even more rocks and detail in the foreground, adding tumbleweeds and smaller details you might find in the desert.

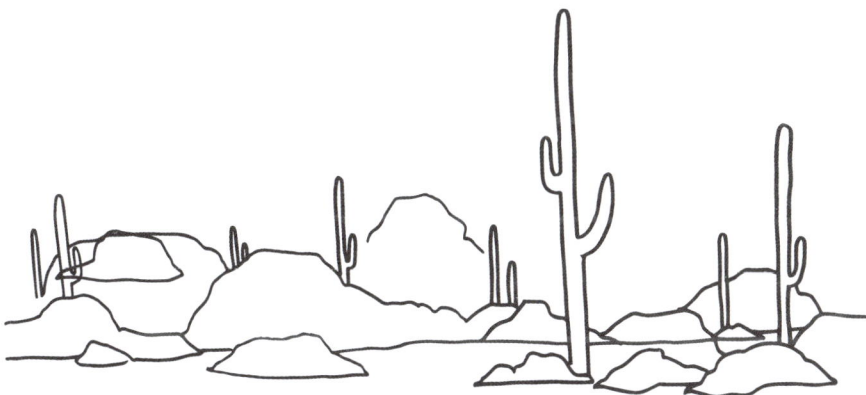

STEP TWO:
Choose a color palette

A desert sunset calls for a range of soft, glowing colors. The way Opera Rose bleeds into Lemon Yellow Deep is absolutely stunning and creates a really beautiful explosion of colors, perfect for a sunset. For the foreground, we'll be painting our subjects using the natural colors you'd find in the desert. The sunset is still casting a good amount of light throughout the landscape, so we can see the cacti, rocks, and desert floor in mostly full light. We'll use Sap Green and Olive Green for the cacti, varying hues of browns and gray for the rocks, and Burnt Umber for the tumbleweeds. For the desert floor, we'll use a mixture of Yellow Ochre and Burnt Umber. These colors will be gorgeous together!

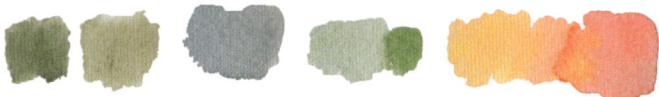

STEP THREE:

Put paint to paper

FIRST LAYER

Using the tip of your size 2 brush, begin by lining the skyline with a wet, full-strength amount of Opera Rose, about 2 inches of the horizon at a time. After each section, with your size 6 brush pull this color up with water into the sky for an even gradient wash using WOW. Now add touches of Lemon

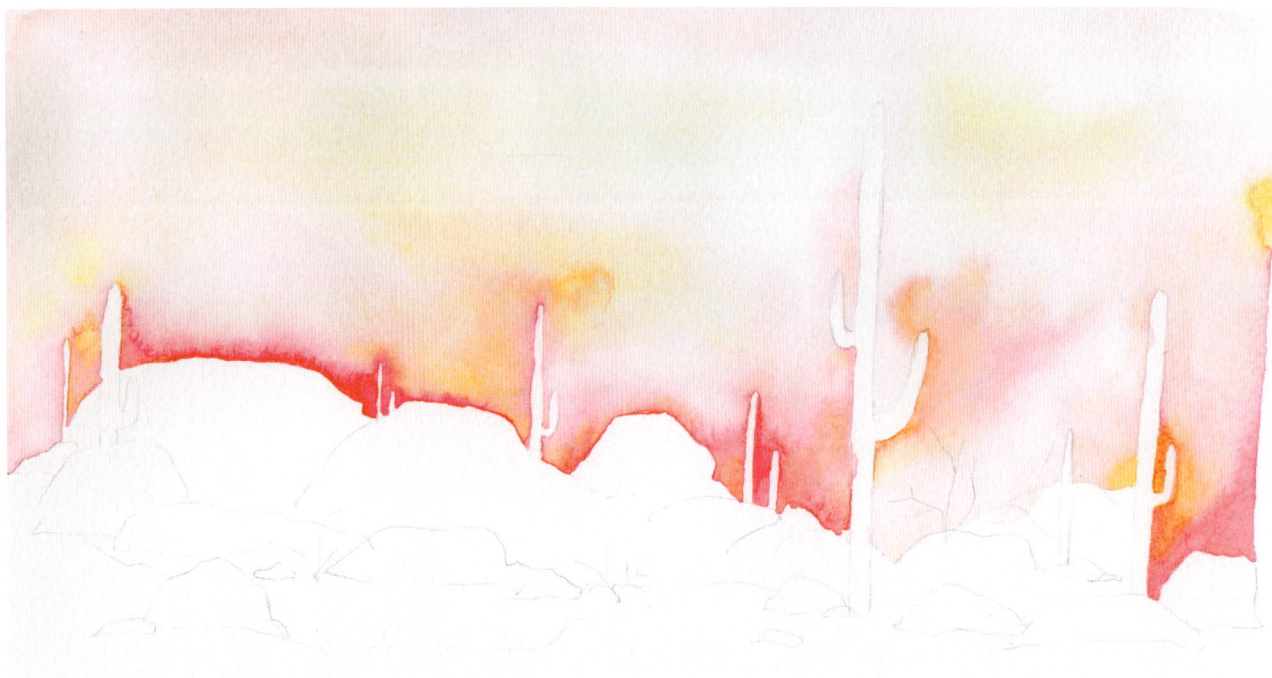

Yellow Deep for bursts of light and watch that color explode into the wet pinks. Continue to work your way across the painting, lining the horizon with a deep pink, then pulling it up with water and dabbing in yellow. Instead of lining the entire horizon with pink all at once, it's crucial to do this in sections, so you can work with wet paint for an even blend. If some sky areas have hard lines or need more color, go back and correct them by adding water and swirling your brush around to help them blend, or add more color to wet areas to add more hue throughout. Wait for the first layer to completely dry before you add the next layer of the background.

SECOND LAYER

This next layer includes a few pale mountains in the background and distant cacti, so load up your size 2 brush with your lightest value of green and add this to all the cacti on the horizon line. Match this lighter value in your cacti for the mountain color showing farthest away with a light mixture of Yellow Ochre and Burnt Umber. Add slightly darker values to the base of these mountains, brushing on this color while the base layer is still wet for a soft blend.

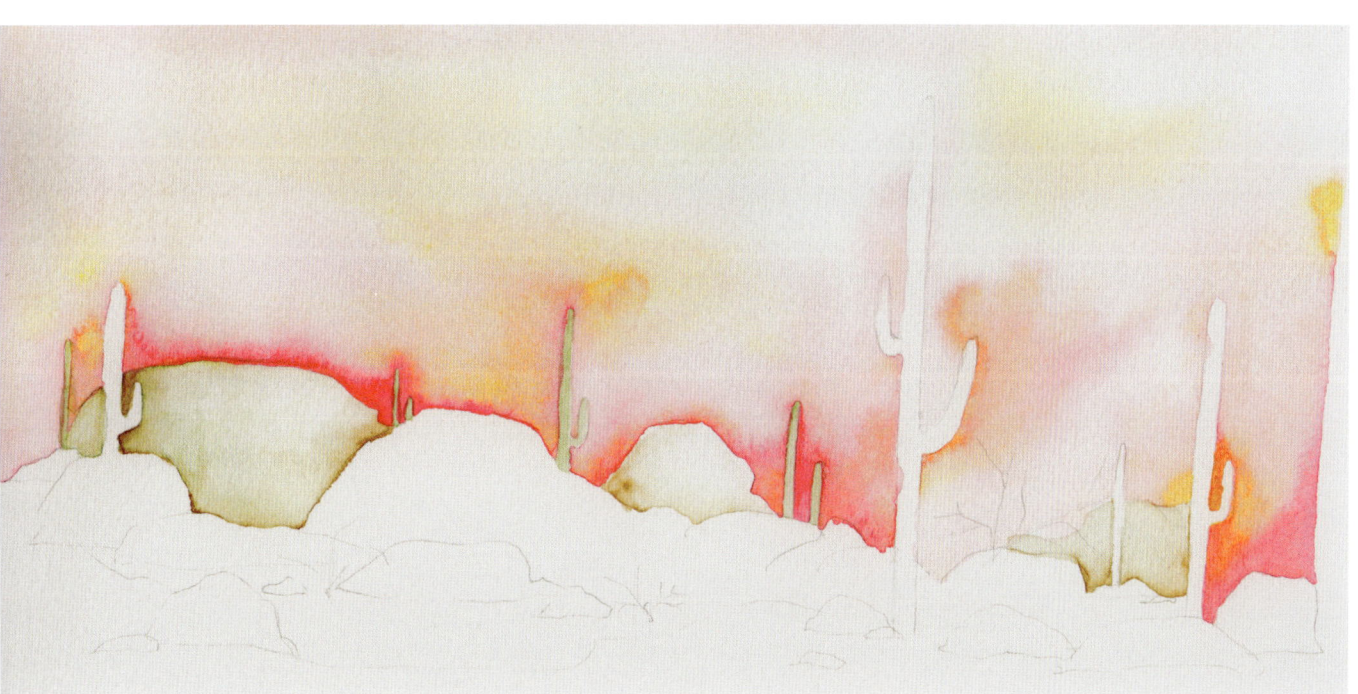

THIRD LAYER

Are you getting the hang of this? We're moving through the piece one layer at a time, getting closer to the foreground. For this next layer, mix up a darker value of the green mixture you've been using and add the next, nearer rank of cacti. Make sure these are slightly fuller-strength in hue and darker in value to distinguish them from those in the previous, more distant layer. Next, mix up a value of Yellow Ochre and a touch of black to add a wash to the desert floor and the larger rock just in front of the horizon line.

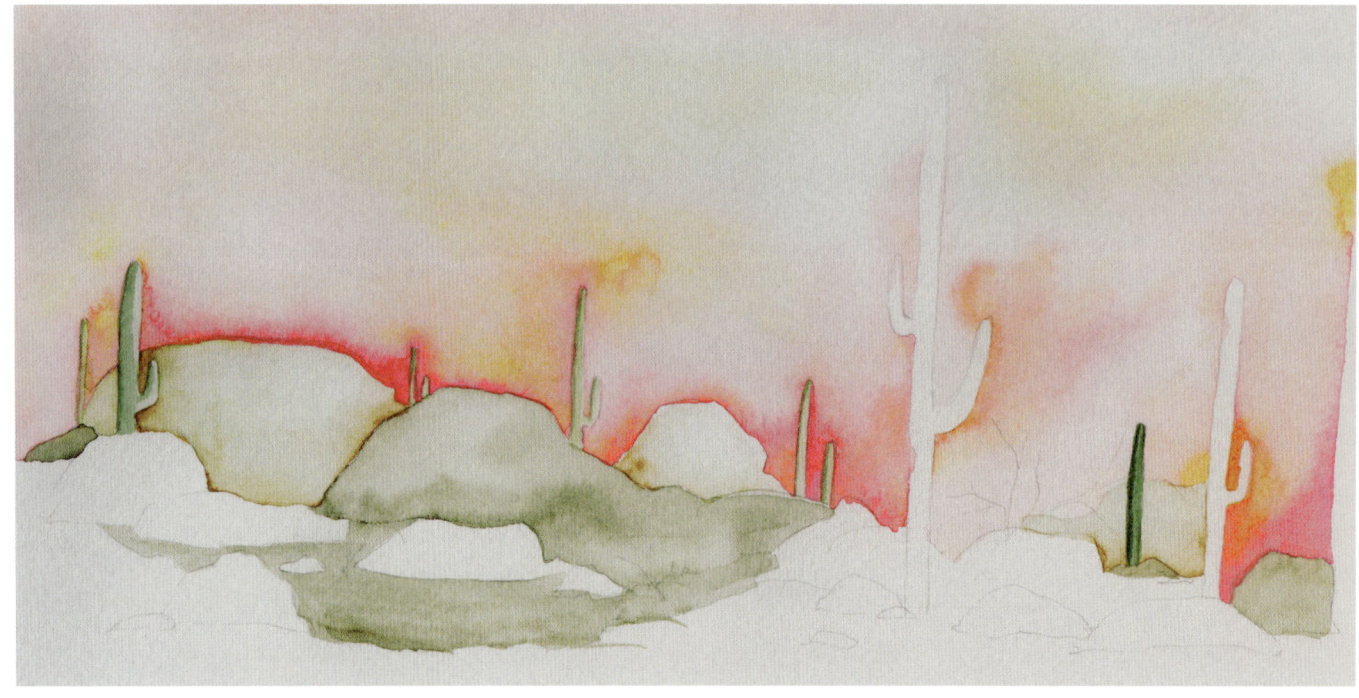

FOURTH LAYER

While the rock dries, add the richest green color to the cacti in the foreground. You can also begin adding rocks to the foreground. Vary their hues, ranging between browns and blacks, but make sure the values found in these rocks are the darkest throughout the piece to bring them forward. (We're really making use of that word "value" here, aren't we?) For landscapes with a long depth of field, value range is absolutely key. The range from light to dark within one hue can add so much complexity to a painting. Lastly for this layer, add a lighter color for the desert floor to help create a pop and contrast against the darker rocks.

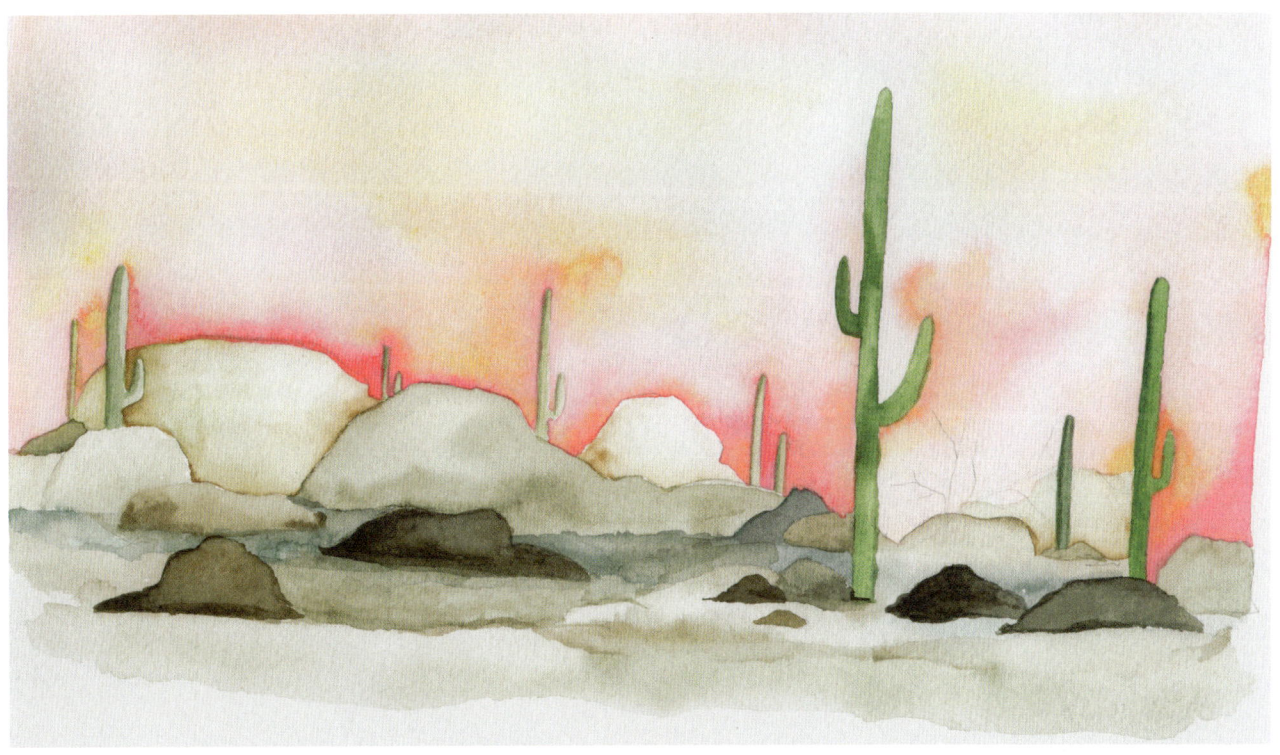

FINAL LAYER

Finally, add tiny details like the tumbleweeds, rocks, and low plants in the foreground on the desert floor. Continue to add depth with each added detail, and remember to assess after each addition in this last step, to make sure you don't overdo anything. Overall, composition, color, and depth of field are the main focus of this piece. Adding too much detail would distract from the beauty and expansiveness of the desert sky, so let that be the feature.

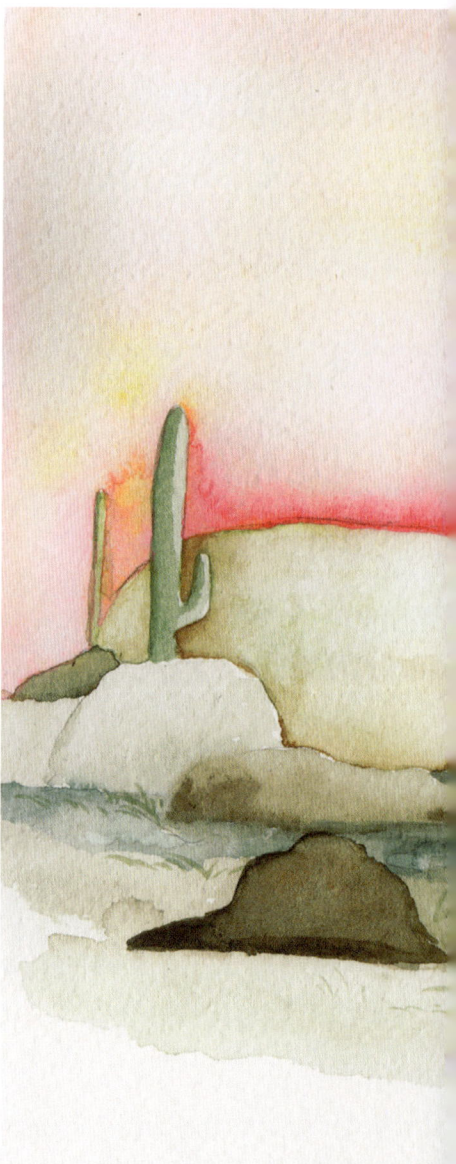

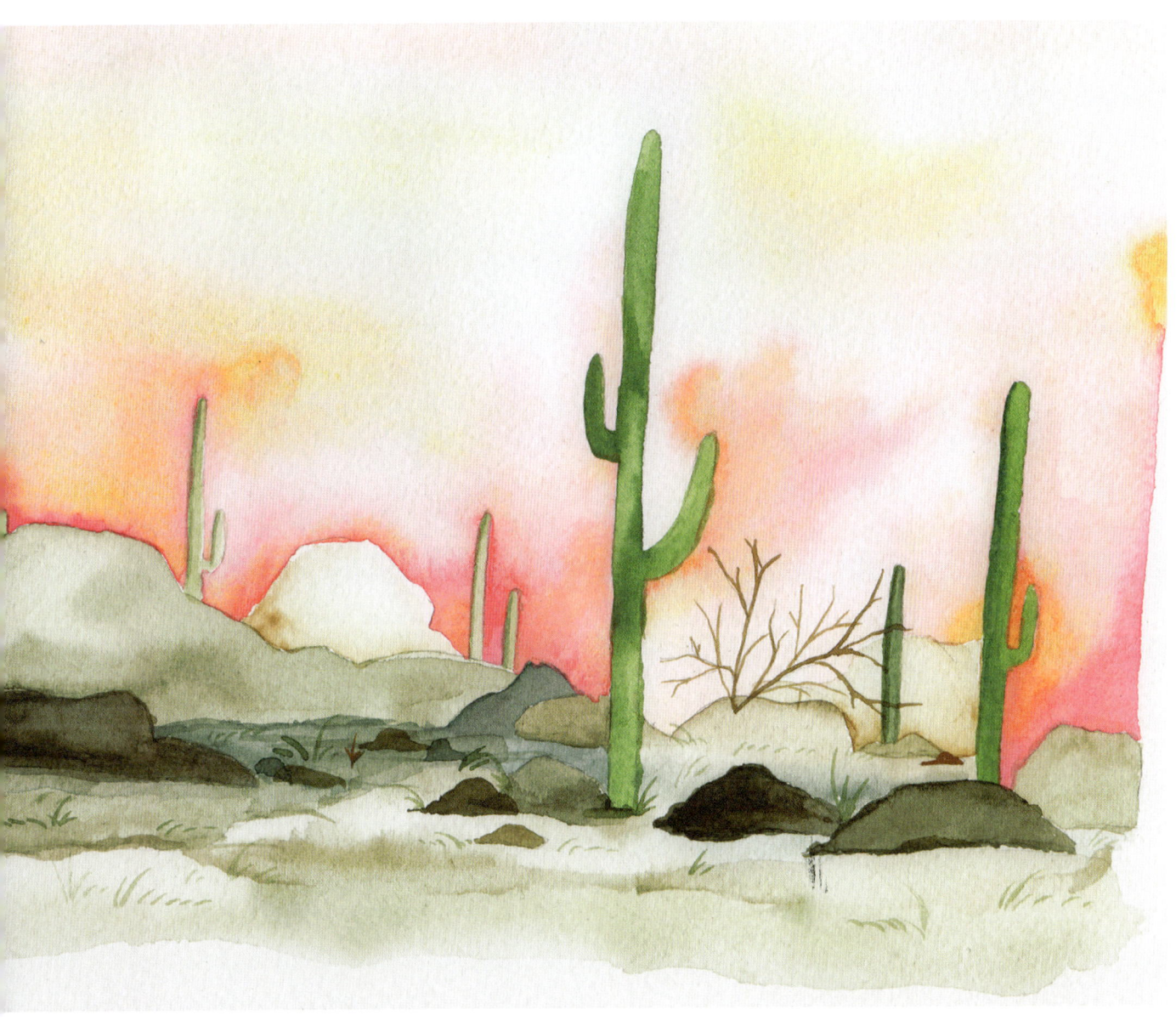

Day Twenty-Six

WIDE LANDSCAPE: JUNGLE

Practice patience and painting with restraint with multiple layers using WOD for a wide jungle landscape.

Estimated time: 1½ to 2 hours

STEP ONE:
Sketch

For this next piece, we're going to step back even farther for an aerial view of a jungle in the mist. This is a fun one! It may seem very intimidating, but I'm going to teach you a few simple tricks for creating the misty look. Our sketch for this piece will be incredibly basic, just highlighting areas where you want trees to poke out of the mist. Don't define any subjects with your sketch, and make sure to apply very light pencil marks. For my example piece, I've made pencil marks in the top left of my paper and over on the right where I'm going to place tiny mounds of treetops poking up out of the fog. You can place these above your horizon line by just adding two smaller "C" curves. Other than that, all you need is just a little pencil mark here or there to show where you want more definition versus water or mist.

STEP TWO:
Choose a color palette

Because this painting depicts a dewy jungle, we're going to use varying hues of greens, ranging from blue-greens to rich full greens, with very pale and light yellow-greens and gray-greens. For this piece, water is your absolute best friend. It will help you soften color to diffuse into the mist—the mist itself is really just a swath of water that treetops and colors can dissolve into.

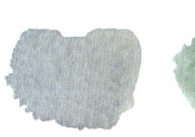 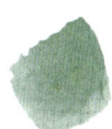  

STEP THREE:
Put paint to paper

FIRST LAYER
To dramatize the mysterious mistiness of this jungle scene, grab your size 16 brush, load it up with lots of water, and wash it across the entirety of your paper. Leave a few gaps toward the top where you want a ridge of

treetops poking out of the mist, but other than that, cover the paper with water. Now add varying green hues throughout the wash. This really helps bring out sections of trees in the mist, so make sure to leave sections of just water wash weaving through the middle, and don't daub any color onto that portion. Add richer greens toward the foreground and fainter greens and blue-greens toward the background.

Next, while your wash is still wet, with the point of your size 2 brush add some faint green trunks in the plain paper gaps, allowing the ends of these trunks to diffuse into the wash. To create the leafy parts of these trees, use the point of your size 2 brush to create "C" curves for branches coming out of the trunk, then create dashes, similar to what we practiced on day 8, for the palms. At this point, add only a few trees in the background, as the rest of the trees will be painted using WOD. I know it just looks like a bunch of color blobs right now, but trust me, we will take this somewhere very special. Just be patient, as these next two layers require some extra time and attention to detail.

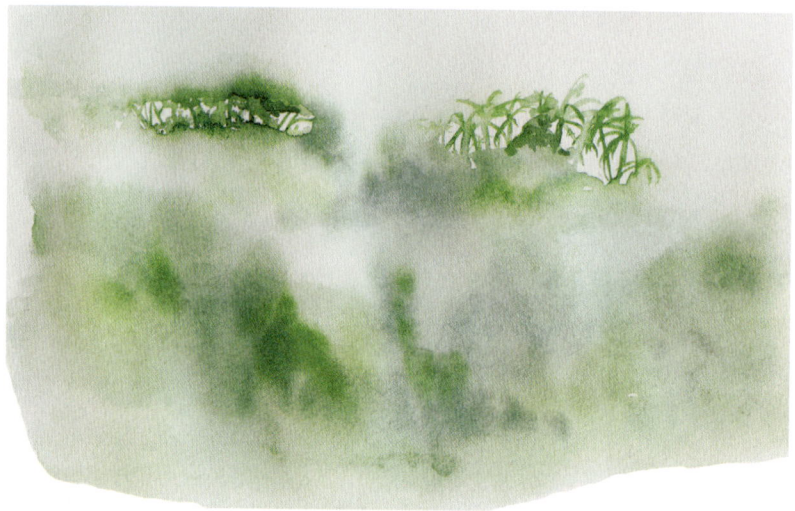

SECOND LAYER

While you wait for most of your paper to dry, add soft texture and marks to indicate leaves surrounding the treetops. Use values to add drama. The closer a tree is to the mist, the lighter the value should be. For some trees, that means that only the trunk is light and the leafy parts are darker, as they're completely out of the mist. But while adding these trees, remember to gradually work your way into the misty areas with lighter hues, and don't cover the entire misty area with trees. Cover up all the blobs of washy color from your base layer with palm trees in similar hues, so that they seem more faint and covered by a light mist. You also want a section of just plain water wash below the treetops to show the dense fog moving through the jungle. Make sure that the closer subjects are to the foreground, the more detail, color, and darker value you're showing. You'll also want these trees to be a bit larger so that they appear closer.

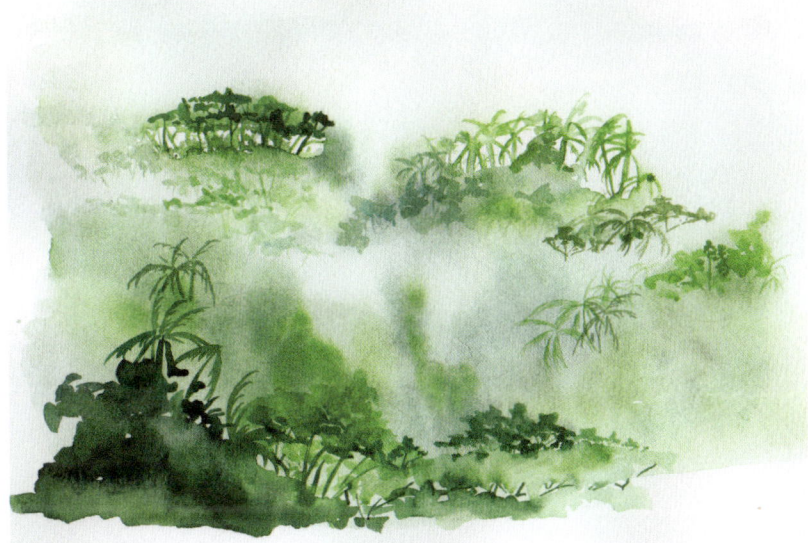

THIRD LAYER

I wasn't joking when I said it's a practice in patience! This piece is good for you. It's character building. You can't avoid stuff like this, because it will help you develop and grow as an artist. Don't rush yourself, but also don't spend too much time on any single little detail or section. Continue adding tiny palm trees fading into the distance and around the mist. The trees at the very bottom left-hand corner are a really dark Winsor Green and Mars Black, bringing these details forward.

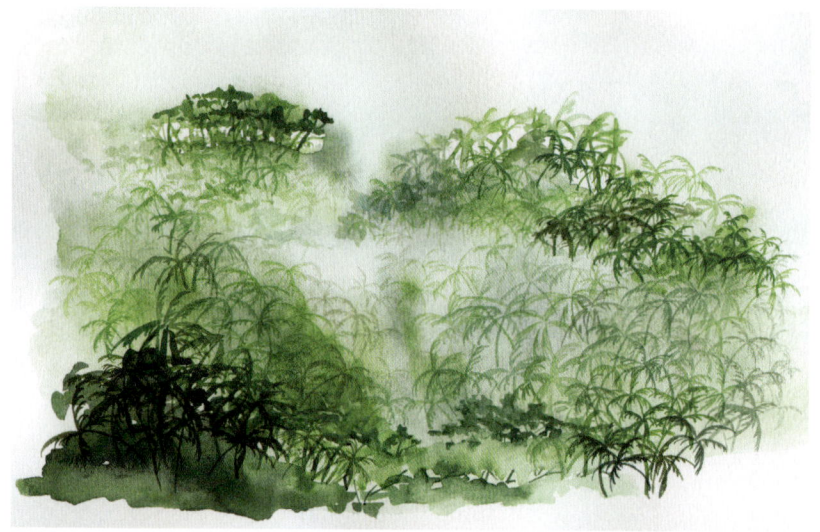

FINAL LAYER

Lastly, line the bottom right section of your page with darker foreground trees. Analyze what you've done and add any final details to the piece. If you're unsure about it, step away from it for a while, then come back with fresh eyes and see what it needs.

Don't be afraid of pieces like this that require some creative thinking. Keep practicing, and remember that patience is what separates the great artists from the amateurs.

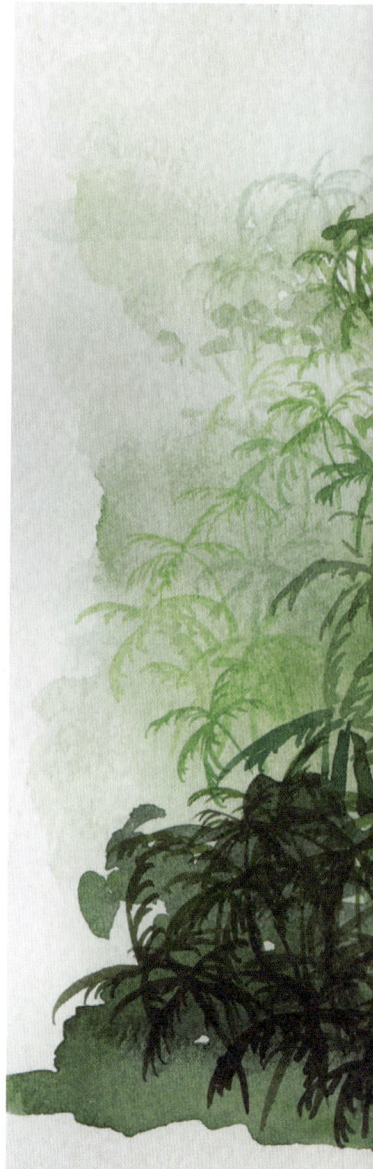

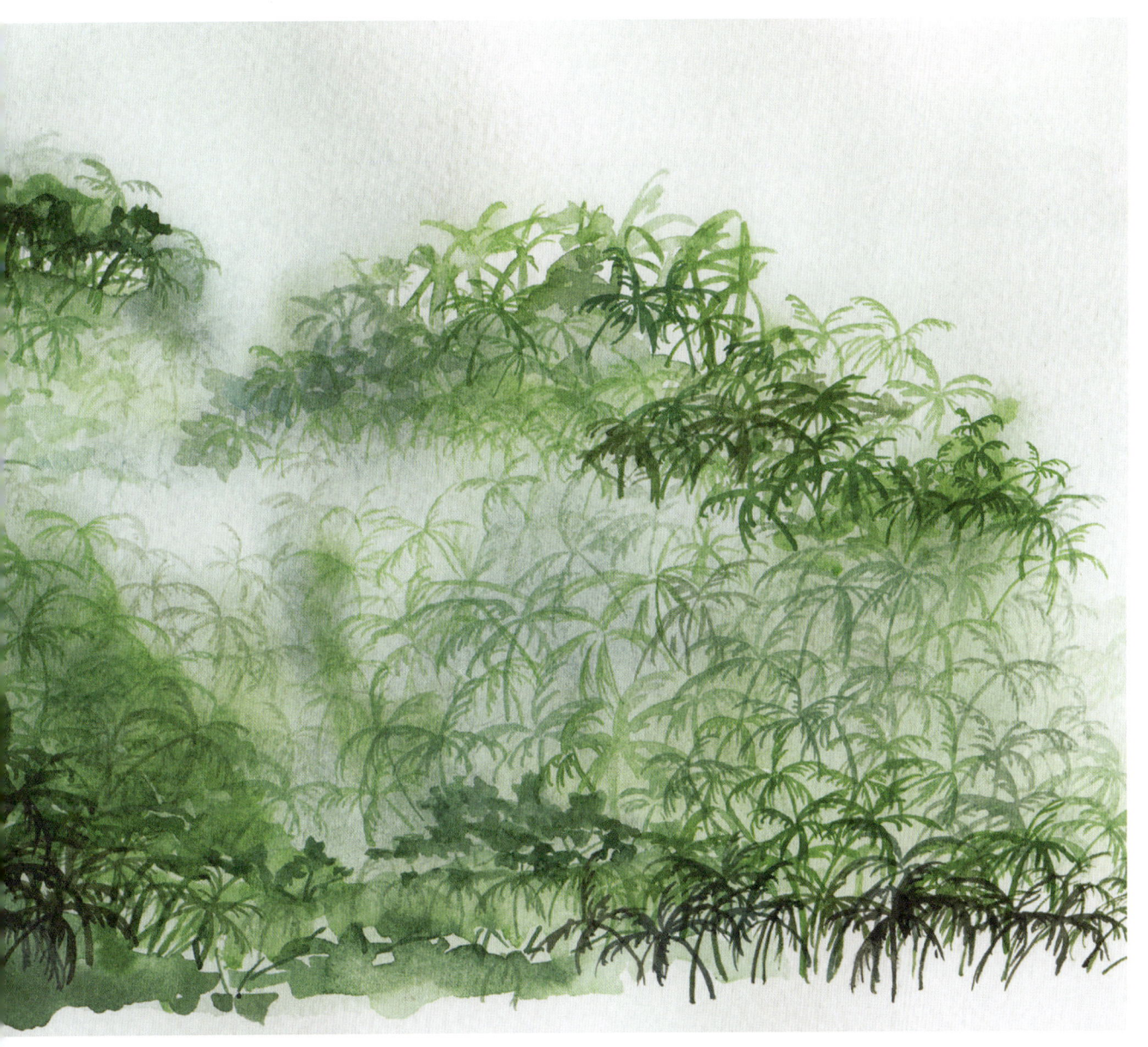

Day
Twenty-Seven

FINAL DESERT PIECE: PART ONE

Understand color harmonies and first layers of a
desert landscape incorporating multiple subjects.

Estimated time: 1 to 1½ hours

STEP ONE:
Sketch

For our final desert piece, we're going to incorporate lots of detail by adding different cactus varieties, flowers, and backgrounds for a lovely range of colors and textures. We'll have more detailed floral subjects, similar to what we painted on day 17, and we'll also focus on points of shading foreground elements as we did on day 24. For your sketch, take each subject one step at a time, and be patient with it. I know I keep saying that, but it really does pay off to put in the time and effort beforehand with your sketches.

The agave plants are simply longer leaf shapes forming a flared cone structure. Outline each leaf of the agave plant with "S" or "C" curves, coming to a really fine tip at the end. Take time to add each layer of every flower so you have guides for making these more detailed. Add rocks and more plants to the foreground as we did on day 24, and think about the overall composition of your piece while you're sketching, using the example on the following page for reference. As you'll notice in my paintings, the composition of this piece steps downward at an angle from the top two-thirds of the paper through the bottom, with varying points of focus. The composition tricks of day 3 can help.

STEP TWO:
Choose a color palette

For this piece, I was inspired by the color palettes found in a Palm Springs landscape. Think art deco, mid-century modern meets the pale, dusty palette of the desert. I'm incorporating bright pinks and vibrant yellows and greens for the mid-century modern vibe, but balancing that out with soft natural colors of the landscape. Agave plants have a similar hue to eucalyptus leaves, using Phthalo Turquoise and a touch of black for a smoky blue-grey color. I'll incorporate dusty pinks and Yellow Ochre for the more detailed flowers and take it up a notch with small amounts of Opera Rose for the more spiky, prickly flowers. This palette is a feast for the eyes!

STEP THREE:

Put paint to paper

FIRST LAYER

For our first layer, we're going to start with the background, applying a light wash of Phthalo Turquoise with a touch of black and yellow for a soft, muted blue-green. Use your size 16 brush to work your way across the bigger sections quickly, then smaller brushes for tighter areas. Wait for this layer to completely dry, then pick it up with the second layer.

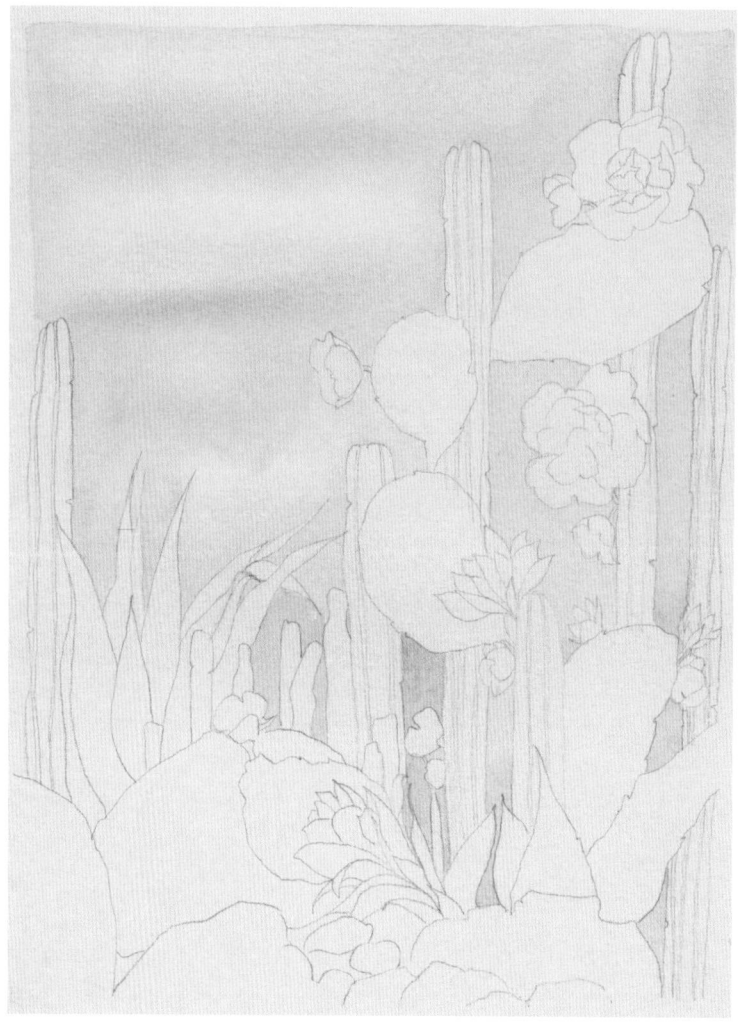

SECOND LAYER

For this next step, we're going to paint mid-tones and highlights for the flowers, using techniques discussed on days 17 and 20. Add blobs of mid-tones and shadows near the crease of a petal and bring in a wash to the petal for WOW and gradual blending. I know this is a lot of layers and petals, but, as with the roses we've painted, treat each section like its own individual painting, moving from one petal to the next. For the side-facing flowers, accentuate the insides of the petals or cone shape by making this section your darkest hue.

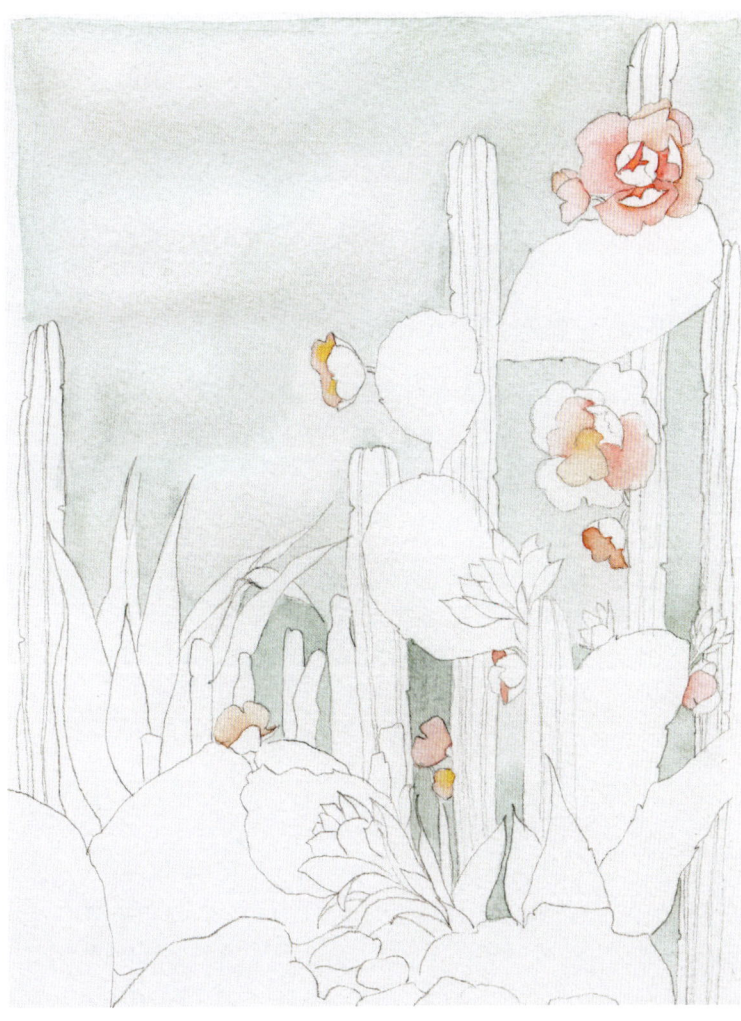

THIRD LAYER

While the mid-tones and highlights dry on your fuller, round flowers, turn to the saguaro cacti, working your way from one side to the other, laying down a really vibrant light hue of yellow-green. This almost chartreuse, neon color is a mixture of Lemon Yellow Deep and a touch of Winsor Green. After painting all of these, add a deep Opera Rose to the flowers. Alternate between petals and sections so that these values don't bleed into one another to create one big blob.

Next, wait for the surrounding areas to dry, then add a light layer of Sap Green to the prickly pear cactus. Finally, take a deep breath and put down your brushes for today. That was a lot of painting! We're going to return to this piece tomorrow for its remaining layers.

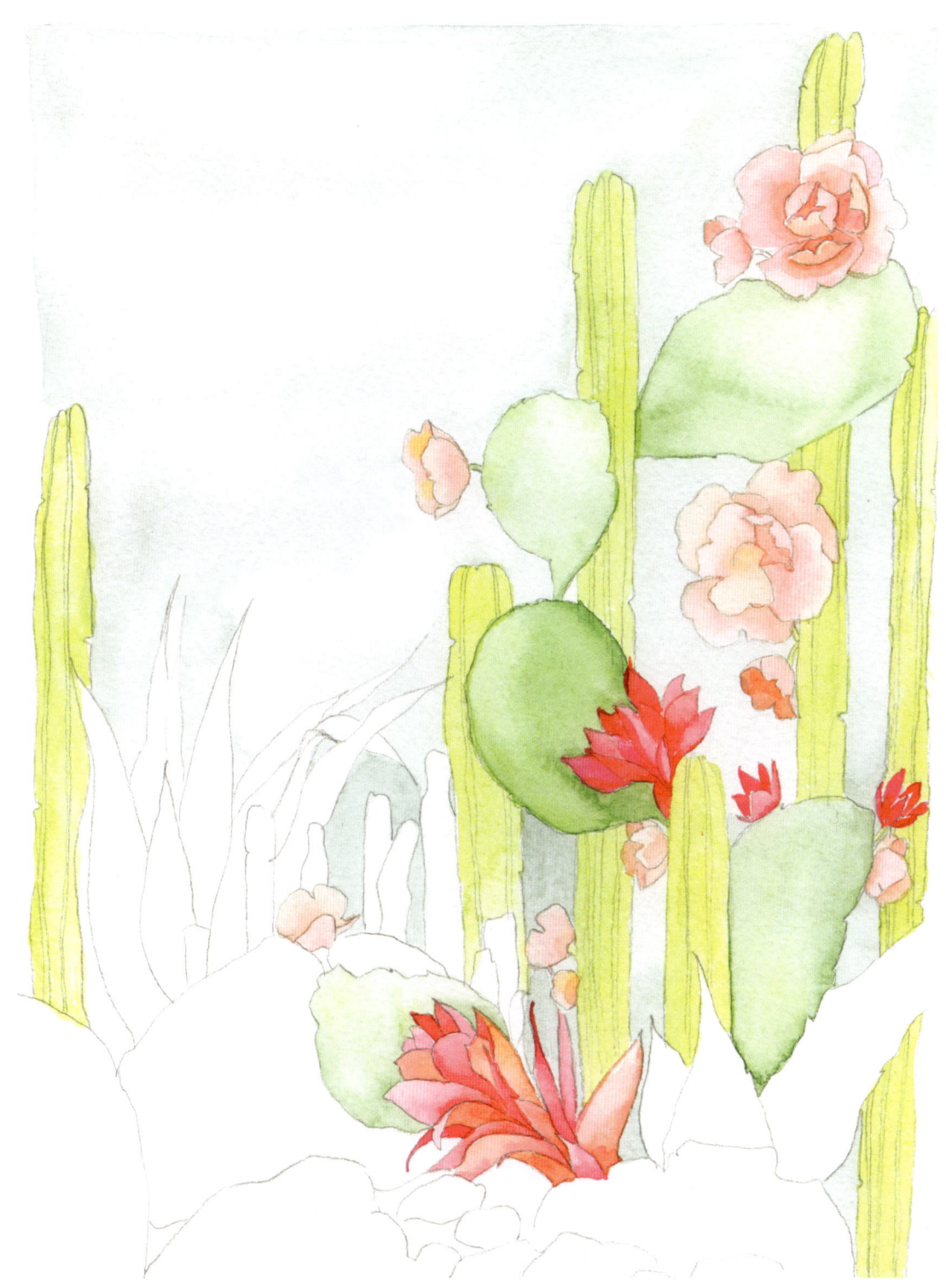

Day
Twenty-Eight

FINAL DESERT PIECE: PART TWO

Paint last steps for the final desert piece. Learn how to incorporate color balance within a desert motif.

Estimated time: 1 to 1½ hours

STEP THREE:

Continued from Day Twenty-Seven

FOURTH LAYER

Welcome back! It's time to complete this piece by adding the final layers and details. To start, paint the agave plant on the far right. Similar to how you would paint petals on a rose, start with your darkest value of a grayish turquoise hue—lining right where the visible edge of the plant meets the top of the rocks. Apply this to the far right leaf first, then wash your brush off completely and gradually work your way down the leaf with water to meet the darker value for a gradual bleed. Using your size 2 brush, add a dash of Burnt Umber at the very tip of the leaf and allow this color to just barely bleed into the turquoise. Then apply the same steps for the rest of the leaves, skipping the one right next to where you've just painted so these don't blend into one another. Do the same for the other agave plant. Vary the hues and values among these leaves so they come to life believably.

Next, add a darker green to the saguaro cacti. Apply it only in lines, with gaps between the lines for the bright yellow-green color to show through as highlights on the ridges. To finish up this layer, apply a combination of Yellow Ochre and Burnt Umber for the sand/dirt area, avoiding the rock sections.

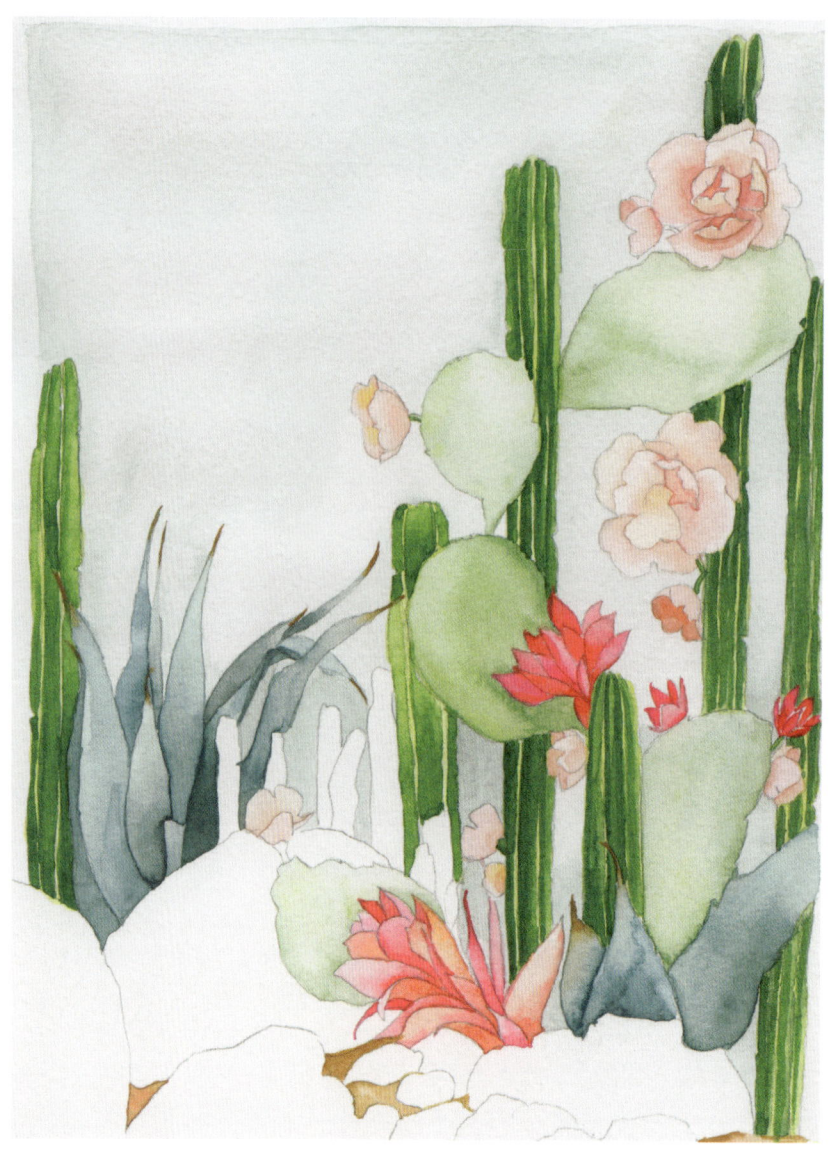

FIFTH LAYER

For this next step, I decided this piece needed more pink to complement the greens and make them pop. So for those smaller saguaro cacti, apply a dusty rose color using WOW. Next, add a lighter wash on the rocks—starting with a light value of Yellow Ochre on the rocks farther away from the foreground to create distance, and giving the rocks directly in the foreground a light gray for their first layer.

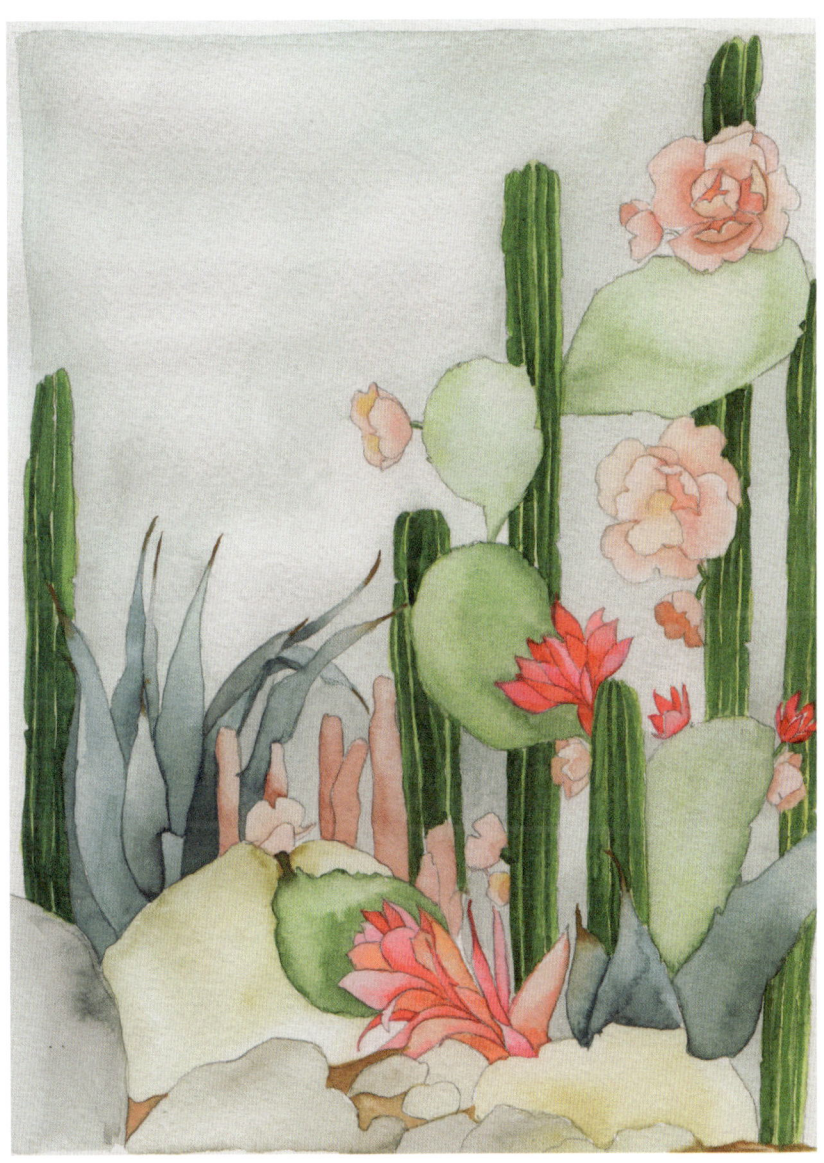

FINAL LAYER

Last but not least, it's time to add final details. We're in the home stretch! With the fine point of your size 2 brush and a darker green hue, add prickly texture to the prickly pear cactus. If any of the flowers need their form accentuated, add this with darker values. Finally, add some shadows to the rocks, applying a couple of shadow varieties and shading them, similar to shading the trunks on day 24. Before signing your name and declaring this piece finished, look over each element and see if it calls for any further detail.

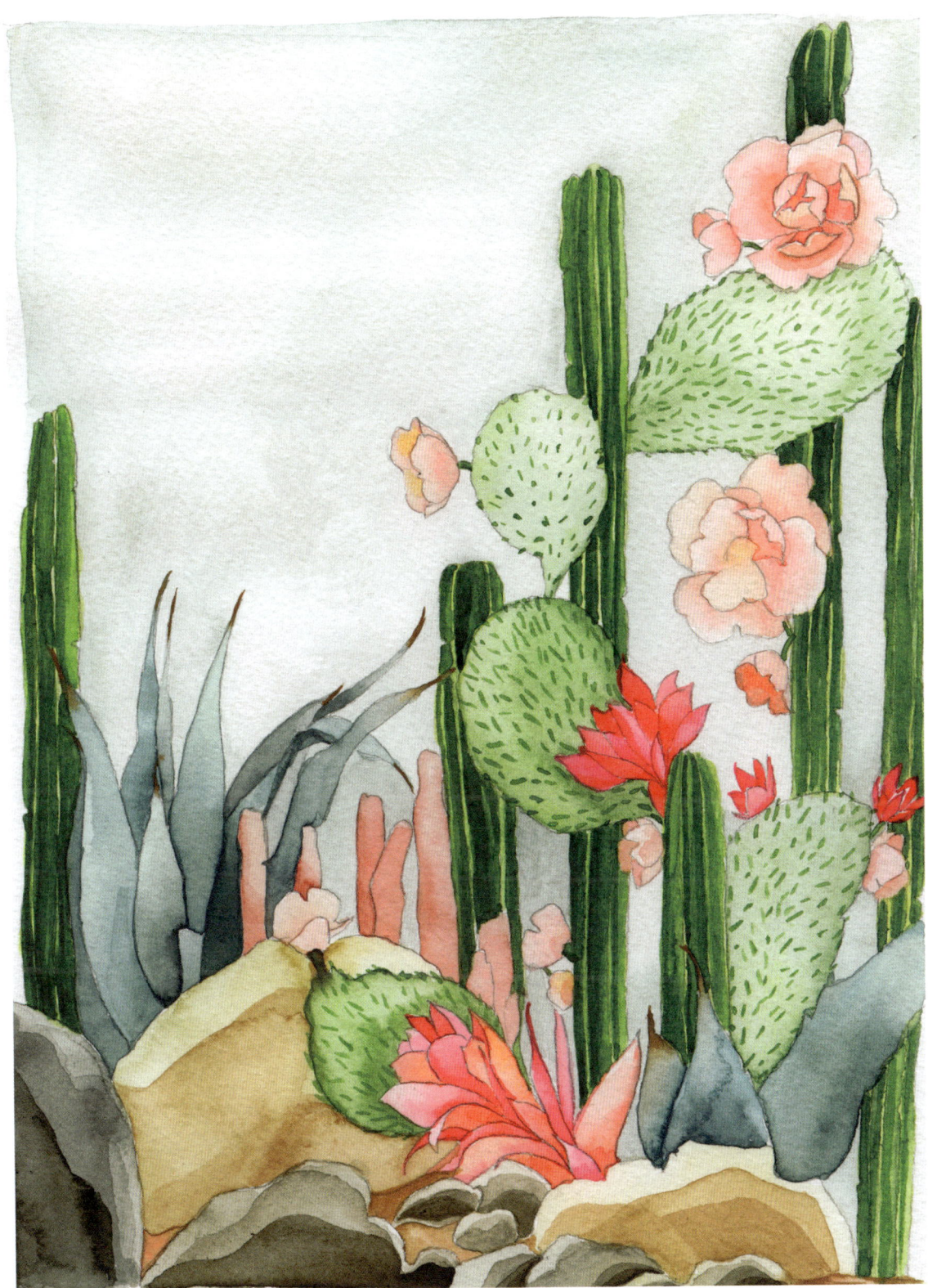

Day Twenty-Nine

FINAL JUNGLE PIECE: PART ONE

Understand color harmonies and first layers of a jungle landscape incorporating multiple subjects.

Estimated time: 1 to 1½ hours

STEP ONE:
Sketch

Today we'll be painting a glimpse into a jungle scene. This isn't going to be a wide landscape painting, but more of a close-up look. Picture walking through a tropical rainforest and brushing aside vines, monstera leaves, and flowers to find a parrot peering back at you. This is our last painting together, so we're going to get wild with it! We'll be using techniques we've already learned, while practicing the discovery of your own style and voice by trying new things. Let's start with mapping things out.

This piece will take up most of your paper, so make sure to sketch and paint with this in mind. We'll start with sketching the macaw. Because this is our focal point—in fact, it's a portrait—we want it to take up a good amount of the picture, but not too much, so we can show the overgrown nature of the jungle. We're going to sketch the macaw like it's peeking into view from the bottom left side, its beak and neck emerging toward the middle. This helps lead the viewer's eyes across the picture.

To sketch the parrot, we'll start with two basic shapes as you did for the toucan. Because the lower half of the parrot's body is out of view, we'll need only two circles to construct this subject. Lightly sketch a smaller circle for the head, then a larger oval for the body just below the circle and to the left. The bottom half will be cut off, as this portion disappears out of frame.

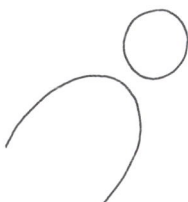

The size and direction of this oval will determine the bird's stance.

From here, you'll wrap a "C" curve around the top of the circle and down toward the oval on both sides. On the right side, connect the base of the circle to the oval with a "C" curve for the neck. You'll sketch in the beak using a "C" curve for the top, "S" curve for the middle, and another "C" curve for the bottom portion.

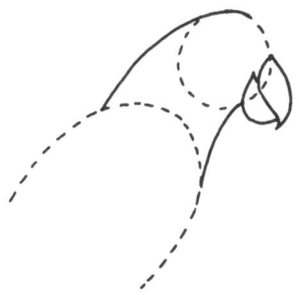

You'll place the eye in line with where the base of the beak opening curves up. Draw a little circle there for the eye, with a pupil dot. Next, we'll start adding light feathers and guides to where the wing will end. The wing (left side of our initial oval) or shoulder curves just below the neck and just slightly forward of it. Finally, erase any unnecessary marks from the basic shapes so they don't distract you when you're painting—leave only the marks of the actual contour sketch you'll need to follow when you paint.

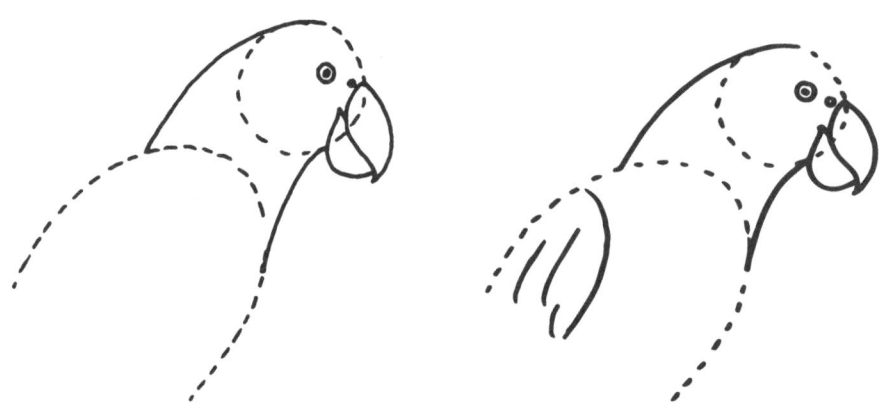

For the rest of this painting, use what you've already learned from previous days to sketch out the monstera leaves and florals. The palm leaves will be added at random, without sketching beforehand, as these are easily constructed with compound strokes. The only items you'll be sketching beforehand are the more complex shapes. Have fun with this part; allow yourself to construct this piece on your own, thinking of shape, proportion, and composition while you're sketching.

STEP TWO:

Choose a color palette

Because this piece has so many elements, you want to make sure that each
item can stand out on its own. You'll do this by adding contrasting colors, or
using lightness and darkness to add depth of field. Remember, the farther
away the subjects are in the background, the lighter they'll become. We'll
be using lots of bright greens, deep reds and pinks, yellows, and turquoise.
It's going to be a bold, bright piece, so make sure to balance that out by
adding analogous color palettes to temper the contrast between colors.

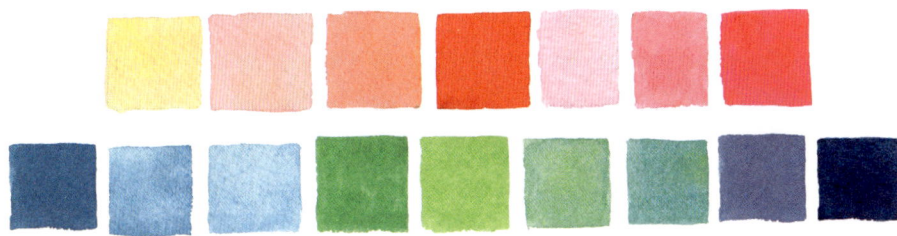

STEP THREE:

Put paint to paper

FIRST LAYER

To start, lay down the first layer of the parrot using a light wash of Lemon
Yellow Deep at the back of the parrot's head, avoiding the beak and the
area around the eye. Similar to how we painted the bird of paradise flower
on day 15, we'll gradually add varying hues, using the WOW technique
so there's some fun blending going on. While the yellow is still wet, add in
Scarlet Lake near the eye section, beak, and most of the belly area. Next,
add turquoise across the wing. Do this quickly so each color you add stays
wet and can create a bleed. Go back and apply more yellow wherever
you want a bright contrast against the darker reds and turquoise.

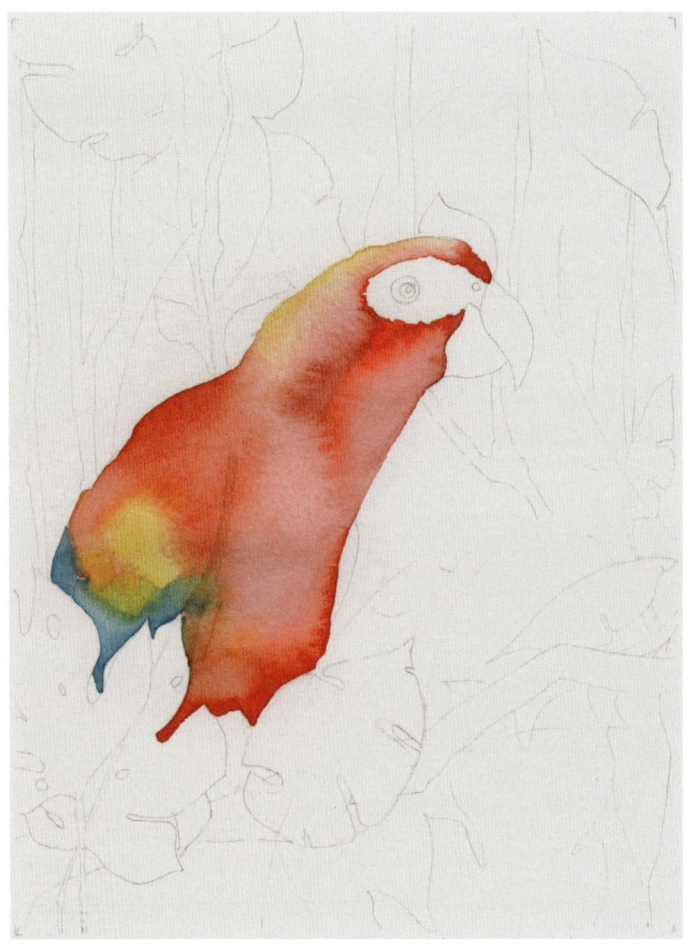

SECOND LAYER

While the first layer on the bird dries, move on to painting the background in a light wash of Opera Rose. A pink background? Absolutely! Traditionally you'd probably see more greenery or a sky color off in the distance, but we can take color harmonies and theory to the next level by switching things up. This pink hue will balance nicely against the turquoise and will contrast with the green colors we'll add later on. We're also putting analogous color to work by mixing up varying shades of pink for the background, including pink to yellow-pink to a more yellow color. Your color combinations are one of the artistic expressions that will catch a person's eye and have them saying "Oooooh!"

Until the parrot's first layer is dry, make sure to paint sections that aren't adjacent, so they don't bleed together. Paint those bordering sections last.

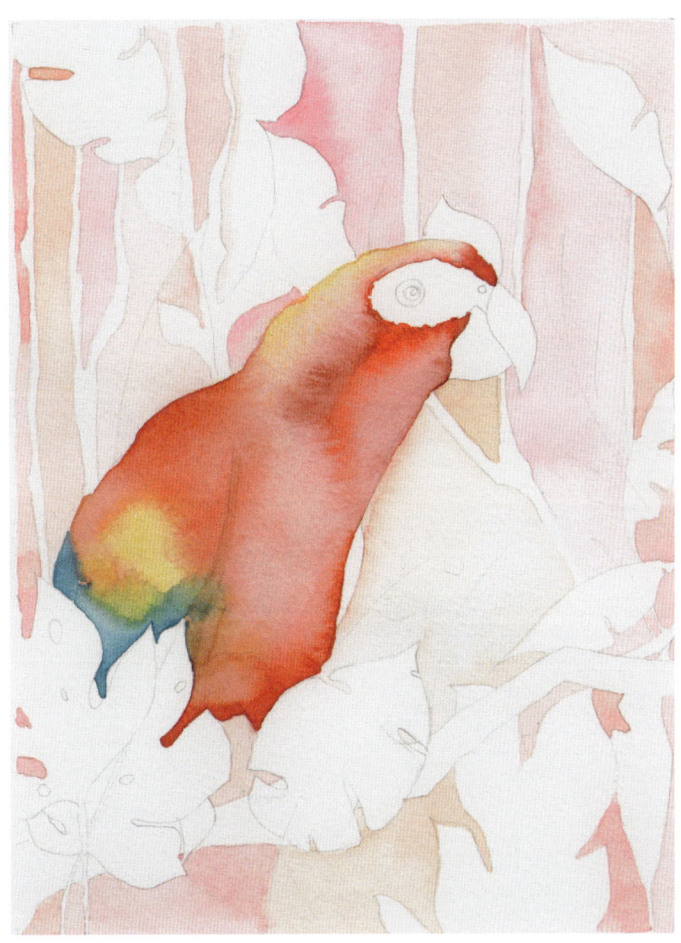

THIRD LAYER

Next, we're going to add more details to the background, like the narrow tree trunks. We'll start painting just one layer of shadows on each trunk, then go back and add thinner lines for details as we did on day 24. Before doing this, make sure the sections next to each trunk are dry. For the trunks I used a pale Phthalo Turquoise for shading. Look at that turquoise color next to those pale pinks. Striking!

Once you've applied your shadows to the trunks, go back with your size 2 brush using a thicker turquoise and add details. Keep in mind the curve of a cylinder for these lines. If you look at the second example, you'll notice that for the trunk in the foreground I switched the color to a cobalt. This adds variety and brings this branch more into the foreground—and hey, why not? The color creates a lovely balance, and we'll be tying this hue in with our next layer.

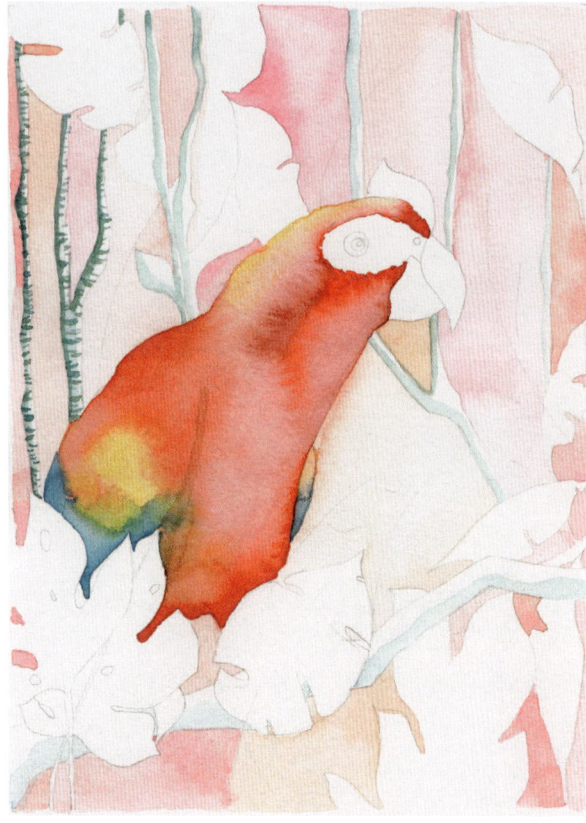
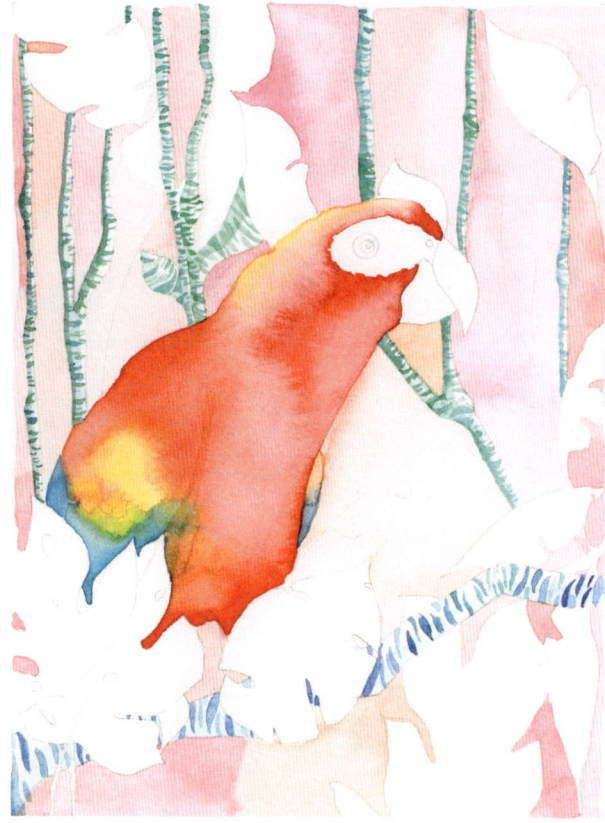

FOURTH LAYER

Once the pink background has had time to dry, we can start adding detail to the foreground using WOD. Paint in fun, leafy details for a funky flair, while also harmonizing with the other hues. I've used a deep cobalt hue for these leaves, and after painting a few, I began adding the first layers of some monstera leaves. Continue adding these blue leaves throughout the piece, varying the values a bit to show some farther away than others, in the background.

Now that we're starting to see some separation between foreground and background, let's take a break and pick up with the final steps tomorrow. You don't want to paint yourself into the ground. Taking a break from such a detailed painting is good to help rejuvenate those creative senses. I'll see you back here tomorrow for our final day together.

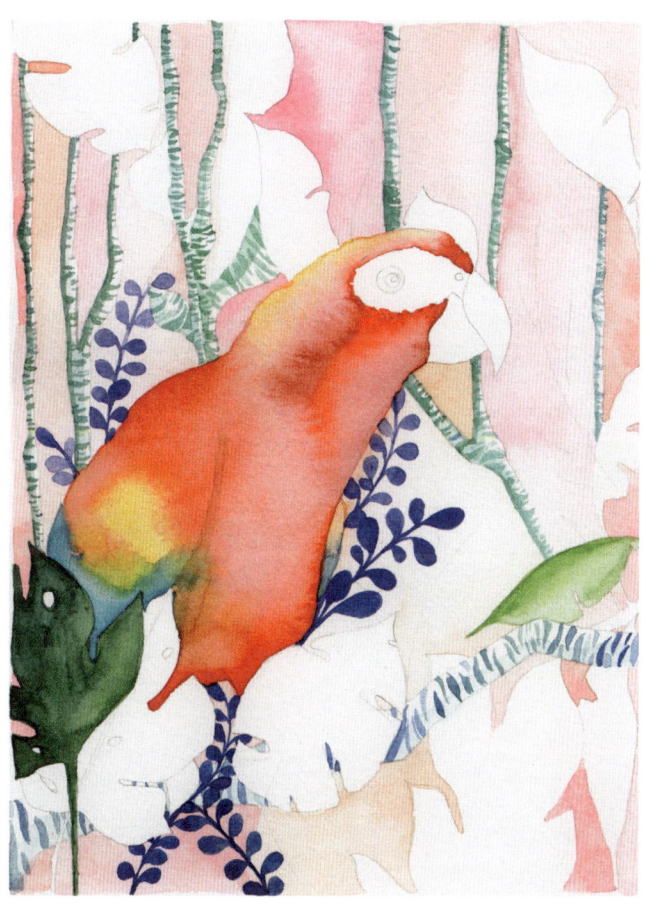

Day Thirty

FINAL JUNGLE PIECE: PART TWO

Paint last layers of the final jungle piece.
Learn how to incorporate color balance
within a jungle motif.

Estimated time: 1 to 1½ hours

STEP THREE:

Continued from Day Twenty-Nine

Do you feel refreshed and ready to paint again? I know it's hard to pull away sometimes, but trust me, your eyes will thank you for it. Now let's pick this back up with our final layers.

FIFTH LAYER

To make the greens of the monstera leaves pop even more, I've used Opera Rose, full strength, to add some free-form grassy blades around the base and sides of the painting. To paint these palm leaves, use the point of your brush for the stem and compound curves for the leaves, as we discussed on day 5. Don't be afraid to overlap some of the leaves and point them in different directions. Continue adding paint to the sketched areas and bringing all the botanical elements into the painting before continuing with the next few steps.

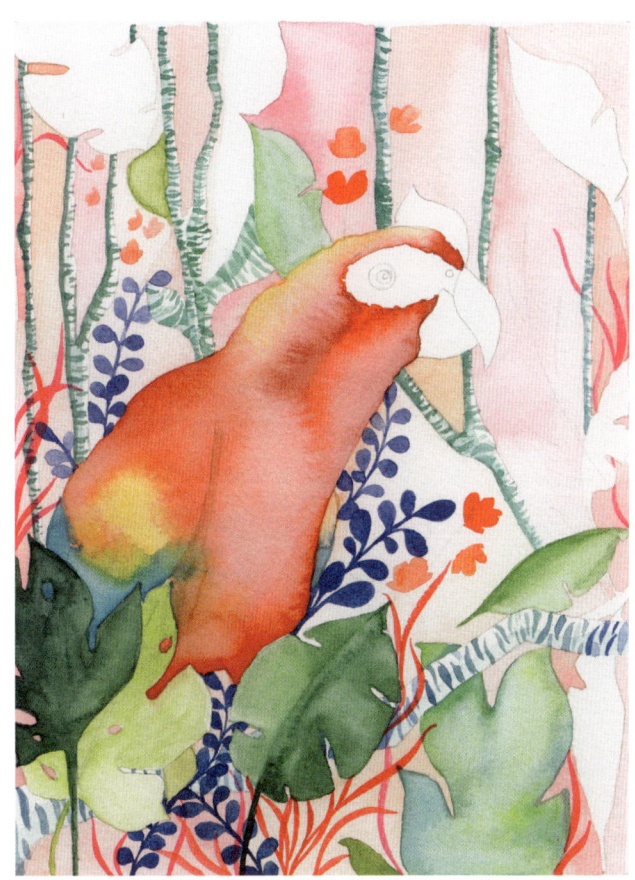

SIXTH LAYER

After laying down the base layer for the rest of your monstera and banana leaves, it's time to let loose. Up until this point we've studied all the rules when it comes to composition, what works in a painting, and so on, but I want you to use this next step to forget all that and just allow yourself to paint. Break the rules! Set yourself free to play with detail; let yourself paint for the process and not the outcome. Of course, every artist's hope and wish is that their paintings will look fantastic when finished, but when you're able to get in a state of creating where you're trusting yourself enough to enjoy every bit of the process, I can assure you that your eye and paintbrush can help show you exactly what a painting needs. And what if you mess up? Do what you can to cover it up or fix it, but if it just can't be mended, that's OK. That's how we learn; you probably won't make that mistake again in the future. Keep adding layers of foliage with more simple strokes, and lighten these elements to add depth to the painting.

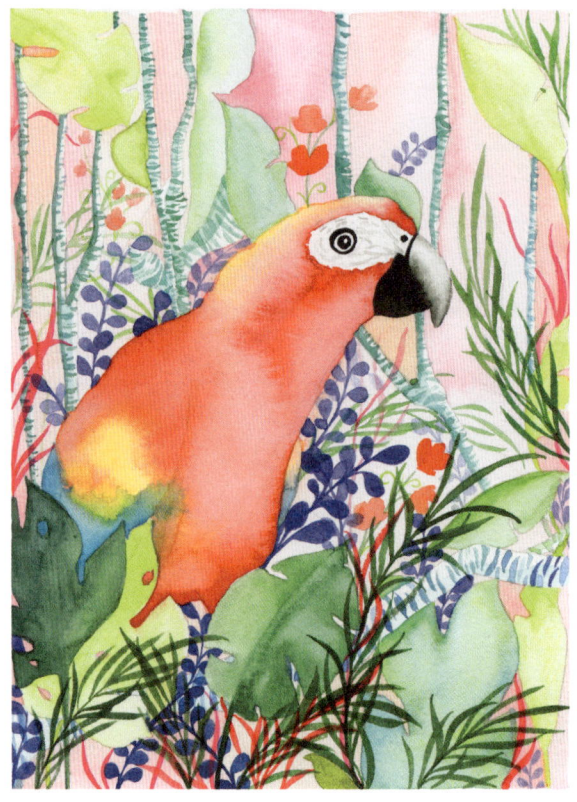

FINAL LAYER

Now that you have all of the elements of your painting mostly done, you can add the final details. Use your size 2 brush to fill in the parrot's eye. For the beak, paint a thick mixture of black for the bottom half, then with just water on your brush, graze across that top edge of paint and pull it into the top half of the beak for a gradient wash from black to gray, from bottom to top. Next, go in with a darker mixture of Scarlet Lake to add feather details to the red portion of the bird and turquoise details on the turquoise portion of the wing. Remember to use "C" curves and don't overthink their placement.

Now take a step back and look at the whole painting. Are there any areas that you think need help bringing forward? Use shading to add dimension and more foliage details if needed, but remember not to overdo it. Trust yourself and what you've learned and practiced from day 1 until now for this final piece.

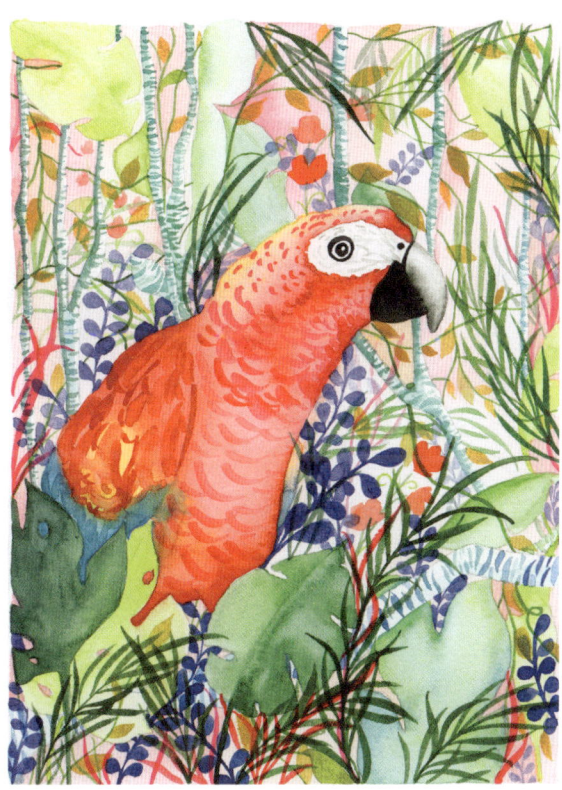

Day Thirty-One and Beyond

Whoa. You did it! Thirty paintings in thirty days. Or maybe it took you more than thirty days (hey, life happens), but you stuck with it anyway! From starting with basic shapes and techniques, to incorporating balance and color harmonies, to adding proper shading techniques and form with WOW and WOD, you've painted it all. I really hope you've enjoyed our process and journey together. With the medium of watercolor, the magic of blending and the luminous quality of the colors are unparalleled. This book was meant to help you discover and grasp the beauty of this medium and the qualities that make you want to paint nonstop. In covering the basics and how to approach watercolor with a different interpretation, I hope I've opened your eyes to the accessibility of watercolor and most importantly, helped you fall in love with the process.

If you were disappointed with how any of your paintings turned out along the way, realize that without mistakes and failed attempts, no artist would be able to grow and develop mastery. Every single artist has those pieces crumpled up in the trash and wasted tubes of paint and canvas, but what separates the developed artist from the amateur is perseverance and patience. This is the rich and powerful energy that will nourish and sustain your creativity—helping you to devote the time and dedication to paint every day, overcome obstacles, and accept failed attempts as opportunities for growth. Once there, you'll realize that fighting and striving for a one-off masterpiece is a minor effort in comparison to learning to paint for the process. Through this, you will paint more, learning from more mistakes, developing and strengthening muscle memory. That's where a "masterpiece" can be found.

I hear so often from students or people in conversation saying how they don't believe they're creative or that they can't paint. I wanted to challenge that crippling mind-set with this book. We all are born with the ability to create—to problem solve and see things differently. Some of us may need more time and patience than others, but don't get caught up in comparing your art with someone else's or wishing it looked more like the examples in this book. The difference could be years of experience and patience. And don't stop here! Use these techniques and foundations you've learned to sketch and paint *anything*! A cityscape or an ocean landscape, or inanimate objects like a vase or cello—for all of these, you use the same steps and techniques we've practiced in this book. Starting by sketching basic shapes, taking time beforehand to choose color combinations, will make all the difference. Keep painting and dedicating this practice to yourself as an artist and creative individual.

As you continue beyond this book, I hope you carry on with applying everything you learned here. Continue this journey of #everydaywatercolor, pursuing your passion for the process and finding your own gifts and creativity.

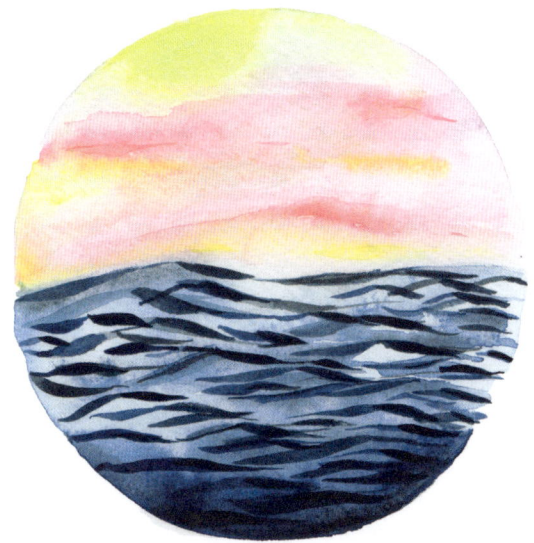

Acknowledgments

First and foremost, I am grateful to the ultimate Creator and Artist—God. Thank you for writing my story and showing me how to spread my wings.

Thank you to my amazing husband, John. Your support and love is everything and you somehow never seem to tire of encouraging me to be my best. And to both of my grandmothers (El and Re), who taught me to paint without knowing it, and to my parents, Clint and Jill, for always inspiring me and supporting me even in my failures.

I would also like to thank the incredible team at Ten Speed, my editor Lisa Westmoreland and designer Angelina Cheney, and my agent, Kimberly Brower. This wouldn't have been possible without you!

About the Author

Jenna Rainey is the founder and self-taught designer, illustrator, and calligrapher behind Mon Voir, a small but mighty illustration and design agency she started out of a love for art and illustration that began when she was very little. With a passion for originality and a background in psychology, she strives to bring out the creativity in each student in a workshop and unique and elegant quality in every design and client project. Jenna's work has been featured in countless publications and wedding blogs—including Nixon, Brit+Co, BuzzFeed, Design Milk, Martha Stewart Weddings, The Knot, and The Lane—and she is now sharing her talent and stories in various keynotes throughout the country, including Connecting Things, Brit+Co's Re:Make Summit, and more. She lives in Costa Mesa, California.

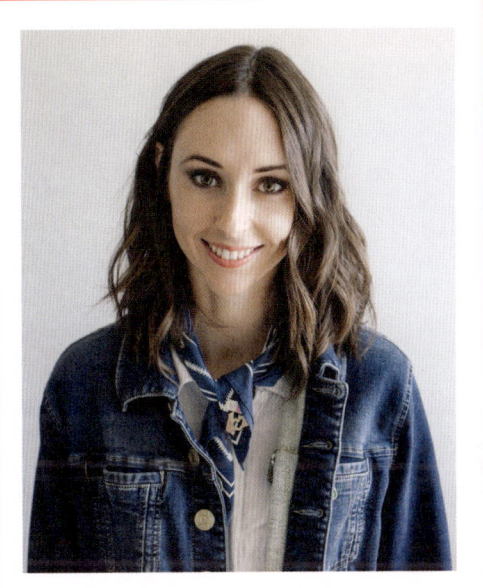

©Michael Radford

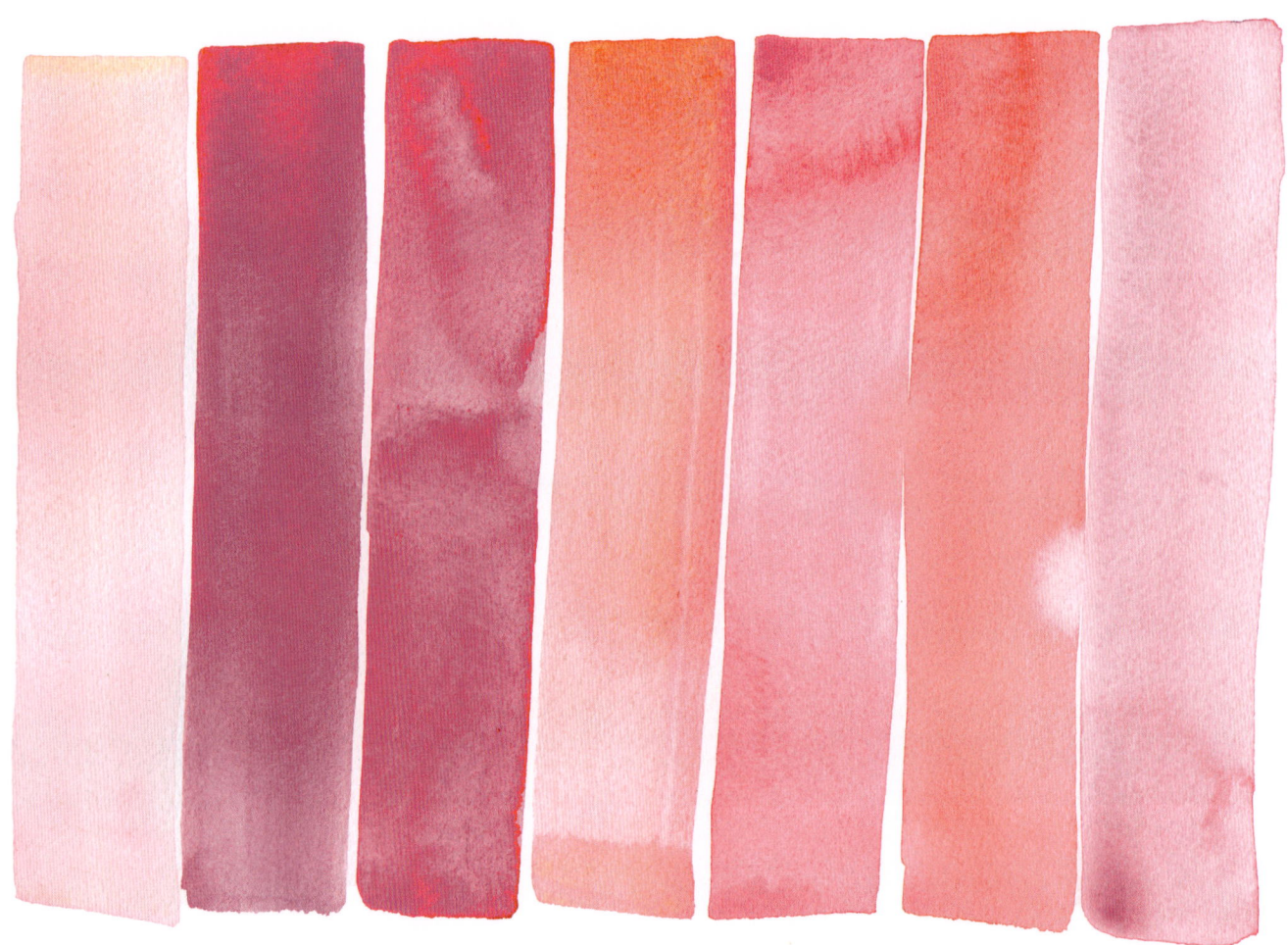

Index

A

Aerial perspective. *See* Atmospheric perspective
Agave plants, 187, 193
Analogous colors, 11–12, 28–29, 34–36, 78
Atmospheric perspective, 146–52

B

Background, 63, 65
Banana leaves, 72–75
Bird of paradise, 102–5
Bleeding, 14, 27–28, 36, 74
Blue, 9
Brushes
    loading with water and paint, 5, 19, 41
    rinsing off with water, 5, 41
    sizes of, 7
    types of, 6–7

C

Cacti, 83–87, 107–9. *See also* Desert landscapes
Cast shadows, 82–87
"C" curves, 25, 45–46, 47
Chickens, 119–23
Circles, 25–28
Colors
    analogous, 11–12, 28–29, 34–36, 78
    complementary, 12, 40–41, 68, 102–5
    muddy, 4, 5
    primary, 9
    role of, 8
    saturation, 10
    secondary, 9

tertiary, 9
tone, 10
warm vs. cool, 13, 34–35, 40–41
See also Hue; Palettes; Value
Complementary colors, 12, 40–41, 68, 102–5
Composition, 13–14, 22, 30
Cool vs. warm colors, 13, 34–35, 40–41
Core shadows, 83, 86
Curves
    "C," 25, 45–46, 47
    complex, 52–53, 90–95
    "S," 45, 46–47

D

Depth
    adding, 63–65, 162
    of field, 146–48
Desaturation, 10
Desert landscapes, 146–52, 172–78, 186–96
Dots, 57
Dragon fruit, 96–101

E

Elephants, 155–59
Eucalyptus leaves, 52, 53

F

Focal point, 13
Folds, 90–95
Foreground, 63, 65, 147

G

Gesture, 118–23, 126–31
Graphite pencils, 8

Grayscale value, 154–59
Green, 9

H

Hexagons, 39
Highlights, 10, 47, 61, 75, 83, 107, 108, 113, 116
Horizon line, placement of, 147, 173
Hue
    blending, 76, 78–81
    description of, 10
    tone and, 10
Hummingbirds, 126–31

J

Jungle landscapes, 161–68, 180–84, 198–209

L

Landscapes
    desert, 146–52, 172–78, 186–96
    jungle, 161–68, 180–84, 198–209
    subjects in, 138–44, 198–99
Layering
    adding depth with, 64–65
    creating patterns with, 66–70
    light to dark, 56–61
Leaves, 46–49, 51–53, 72–75, 91–95
Light source, 72–75, 84–85, 86
Lines
    fine, 106–9
    straight, 33

M

Marks, 57, 60
Materials. *See* Tools and materials
Mid-tones, 61, 74, 83, 86, 92–94, 98, 104, 107–8, 113, 116
Mist, 181–82
Mistakes, learning from, 208, 210–11
Monochromatic palettes, 11, 20
Monstera leaves, 91–95
Movement
  creating, 13, 36, 48, 53, 70
  gesture and, 118–23, 126–31

O

Orange, 9

P

Paints
  composition of, 4
  loading brush with, 5, 19, 41
  number of, in palette, 5
  quality of, 4
Palettes
  analogous, 11–12, 28–29, 34–36, 78
  complementary, 12, 40–41, 68, 102–5
  monochromatic, 11, 20
  mood and, 98
  number of paints in, 5
  split-complementary, 12
Papayas, 77–81
Paper
  thickness of, 6
  types of, 5
Parrots, 199–205, 209
Patterns, 66–70
Pencils, 8
Peony leaves, 51, 52
Perspective, atmospheric, 146–52
Pigments, 4–5
Poppies, 67–70
Primary colors, 9
Purple, 9

R

Red, 9
Roses, 111–16, 132–37
Rule of thirds, 13
Rules, breaking, 208

S

Sage leaves, 51, 53
Saturation, 10
"S" curves, 45, 46–47
Secondary colors, 9
Sections, painting in, 96–101
Shading, 10, 72–75
Shadows
  cast, 82–87
  core, 83, 86
  hues for, 113, 115–16
Sketching
  basic techniques for, 39
  examples of, 39, 57–58, 77, 103, 107, 111–13, 119, 127, 133–34, 139, 147, 155, 161, 173, 199–200
  tools for, 8
Split-complementary palettes, 12
Strokes
  basic, 18–22
  compound, 44–48, 50–53
  varying widths of, 33
Style, developing, 3
Sunsets, 173–74
Swatches, 19

T

Tertiary colors, 9
Thyme leaves, 51, 53
Tone, 10
Tools and materials, 3–8
Toucans, 138–44
Trees, 57–61, 63–65
Triangles, 33, 36

V

Value
  grayscale, 154–59
  picking out, 132–33, 135
  scale, 10–11, 133, 155
Visualizing, 30
Volume, creating, 160–68

W

Warm vs. cool colors, 13, 34–35, 40–41
Water, 5, 19, 41
Watercolor
  characteristics of, 1
  learning, 2–3, 15, 210–11
Wet on dry (WOD) painting technique
  accentuating details with, 76, 142
  from light to dark, 75
  overview of, 14–15
Wet on wet (WOW) painting technique
  blending hues with, 76, 78–81
  overview of, 14, 15
  shading and, 74, 75
White, 5

Y

Yellow, 9

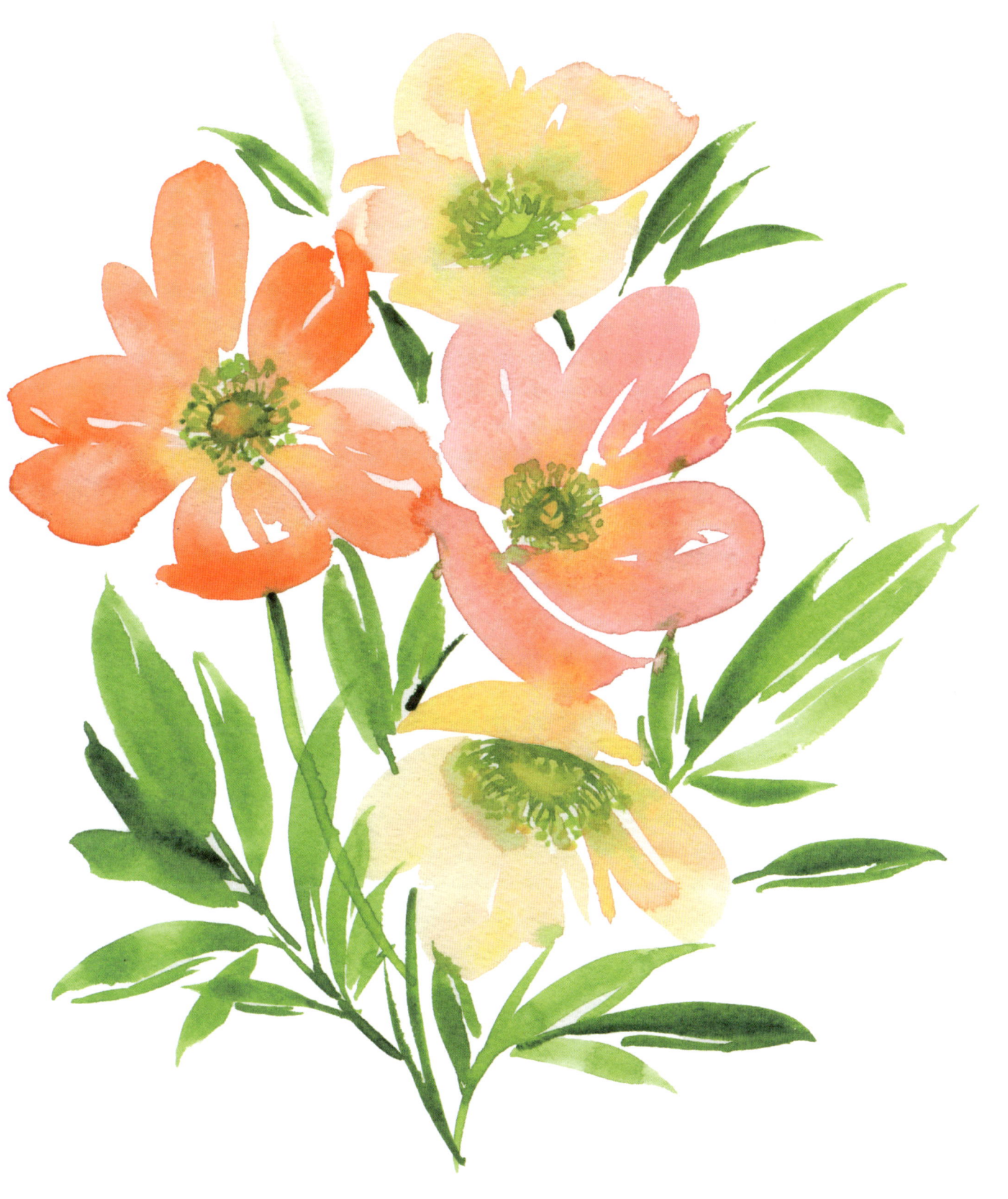

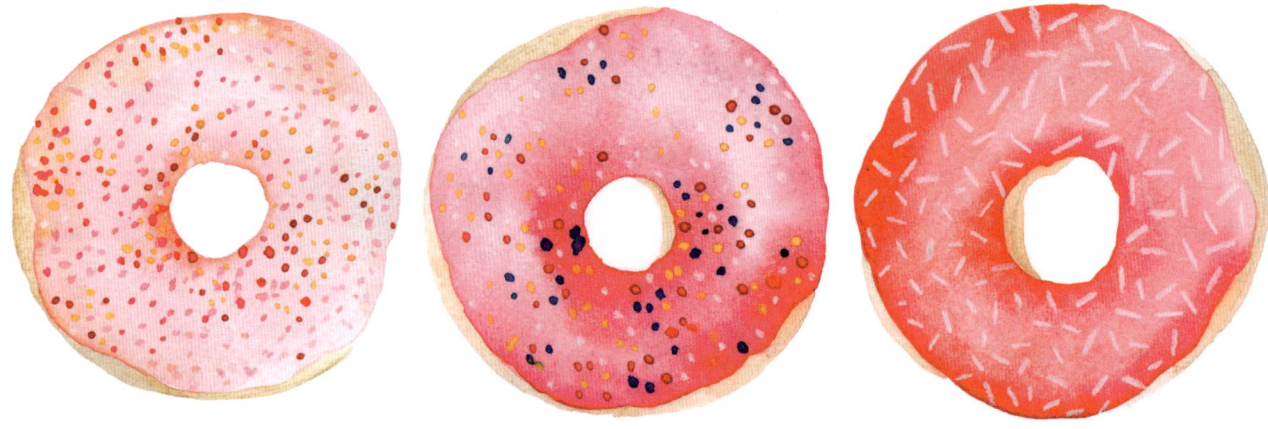

Published in the United States by Watson-Guptill Publications,
an imprint of the Crown Publishing Group, a division of
Penguin Random House LLC, New York.
www.crownpublishing.com
www.watsonguptill.com

Watson-Guptill is a registered trademark and the colophon
is a trademark of Penguin Random House LLC.

Library of Congress cataloging-in-publication data is on file
with the publisher.

Trade paperback ISBN: 978-0-399-57972-1
Ebook ISBN: 978-0-399-57973-8

Printed in China

Design by Angelina Cheney

18

First edition